Dear Rob & Andrea,

Your excitement about the book feels really great.

All the best,

Peter & Drew

MASTERING THE FINANCIAL DIMENSION OF YOUR PRACTICE

MASTERING THE FINANCIAL
DIMENSION OF YOUR PRACTICE

The Definitive
Resource for Private
Practice Development
and Financial Planning

Peter H. Cole, Chartered Financial Consultant, LCSW
Daisy Reese, LCSW

Brunner-Routledge
Taylor & Francis Group

NEW YORK AND HOVE

Published in 2004 by
Brunner-Routledge
270 Madison Avenue
New York, NY 10016
www.brunner-routledge.com

Published in Great Britain by
Brunner-Routledge
27 Church Road
Hove, East Sussex
BN3 2FA
www.brunner-routledge.co.uk

Brunner-Routledge is an imprint of the Taylor & Francis Group.
Printed in the United States of America on acid-free paper.

10 9 8 7 6 5 4 3 2 1

Library of Congress Cataloging-in-Publication Data

Cole, Peter, 1955-
  Mastering the financial dimension of your practice : the definitive resource for private practice development and financial planning / by Peter Cole, Daisy Reese.
     p. ; cm.
  Includes bibliographical references and index.
  ISBN 0-415-94838-X (hardback : alk. paper)
  1. Psychotherapy—Practice. 2. Psychotherapy—Practice—Finance. 3. Psychotherapists—Finance, Personal.
  [DNLM: 1. Practice Management. 2. Psychotherapy. 3. Financial Management. WM 21 C689m 2004] I. Reese, Daisy, 1947- II. Title.

RC465.5.C64 2004
616.89'14'0681—dc22

                                                                    2004002154

Dedication
We dedicate this book to our children: Emily, Joanna, Alex, Elizabeth, and Hannah. You are amazing people and we love you with all our hearts.

Acknowledgments

First, thank you to George Zimmar, PhD, Executive Editor at Brunner-Routledge. This book could never have come into being without you. Your unflagging support, encouragement, and valuable feedback have meant a great deal to us. Also at Brunner-Routledge, Dana Bliss and Shannon Vargo deserve acknowledgment. You both have been incredibly helpful every step of the way—thank you!

We would like to thank the mental health professionals who generously gave of their time, knowledge, and insight in agreeing to be interviewed for this book: Claude Arnett, MD; Allison Buckley, MFTI; James Hansell, PhD; Phillip Littman, LCSW; Karin Nilsson, PhD; John Robinson, PhD; Leslye Russell, MFT; and Shani Simon, LCSW. In particular, we appreciate the wisdom of the elder therapists we interviewed: Hilde Burton, PhD; Joan Cole, PhD; and Betty Russell, LCSW. Your insights and example were truly inspiring.

We would also like to thank the folks at Securities America for their support and encouragement on this project: especially Peter's mentor, Bob Binn. Bob, your generosity, coaching, advice, and no-nonsense approach have been deeply appreciated. Theresa

Ochs—you have kept us honest and have been a pleasure to work with. Thanks for all the time you put in and for your intelligent feedback.

A special thanks goes to our loyal staff at Insight Financial Group, especially Gail Aguilar and Volodymyr Osadchuk—we truly could not have done this without you. Thanks also to Bob Wendlinger—your wisdom about publishing and writing has been a big help along the way.

To the many therapists who have chosen Insight Financial Group for their financial planning and investing needs, we thank you for placing your trust in us. We hope to earn it every day.

Tables and Figures

Contents

ADDENDA

Introduction

WHY A FINANCIAL PLANNING BOOK FOR THERAPISTS?

Most psychotherapists enter private practice with a sense of excitement—a feeling of fulfilling a long-held dream. It's true. Private practice can be a source of tremendous satisfaction, intellectual stimulation, and personal enrichment. Private practitioners can set their own hours, create their own environment, and connect with stimulating people—both colleagues and clients. Private practice offers rich opportunities to follow one's own path.

For private practice to be viable, however, it must pay the bills. It must cover overhead expenses, support a comfortable lifestyle, and ensure a secure financial future for therapists and perhaps their families as well.

Many psychotherapists, however, feel uncomfortable with and ill-equipped to effectively handle the business aspects of their practices. It is this recognition that led us to write this book. We have dealt with hundreds of therapists during our years in practice. We have acted as therapists, trainers, and mentors. Peter has worked with many therapists as their financial planner. Having struggled to establish a successful private practice and having helped many others to do so, he has a unique understanding of the necessary steps for making a practice thrive—personally, professionally, and financially.

Our goal with this book is to address the financial issues specific to psychotherapists:

1. Therapists' careers are often lifelong, with new professional and financial goals emerging into the foreground as their practices develop.

    The first section of this book ("Life Cycle of a Psychotherapy Practice"; Chapters 1–5) takes an in-depth look at the life stages of therapists along with the developmental tasks and financial planning strategies appropriate to each stage.

2. Therapists are attuned to the emotional dimension of human experience, including the emotional dimension of finances.

    We recognize that emotional issues can sabotage the best intentions. In working with this book, you will come to a clearer understanding of your own emotional issues around money and be better able to avoid the unconscious pitfalls that may have hindered you in the past. The second section of this book ("Psychological and Therapeutic Considerations"; Chapters 6–12) covers a range of issues concerning the powerful influence of our emotional lives on our financial behavior.

3. Therapists must deal with money as an issue in their psychotherapy practices.

    We understand that the private practice of psychotherapy necessarily involves a complex interweaving of a service business with deeply intimate work. Section II also explores the fascinating terrain of money as an issue in psychotherapy.

4. Many therapists are highly skilled clinicians but have underdeveloped financial skills.

    We offer comprehensive financial information designed to help you develop the essential skills to be financially successful in private practice. Section III ("A Therapist's Money Guide"; Chapters 13–21) is designed to be both a crash course and an ongoing resource for understanding the fundamentals of personal financial planning.

5. Therapists in private practice do not have the safety net of benefits provided by an employer.

You must recognize the fact that you are your own employer, with all the responsibilities that being a good employer entails. We provide extensive information on arranging an appropriate benefits package for yourself. Chapter 15 takes you through the pros and cons of every major tax-advantaged retirement vehicle open to sole proprietors in private practice. Chapter 20 provides essential insurance information.

6. Since most therapists' retirement plans are self-directed, therapists need input about appropriate investment choices.

Throughout the text, we address appropriate investment strategies for the life stages and financial situations of therapists and their families. In section I, we discuss appropriate asset allocation and investment choices for each phase of the therapy practice life cycle. Chapter 17 is a guide to common investment options for today's retirement plans.

7. Many therapists are reluctant to seek professional financial advice and thus have assembled informal financial plans without an in-depth understanding of what this requires.

We provide a roadmap to sound financial and estate planning that can be tailored to fit your unique situation. Section IV ("Your Money Pages"; Chapters 22–24) provides worksheets designed to help you establish an individualized financial plan. In Chapter 11 we address how to find a qualified and suitable financial planner.

8. Due to financial constraints, many therapists are responsible for their own bookkeeping.

This book will help you put your practice bookkeeping in good order. In Addendum III, we provide a step-by-step guide to getting started with QuickBooks®, an essential accounting package for small businesses.

9. Therapists, who earn most of their money by providing psychotherapy in the 50-minute hour, have difficulty leveraging their time-to-money ratio.

Throughout the text, we look at ways of adding to your income by making your money work for you.

This book is organized into four distinct sections:

1. Life Cycle of a Psychotherapy Practice
2. Psychological and Therapeutic Considerations
3. A Therapist's Money Guide
4. Your Money Pages

We hope you will use the book interactively—in a way that best fits your individual style and particular needs. For the reader who is a novice in financial matters, it might be helpful to look first at section III to get an overview of financial planning terms and concepts. If you feel relatively comfortable with your general financial knowledge, you might choose to start with section I or II. Please note that section IV contains a number of "Process Pages" on which you are encouraged to journal your emotional responses as you work through the process of developing an individualized financial plan. We hope you will not confine yourself to writing only on the process pages. The entire book is meant to be used interactively. Make notes in the margins, skip forward and backward—make it work for you. This book is packed with a wealth of financial information. The more engaged one is with the material, the more meaningful and useful it will be.

To be an effective therapist requires compassion, knowledge, insight, patience, humor, and generosity of spirit. It is our hope that this book will help you to provide well for yourself so that you can continue offering these qualities to your clients.

Daisy Reese, LCSW

Life Cycle of a Psychotherapy Practice

CHAPTER 1

Moving Through the Seasons

More than any profession one can think of, psychotherapy involves the whole person. Who the therapist is—his or her dreams, fears, strivings, and Achilles' heels—directly impacts how, and how well, he or she will perform the work. As therapists ourselves, we have had an insider's view of therapist professional development. In observing our own development over the course of our careers and observing friends, colleagues, interns, and trainees, we have become interested in trying to define the "life cycle" of a therapist—from graduate school through retirement. What are the clinical, personal, and practice development tasks of each phase? What are the pitfalls? We have paid particular attention to the financial planning issues at each phase and looked at the way they are integrated into the larger picture.[1] Certainly, we cannot claim to have found the definitive answers to these questions. However, we hope you will share some of our fascination with the questions themselves. We hope this section will be a springboard for reflection on where you are in your own professional development, so that you are in a strong position to plan for your future.

---

[1] Although we have considered practice development issues without regard to chronological age, by necessity the financial planning questions will be addressed with age as an important factor.

In writing this chapter we interviewed therapists across the spectrum—from a 32-year-old intern to a semi-retired therapist in her 80s. We came away from these interviews with a heightened respect and affection for our chosen profession and the people who practice it. Our sincere thanks to our thoughtful and generous interviewees.

LAUNCHING PHASE—LAYING A SOLID FOUNDATION

Tell me, what is it you plan to do with your one wild and precious life? [2]

Mary Oliver

Characteristic Tasks and Goals

- Creating a space of one's own—leasing and furnishing an office
- Finding or creating a particular niche
- Learning how to market—developing a plan for referrals
- Finding and developing relationships with mentors
- Finding a professional community that fits
- Setting up a bookkeeping system
- Initiating a financial/retirement plan—asset allocation could be rather aggressive at this stage
- Arranging the necessary health and disability insurance coverage

ESTABLISHING PHASE—BEGINNING TO BUILD

The slow and difficult trick of living and finding it where you are. [3]

Mary Oliver

Characteristic Tasks and Goals

- Balancing work and family commitments without losing a sense of self

---

[2] Oliver, Mary. (1993). The summer day. *New and selected poems.* Boston: Beacon Press.
[3] Oliver, Mary. (1993). Going to Walden. In *New and selected poems.* Boston: Beacon Press.

- Developing a reputation with centers of influence and referral sources
- Learning to value increased expertise and reflecting that in the fees you charge
- Beginning to assume leadership roles in the professional community
- Keeping on track with retirement funding—asset allocation should probably become somewhat less aggressive with the inclusion of more investment-grade bonds
- Purchasing or upgrading a life insurance policy
- Considering the possibility of buying real estate—a home, rental property, maybe an office building in which to practice

PRIME PHASE—REAPING REWARDS

To everything there is a season ... a time to sow and a time to reap.

Ecclesiastes

Characteristic Tasks and Goals

- Sharing wisdom—becoming a mentor
- Developing skills at writing and speaking
- Shaping a satisfying practice—working at what interests you and learning to say "no" to what does not
- Giving back to the community—through pro bono work and leadership in professional organizations
- Maintaining the discipline of amply funding a retirement plan—moderately conservative asset allocation is appropriate at this stage
- Seriously evaluating long-term care insurance by your mid-50s
- Paying off the mortgage on earlier real estate purchases

ELDER PHASE—REWARDS FOR WORK WELL DONE

To live so that that which came to me as seed goes to the next as blossom and so that which came as blossom goes on as fruit.

Dawna Markova[4]

---

[4] Markova, Dawna. (2000). *I will not die an unlived life: Reclaiming purpose and passion.* York Beach, ME: Conari Press.

Characteristic Tasks and Goals

- Determining how much work feels right at this phase—because most therapists love what they do, they often do not want to relinquish work completely
- Aligning spending with retirement income so that work is by choice and not financial necessity
- Developing a new lifestyle that feels satisfying—redefining what a balanced life means for you personally
- Attending to estate planning issues
- Making sure that appropriate advanced medical directives are in place
- Ensuring that asset allocation is increasingly conservative, with the majority of holdings in income-producing securities and growth securities de-emphasized.

CHAPTER 2

Launching Phase

You've made up your mind! Maybe you are like the psychiatric residents in our fourth-year seminar—fresh out of training, with all the energy and enthusiasm of youth. On the other hand, maybe you are more like many of our interns—making a midlife career change or gradually transitioning from agency work to private practice. Whatever your chronological age, your practice is just beginning. So let's take a look at some of the nuts and bolts of establishing a successful therapy practice.

TO SHARE OR NOT TO SHARE—THAT IS THE QUESTION

It may seem obvious, but before seeing that first client there must be an office available in which to do so. Do you want to sublease from another therapist or look for an office that would be wholly or primarily yours? The answer to this may also seem obvious—it is a significantly greater financial commitment to lease your own office. Consider for a moment, however, which feels more comfortable—your own living room or a furnished apartment (even a lavishly appointed one)? Just like your living room, your office expresses who you are. Your books are on the shelves, your pictures on the walls. Along with its effect on you, your office also sends a powerful nonverbal message to your clients. We once had a client drop by in hopes of an emergency appointment. She told us: "If you hadn't been here, I would have just sat in the waiting room for a while—that would have been enough." Our bias is clear by now—better a more modest office that is truly "you." If paying rent is not manageable at this point, you might consider seeking a colleague who would like to sublease from you.

Office location is also important. Some things to consider:

- Is the location convenient—easy access to freeways, close to downtown, etc.?
- Is parking available—both for you and your clients? Do you need a handicap-accessible space?
- Do you want to be in a building with other therapists for mutual support, consultation, etc.? Or would you rather be in a building with allied professionals (physicians, attorneys) who could become referral sources?
- Is the building secure and well-lit for after-hours clients?
- Is the building quiet and conducive to the work you do?

Keep in mind that your first office is where you will form some of your first professional connections. Although it is unlikely that you will stay in the same office over the course of your career, those connections can last a lifetime. We still do much of our cross-referring with original officemates from 20 years ago.

MANAGED CARE—KEEPING YOUR BALANCE ON THE SLIPPERY SLOPE

Fifteen years ago, when managed care first began making serious inroads into California, we had frantic conversations with colleagues. How could we get ourselves included on as many panels as possible? Managed care seemed to offer limitless referrals and guaranteed reimbursement. What more could a beginning therapist ask for? Unfortunately, the reality has not quite lived up to expectations. Yes, managed care does offer ready-made referrals—sometimes more than you really want. However, reimbursement is invariably lower than standard fees, often substantially lower. Although theoretically guaranteed, reimbursement can be slow to arrive and often requires repeated billings. It always involves significant paperwork, ranging from annoying to infuriating in its complexity. Most importantly, managed care inserts a third party into the intimate space between therapist and client. Therapists can no longer make decisions solely based on what they consider to be best for the client. Rather, treatment decisions and options are often dictated by what the insurance company allows or requires.

Does this mean that one should steer clear of managed care altogether? Probably not—at least not in the early days of practice. Rather, think of managed care as a temporary measure, providing income and a client base to help you develop your skills as you work to establish yourself and build referral sources.

One caveat: Be sure to read all managed care contracts thoroughly. Ask the following questions:

What is the reimbursement schedule?
What is required for authorization?
How many visits are typically authorized?
Once you sign on, are you obligated to see whatever patients are referred to you?
Are you obligated to see patients who might be "at risk," even after authorized visits have been exhausted?

Protect yourself in the beginning and you may save a lot of legal and ethical trouble in the long run.

IF NOT MANAGED CARE, THEN WHAT?

It has been said, "a business with no sign is a sign of no business." In a metaphorical sense, this is as true for a psychotherapy practice as it is for Macy's or Barnes and Noble. Although you likely will not want to put up a billboard or run a full-page ad in your local newspaper, you do need to focus on developing your marketing skills. You may have become a therapist for any number of idealistic and altruistic reasons. The reality, however, is that you must make a profit from your therapeutic work. "Profit"—it is really not a four-letter word. There is nothing shameful or embarrassing about wanting to make a comfortable living from doing the work you love. Simply acknowledging this to yourself is the first step.

COMBINING PASSION WITH NONATTACHMENT

As a psychotherapist, rather than selling shoes or books, you are selling expertise. No one can possibly be interested in your expertise if they do not know about it. This means you must become comfortable selling yourself as an expert. In other words, you must bring your work to the marketplace. You may ask how, in a marketplace that is so vast and so complex, are you going to find a voice that is heard? The answer is by following your passion, and bringing to the marketplace a public offering of that which you are passionate about.

A helpful complement to passion is the Buddhist concept of nonattachment. If you present to the marketplace what you love, without attachment to the outcome, it is possible to reap rewards in surprising ways. For many years, we did huge, regional mailings of brochures for our Gestalt training group but received minimal response. Each spring we would look at each other and question, "Is it worth doing again?" Nevertheless, we kept on, with the faith that we were sowing important seeds even though we could not yet see many sprouts. Then some interesting calls began to come in: "I've been saving your brochure for a long time. Now I'm ready to do the training." "I've seen your name around for a long time. You must be pretty well established." By sticking with something that excites and satisfies us and practicing nonattachment to immediate outcomes, we have succeeded in having our voices heard in the clamorous marketplace.

So where does your passion lie? Your answer will be a guide to the segment of the marketplace that will be responsive to what you have to offer. The focus may be on a theoretical approach:

Gestalt
Psychoanalytic
Transpersonal
Jungian
Cognitive-behavioral

If this is the case, it will be important to associate yourself with professional organizations that train and mentor therapists in the particular approach. Many early referrals will probably come from supervisors and colleagues in these organizations and from networking at seminars and conferences.

Another avenue is to focus on working with specific types of clients:

Women
Men
Adolescents/children
Gays and lesbians
Senior citizens
Couples

If you focus on a particular client group, it makes sense to go to venues where members of that group congregate. Connecting with counselors and teachers at schools, speaking at a senior citizens' center, or making a presentation to your church's Sunday school class for couples are examples of ways to practice enlightened self-interest—in other words, "doing well by doing good." Your marketing efforts must be valid in their own right, rather than merely an advertisement for your practice. If you bring something of value to the community, you will find that the community responds.

Yet another approach is to focus on specific issues:

Anxiety and depression
Women in the workplace
Parenting
Relationships
Adults abused as children
Addictions
Midlife issues
Eating disorders

Focusing on a particular issue can make successful marketing much easier. One of our former interns, Donna, has chosen to work with people who have eating disorders. She has sent letters to physicians, given presentations at high schools and colleges, listed herself as a referral with the Mental Health Association, and done extensive networking with other therapists. Although she has been licensed for only a few years, she now has a successful practice and runs several eating disorder groups per week. Whenever we need to make a referral for a patient with an eating disorder, hers is the first name that comes to mind.

KNOWING YOURSELF

Donna is the exception; she feels comfortable with a wide variety of marketing approaches. Most people are a little less versatile. If you are someone who freezes at the thought of speaking in public, forcing yourself to speak to large groups will be painful and probably nonproductive. If you suffer from terminal writer's block, do not offer to write a monthly column for your organization's newsletter. In short, play to your strengths rather than your weaknesses. There are many paths to building a successful practice. The trick is finding the one (or two) that work with who you are.

We have focused much of our practices on training and group work. We are both sociable and find teaching to be exciting—a great way to keep ourselves and our work fresh. A more introverted therapist may look for a mentor to work with one-on-one (a mentor who can also become a referral source), or talk with the local newspaper or a special-interest publication about writing an article or column. If you like to organize and do public presentations, innumerable organizations (e.g., schools, PTAs, service clubs, churches, and synagogues) would love to have you volunteer to give a talk or present a workshop for their members. Do you have contacts or interest in the media? Newspapers have a lot of column inches to fill, and radio and television stations have plenty of airtime. Contact the local media with ideas for timely topics (e.g., dealing with stress, making your step-family work, parenting teenagers) and you may find yourself becoming a minor celebrity—the expert they call for thoughts on the topic of the day.

Another, sometimes more sensitive, aspect of knowing oneself as a therapist is understanding where one's wounds and weaknesses lie. It can be tempting to specialize in a problem that touches a personal chord. The archetype of the "wounded healer" is a powerful one, and many significant contributions have been made by therapists working in the area that is closest to home for them. However, for this to work well the therapist must have worked with his or her own issues to a significant extent. If a therapist enters into the area of sexual abuse, for instance, as a crusader—determined to rescue victims and right wrongs—that therapist can do unintended harm to patients by imposing a personal agenda. Through personal therapy and consultation, the therapist can come to a place where he or she listens with a "loving neutrality" that allows clients to access their own strength rather than remaining stuck in victimhood. This loving neutrality also allows therapists to take care of themselves in their work life—not working more than they can realistically sustain and not forgetting their own interests (including financial) in their zeal to help clients. As one of our early supervisors said, "Psychotherapy operates on two levels—the emotional and the financial. If one doesn't pay attention to both those levels, the therapy can't be effective. It's the tension between the emotional connection and the financial relationship that gives therapy much of its power."

THE RIGHT MARKET MEANS A MARKET THAT CAN AFFORD YOUR SERVICES

We hope Peter's old social work professors at Bryn Mawr and Daisy's at the University of Texas will not disown us when they read this, but our advice for the beginning private practitioner is to market to people who can afford to pay for therapy out of pocket. It makes sense to direct one's marketing to people who can and will pay for psychotherapy. Most therapists have an altruistic streak, and pro bono work is important for many reasons. However, in order to do pro bono work without becoming resentful and burned out, one must have a solid base of clients who pay the bills. Before you can care well for others, you must care for yourself.

The idea of nonattachment may be helpful here. If what you are bringing to the marketplace is educational, informative, and useful; if you market to people who understand, appreciate, and are willing to pay for therapy; and if your marketing plan is a comfortable fit with your interests and personality, then you can detach from needing to see immediate results from your efforts. The results will come, but often in roundabout and unexpected ways. Sometimes people show up in your office years after they came to a seminar or class. Sometimes they refer a friend years later. In the meantime, your marketing is a way of bringing an important message to the community.

BEYOND THE CONSULTING ROOM

Erving Polster, one of the leading lights of Gestalt therapy, once said, "Therapy is too good to be limited to the sick." With the tensions and conflicts in the world today, the need for therapists to find a voice in the broader society is greater than ever. Psychological thinking addresses a dimension of human motivation that people in the fields of economics, history, politics, business, and even the arts frequently are not attuned to. For example, we serve on the grants committee of a philanthropic organization that funds visionary ideas, and recently, we were assigned to be the evaluators of a very exciting grant application. We started the evaluation full of enthusiasm. The person applying was clearly brilliant and his project was one we thought could have a huge impact on society. Gradually, though, our enthusiasm faded. Our e-mails were not returned, references were lukewarm, and we began hearing distressing stories about the applicant's treatment of people he considered "beneath" him. Because of our psychological backgrounds, we felt confident in saying, "His narcissism is out of control and the chances of his being able to work collaboratively are slim." We were able to take into account not only the intellectual dimension but also the interpersonal and psychological dimensions and make a decision from a holistic standpoint.

If the consulting room, working with one individual at a time, does not fit for you, your ability to think psychologically can stand you in good stead in a wide variety of arenas. Many therapists are thinking "outside the box" of the traditional consulting room and are bringing psychological understanding and expertise to people and organizations at all levels of society.

Turn your creative mind loose to explore alternatives and you may wind up working in realms you never could have predicted. Consider the following examples:

Dr. K. is a psychologist who works with organizations large and small to do team building.

Cassie H., LCSW, has built a successful international business working with the hospitality industry on the issues of sexual harassment prevention and conflict resolution.

Dr. C. is a psychiatrist who serves as a consultant to executives on a broad range of issues.

Dr. E. acts as a psychiatric consultant to adolescent treatment facilities.

Jessie O., an inheritor herself, is a family counselor who specializes in working with inheritors. She works with a major New York brokerage as a "wealth counselor" for their clients.

The rapidly developing technology field can be a tremendous resource for alternative forms of therapy. Ours is an era in which communities of interest are arising without regard for geographical proximity. The Internet and mass communication have created a global village that allows these communities of interest to thrive. Therapy by telephone is already commonplace. Soon it will be feasible to provide therapy via video conferencing.

Some therapists love the 50-minute hour and want a very traditional practice. Others want to teach, consult, write, speak, or market their expertise in creative new ways. The possibilities for expanding a practice beyond the four walls of the consulting room are limited only by the therapist's imagination and willingness to risk.

THE FINANCIAL DIMENSION OF THE LAUNCHING PHASE

Bookkeeping

The process of establishing a practice provides an excellent opportunity to set up one's bookkeeping system correctly. There are a number of therapist bookkeeping programs in the marketplace. However, because many of these programs are high priced, it pays to shop around. The best solution we have found is a mass-market bookkeeping program. The company who makes this product is able to keep the sales price down because of high sales volume and has amassed the large amount of capital necessary to maintain high-quality programming and service. We use QuickBooks®

(see Addendum III) by Intuit, which is economical to use and very well written and supported. The scheduling program we use is Lotus Organizer, which filters into our Palm Pilots for easy hand-held scheduling.

QuickBooks® Health Care version has a mental health setup and template that will take therapists through all the dimensions of bookkeeping and billing they are likely to need. It is easy to use and is considered standard among CPAs, so that when tax time rolls around you will likely be able to e-mail your CPA all the information he or she will need to do the taxes for your practice. QuickBooks® is available online at *http://www.intuit.com*.

SETTING UP A RETIREMENT PLAN

Put the time value of money to work by beginning a retirement plan from the first day of private practice. For many therapists, a good place to start would be to open an individual 401(k) plan. For individuals who are self-employed and organized as a sole proprietorship, the individual 401(k) allows a maximum amount of pre-tax retirement money to be put away. Your financial planner will be able to help with the details of opening and maintaining the retirement plan. If you are in your late 20s or early 30s, you might want to consider an aggressive asset allocation, meaning that the preponderance of your assets will go into stocks rather than bonds. At this phase of the game, many investors trade growth potential for stability because of the long time horizon before the money will be

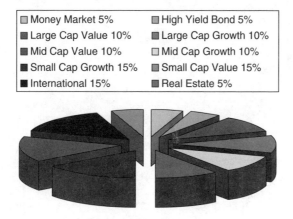

☐ Money Market 5%	☐ High Yield Bond 5%
■ Large Cap Value 10%	■ Large Cap Growth 10%
■ Mid Cap Value 10%	☐ Mid Cap Growth 10%
■ Small Cap Growth 15%	■ Small Cap Value 15%
■ International 15%	■ Real Estate 5%

FIGURE 2.1. Aggressive Model Portfolio.
(This model is provided for illustrative purposes only. Please consult an investment advisor before purchasing.)

needed for retirement. A good place to begin is to earmark 15% of your gross (before tax) income for your retirement plan. As your income rises, so will the amount that goes into your 401(k). Also, you will need to have liability, health, and disability/business overhead insurance (please see Chapter 20). An aggressive asset allocation might look something like the pie chart in Figure 2.1

CONCLUSION

The launching phase is an exciting time, full of promise and hope. It is the ideal opportunity to properly organize one's financial planning, so that a strong foundation is in place on which to build a prosperous career.

CHAPTER 3

Establishing Phase

The seeds have been planted. Now comes the sustaining work of managing what you have sown to provide for a satisfying harvest.

THE IMPORTANCE OF SELF AS INSTRUMENT

"The hardest part for me is balancing my practice and my family. How do I put out emotional energy for my clients all day and still have something left over for my husband and kids?" This is often the central question for therapists at this phase.

Imagine for a moment that you are a concert violinist. You have a beautiful, finely tuned instrument on which you have spent many thousands of dollars. Obviously, you would do everything in your power to protect this violin, giving it all the care and attention it required. As therapists, we have no other instrument but ourselves. We have spent many thousands of dollars on education and training. We have created a beautiful environment in which to work and invested time and energy in our marketing efforts. Doesn't it make sense, then, to treat ourselves with the same respect that a musician would offer the violin?

To function well, we must learn to feed ourselves

Physically
Intellectually
Emotionally
Spiritually

Physical

The physical level is often the most neglected. When it seems there simply are not enough hours in a day, personal well-being can easily be squeezed out. Along with paying attention to eating well and getting enough sleep, finding ways to move your body on a daily basis is incredibly important. Is it possible to walk or ride a bike to your office? Is there a gym or health club near where you work? It can feel great to take a 2-hour break in the middle of the day and go to an aerobics or yoga class. How about massage? Giving yourself the gift of a regular massage once or twice a month is not simply a luxury. It is an important piece of "keeping your instrument in tune." What do you do with those 10 minutes between appointments? When we first started practicing, we routinely let clients run over—often finishing with one just in time to meet the next. Later, those 10 minutes became a time to catch up on paperwork or return phone calls. Today we are much more protective of that space between one client and the next. We keep yoga mats in the office closet, making it easy to sit down for a few stretches in that precious 10-minute break. At other times, a walk outside to reconnect with the larger world can restore perspective. However you choose to do it, it is important to take time throughout the day to refresh yourself—you will find that this leaves you significantly less exhausted and burnt out at the end of the day.

Intellectual

At its best, psychotherapy can be tremendously intellectually challenging. However, this is not automatically true. Do you sometimes find yourself feeling bored by the "same old stories"? Do you have a sense that you have heard it all before and find yourself operating by rote? A colleague once told us, "Oh, I can handle most of my cases in my sleep!" If you start to have a similar feeling, it is time for some stimulation. Look for seminars or workshops that excite you. Too often therapists focus only on "How many CEUs is this worth?" But your continuing education should do much more than provide you with required CEUs. Find a presentation by someone whose writings interest you and make it a goal to read much of his or her work in preparation. Try a workshop on a topic outside your area of expertise. We find that workshops are much more meaningful to us if they include an experiential aspect. Let yourself take some risks and explore an interactive group experience or training that involves personal as well as professional growth.

Consultation is another way to keep yourself intellectually stimulated. Now that you have been in practice for a while, you may have gotten out of the habit of seeking out good supervision. Therapists do not improve their skills through experience alone. Consultation and supervision are important tools for increasing your skill level. The right consultant can help therapists at all levels of experience sort out difficult cases, better understand countertransference issues, and challenge themselves to develop professionally. Over time, the consultant can become an important mentor as well as a valuable referral source. Peer consult groups also serve an important function. Ideally, they can provide social connection, clinical consultation, and professional networking. Be sure to look for a group that feels friendly and supportive but also challenging. If you cannot find the right group, it is worth taking the trouble to start talking to like-minded colleagues and form your own group.

Emotional

As important as keeping yourself well-nourished physically is paying attention to your emotional nourishment. Clients demand a great deal from you in terms of emotional support, and families and friends expect you to be emotionally available to them at the end of the day. Where does your emotional sustenance come from? It must come from many sources. No one person can provide you with all you need. A spouse or partner can be an important resource. Groups of friends who are willing to really listen and really talk are invaluable. Finding a therapist for yourself (even if you thought you were "finished") may be helpful. Carl Whitaker used to talk about his "cuddle group"—a group of professional colleagues who supported each other through difficult clients and the profession's inevitable ups and downs. Some things about our profession can be understood only by another therapist. The energy you put into seeking out and maintaining connections with colleagues you resonate with will serve you well throughout your career.

Spiritual

What can "restoreth your soul"? For some people, traditional religious services are an important aspect of life. For others, spending time in nature is a necessity. Do you love music or art? Concerts, museum exhibits, or joining a choir or amateur chamber music group may be what you need to feel spiritually fed. Meditation, tai chi, or yoga can be both relaxing and centering. It may be that, between the demands of developing your practice and dealing with your personal life, you have not stopped to consider what your particular spiritual food is. If that is the case, take some time now to experiment. Begin by giving yourself some solitude to tune in to what feels lacking in your life. As you begin to attune yourself to your inner wisdom, that wisdom will begin to speak in an increasingly clear voice. It will be a trustworthy guide as you move through the developmental phases of your practice.

FINDING YOUR POWER—BECOMING AN AUTHORITY AND SETTING YOUR FEES

No longer a beginner, in this phase your overall feeling of professional confidence should be growing. In many ways, you are now at the most critical stage of therapist development. You are setting the trajectory that will determine the course of your future practice.

One important aspect of setting your trajectory is charging "market value" for your services. Effective psychotherapy can change the course of a person's life. Far from being an optional luxury, it can mean the difference between a life that is productive and satisfying and one that is sterile, disappointing, and destructive. That being said, the person who makes that difference possible (you!) deserves to be well paid for providing that service.

As an intern or a newly licensed practitioner, it seems appropriate to charge a lower fee and to be accommodating about providing a sliding scale. However, as one of our establishing phase interviewees said, "I'm at a point now where my fee is my fee. If people can't afford it, I'll be willing to see them less often or provide them with a referral."

The question is, of course, how to set your fee. In most communities experienced therapists seem to charge a fairly wide range of fees. Daisy once got a piece of advice that she found very useful. See if it works as well for you. Begin by finding out what the highest fee is in your community (e.g., $150 per hour). Try saying out loud—maybe in front of a mirror—"I charge $150." If this makes you gulp or stammer, as it very well may, try saying, "I charge $140."

Continue in this way, working your way downward, until you arrive at the fee that feels like a comfortable fit for you. You may need to repeat this exercise periodically, when it seems like it is time to raise your fee.

WEAVING THE WHOLE CLOTH

In the establishing phase, the therapist's marketing efforts take on a different flavor than at the launching phase. The initial networking efforts of the launching phase evolve into an expansion of word-of-mouth referrals, as the therapist's expertise gains recognition. By the establishing phase, the therapist has developed a niche in which he or she feels comfortable. Although this niche may change over the course of a career, the wise establishing phase therapist will allow for the time and resources needed to become a recognized authority. As well as providing a source of referrals, it can feel exciting and validating to becoming known as an "expert." As an establishing phase interviewee told us, "I know I do very good work with adolescents. I don't get anxious with them the way I sometimes can with adults. I'm much freer to be myself—to take risks, challenge and tease—and the kids really respond to that." As patients and centers of influence come to recognize and appreciate your expertise, you will find referrals coming from many sources. Indeed, in the fee-for-service therapy market, word-of-mouth is undoubtedly the therapist's best referral source.

Another important source of referrals is other professionals. If you are diligent about maintaining your professional connections, you can tap into a rich mine of referrals. When you get a call from a patient who says, "My husband is seeing Dr. Jones and he suggested that I call you," do you immediately make a call to Dr. Jones? It is important to express your appreciation and also (once you have a signed release of information form) to tap into Dr. Jones' insights about the case. You can even send a written note occasionally. Let other professionals know that you appreciate their referrals and that you are willing to reciprocate. Daisy has been known to cross therapists off her referral list when neither thanks nor reciprocity has been forthcoming!

Clearly, by the time you reach the establishing phase, marketing and networking are threads in the same cloth. Another significant thread is community involvement. One of our interviewees made a most telling comment. When asked about how she decides who to refer to, she replied, "I tend to refer to people who are active in the community—people I know from committees or who I've worked with in my professional organization. People who are involved in the professional community can usually be relied on to be responsible to the ethical standards of the community. There is a sort of accountability that's missing in people who aren't involved."

If you are willing to work for the advancement of the profession and the well-being of your community, you will find that your fellow therapists tend to trust and respect you. Whether you serve on an organizing committee for the American Psychological Association, teach a class at your community college, or donate an hour or two per week to the local free clinic, investing in your community is vital to maintaining a successful practice.

INVESTMENT CONSIDERATIONS IN THE ESTABLISHING PHASE

What about Real Estate?

One of the most important investment decisions to make at this phase is whether and how much you want to invest in real estate. Most therapists in private practice want to own their own homes. How about going further and buying rental property or a building to house your office? To make the decision about whether this is right for you, the following questions should be helpful:

Is your credit good enough to obtain a favorable mortgage rate?
Do you have substantial available cash for a down payment?
Is your cash flow steady enough to carry the property until you find appropriate tenants?
Are you a "handyperson" yourself, or do you know someone reliable to help you with repairs and maintenance?
Are you comfortable maintaining a friendly but businesslike relationship with tenants?
Is your risk tolerance level such that this kind of investment will not keep you awake at night?

If the answers to all of the above are "yes" our advice is to read the more in-depth discussion in Chapter 17. We were at a retirement party recently for a very successful therapist who said, "The only regret I have about my career is that I didn't buy the building where I rented my office." Real estate investing can be a challenge, but it can also bring professional, personal, and financial rewards over the long term.

Other Long-Term Financial Planning

The establishing phase is an extremely important time financially. As we have discussed previously, unless you are expecting a source of revenue apart from what your practice provides, it is important that you think like the tortoise—not the hare. With a long time horizon you can provide well for your future self without undue hardship now. As you get older, it gets harder to put away enough money for retirement because the shortened time horizon diminishes the power of compound interest and the time value of money.

In Table 3.1 we consider the amount one needs to save monthly in order to accumulate $1 million for retirement. Let us illustrate two scenarios from the table. Using simple math, you can determine that a therapist who is 35 years old and plans to retire at age 70 has 35 years to reach that goal. If the therapist were to average a modest 6% return on investment in a tax-deferred retirement account over those 35 years, he or she could theoretically reach the $1 million goal by investing $698.41 per month until retirement at age 70. On the other hand, if a 50-year-old therapist with no current savings wanted to reach the $1 million retirement goal by age 70, it would require investing $2153.54 per month to reach that goal. These examples should underscore that beginning retirement investing in one's 30s requires a significantly less aggressive contribution schedule to reach one's goals than if one waits until later in life.

TABLE 3.1
Monthly Savings Needed to Reach a Retirement Savings Goal of $1,000,000 (assuming a 6% rate of return in a tax-deferred account)

Years until Retirement	Monthly Savings[a] toward $1,000,000 Goal
5 years	$14,261.49
10 years	$6,071.69
15 years	$3,421.46
20 years	$2,153.54
25 years	$1,435.83
30 years	$990.55
35 years	$698.41
40 years	$499.64
45 years	$361.04

Note: See text for examples.
[a]Amounts are invested at the beginning of each month.

Asset allocation at this phase of the game (the establishing phase) can typically be moderately aggressive. With a long time horizon until retirement, many investors feel they can trade volatility for growth potential in their portfolio of stocks and bonds. A typical moderately aggressive portfolio might look something like the one provided in Figure 3.1.

Insurance Needs

The establishing phase is also an important time to evaluate your life, health, and disability insurance needs. Clearly, if you have children or other dependents who rely on your income for their well-being, then life insurance should be a consideration. Similarly, if you and your dependents rely on your practice income for day-to-day living expenses, disability insurance can make a huge difference in the event that you become ill or injured. Health insurance is necessary at every stage of the game, and private practitioners should definitely have coverage in the establishing phase because the cost of a major medical condition or event can devastate one's financial life.

□ Money Market 5%
▨ Investment Grade Bond 10%
■ High Yield Bond 10%
□ Large Cap Value 10%
■ Large Cap Growth 10%
▨ Mid Cap Value 10%
■ Mid Cap Growth 10%
□ Small Cap Growth 10%
■ Small Cap Value 10%
■ International 10%
□ Real Estate 5%

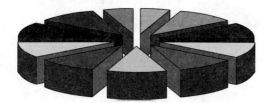

FIGURE 3.1.   Moderately Aggressive Model Portfolio.
(This model is provided for illustrative purposes only. Please consult an Investment advisor before purchasing.)

CONCLUSION

In every way, the establishing phase is full of promise for the private practitioner. It is a time of coming into one's own professionally as well as financially. It is a transitional phase from being a beginner to becoming a seasoned veteran. In the dimensions of professional development, marketing, refining one's niche, and investing, the establishing phase therapist is laying the foundations that will make the prime and elder phases successful and fulfilling.

CHAPTER 4

Prime Phase

The prime phase is a rewarding time—a time when your practice is firmly established and you are reaching your full professional maturity. Your clinical skills are finely honed, you are recognized and respected in the community, and you are at peak earning capacity. Financially, the stakes are higher than ever. You may have college tuition or aging parents to provide for, and certainly there is diminishing time to prepare for retirement.

AT THE CROSSROADS

In the prime phase, you stand at the crossroads. Looking back, you can take pride in how far you have come and also acknowledge your regrets. Daisy's brother once remarked that the definition of a midlife crisis is the time when all the stupid mistakes of our youth become unavoidably apparent! No one reaches midlife without a fair share of mistakes, regrets, and stupidities, and therapists are no exception. However, to paraphrase Willie Nelson, "There ain't nothing we can do about it now." Will you let yourself be consumed by the "might have beens" or will you do the developmental work of midlife and move toward integrating all the aspects of yourself in the effort to become a more complete human being?

Jung said that one could not truly enter into therapy before the age of 40. He was referring, we think, to the individuation process, which is lifelong but which reaches a new level of awareness at midlife. By this point, much of the "dragon-slaying" of the younger years has been accomplished and it is time for self-exploration. This may be a time to consider a return to therapy for yourself—perhaps with an intersubjective or Jungian analyst. Working with a dream group or keeping a journal, even if these things have never appealed to you before, can be important avenues to tapping into the self. Some amount of solitude is an important consideration at this phase. In many traditional cultures, women retreat for a time when entering menopause. When they return from retreat, they have assumed the mantle of the wise woman. A lengthy retreat may not be feasible for you, but even a day or two at the ocean or in the mountains can provide valuable time to pause and reflect.

INTEGRATING THEORY AND AUTHENTICITY

Most therapists, in graduate training or sometime early in their careers, embrace a theoretical orientation that feels valid and useful. For the theory to sustain you in your work over the long haul, it must also fit your personality style. Daisy sometimes entertains herself by speculating about whether like attracts like, in terms of theoretical orientation, or whether opposites attract. For example, is a therapist with a flamboyant, extroverted style more likely to become a psychodramatist (like attracts like) or choose a restrained psychoanalytic approach (opposites attract)? We have yet to arrive at a satisfactory answer to this question, but it seems clear to us that, over the course of their careers, therapists both shape and are shaped by the orientation they choose.

By the time you arrive at the prime phase, you have gained the wisdom and maturity that allow you to interact with your patients in ways that can be deeply healing and, at times, transformative. The prime phase therapist knows that:

- *By sitting in the therapist's chair, one automatically assumes a significant amount of power.* For those of you who came of age in the 1960s, this has perhaps been a difficult lesson to assimilate. You haven't wanted to "power-trip" people, after all! However, recognizing that patients inevitably hand you power and authority enables you to handle that power thoughtfully and effectively—using it for the patient's growth rather than denying or abusing it.

- *Regardless of theoretical orientation, it is the relationship that heals.* It has been said that "therapy is nothing more and nothing less than one human being talking to another." Rather than relying on clever interventions or brilliant interpretations, the prime phase therapist values the humanness of the therapeutic relationship.
- *The authentic self of the therapist calls to the authentic self of the client.* How self-revealing you are as a therapist is an individual decision, but your willingness to be authentically who you are encourages your clients to do the same.
- *The "rules" of therapy are important (e.g., no sexual contact with patients), but the rules must serve as a container for the therapy, not define it.*

Studies have shown[1] that effective therapists from different theoretical schools are more alike than are effective and ineffective therapists from the same school of thought. Prime phase therapists have refined their theory and technique so that they can use them as a bridge between themselves and their patients, rather than as a barrier.

Whatever the theoretical orientation of the therapist, in the prime phase, the integration of theory is now more internalized and expressive of the therapist's authentic life perspective. Theory at this point becomes more an expression of who the therapist is rather than an intellectualized exercise. The theory you have lived with over the years has shaped you, and now you shape the theory to reflect your individual style. It has been wisely said that a truly developed therapist is one who has mastered the tools of the trade and can then leave them outside the consulting room door. At the prime phase this can become reality.

SHAPING YOUR PRACTICE

Another advantage of being in the prime phase of your career is the increased freedom to choose your clients. When you began your practice, you likely welcomed every referral with eager anticipation. The idea of turning down a paying client would never have occurred to you. Even at later stages of one's career, it can seem like tempting fate to say "no." However, if you want a psychotherapy practice that feels deeply satisfying—a true reflection of who you

---

[1] Carkhuff, Robert and Bernard G. Berenson. (1977). *Beyond counseling and therapy, 2nd edition.* New York: Holt Rinehart and Winston.

are—you need to shape your practice. And that means, in one way or another, choosing your patients. Certainly, ability to pay a full fee is one important criterion. It can be helpful to decide how many spaces in your caseload you are comfortable providing to pro bono or reduced-fee clients. Once those slots are filled, you must be willing to provide appropriate referrals to people unable to afford the full fee.

At the prime phase many private practitioners want to limit the number of managed care cases they take. The first time Daisy told a managed care referral that she could not see him, her heart was in her mouth. She asked herself, "Is this hubris that I will pay for later?" Interestingly enough, her willingness to say "no" seems only to have increased the number of referrals she receives.

So is every full-fee referral a good one? Not necessarily. Pay attention to what interests you and give yourself permission to choose accordingly. Daisy had always enjoyed working with adolescents, but when her children were going through their teens the idea of seeing adolescent clients sounded truly awful. It was important to honor her own limits and focus on adults. One of our interviewees told us that she no longer sees couples: "I found it just too exhausting to be required to maintain neutrality." Many psychoanalytically oriented therapists focus their practice on clients who are interested in working analytically.

Private practice can provide you with a good deal of freedom. To truly reap the rewards of your freedom, you must be willing to tolerate the anxiety that can come with open space in your schedule. For instance, if you say, "No, I don't have any sliding scale slots right now," "No, I work only with adults," or "No, I'm not accepting new clients at the moment," there will inevitably be some unfilled appointment times in the schedule periodically. Certainly, this can stir up a lot of anxiety. However, if you can come to consider these spaces as possibilities rather than signs of failure, you will find that your practice will increasingly assume a shape that reflects your individuality.

GENERATIVITY—THE IMPORTANCE OF CONNECTING TO THE LARGER WORLD

Erik Erikson defines the developmental crossroads of midlife as generativity vs. stagnation. In the prime phase, the therapist encounters many opportunities for generativity, and it is the seizing of these opportunities that will make the difference between a life well lived and a life of "quiet desperation."

Mentoring and Training

Each generation has an obligation to pass on its knowledge and wisdom to the next. You may find satisfaction in taking on an intern. As one of our interviewees commented, "It's so validating to work with an intern. It helps me recognize how far I've come in my own professional development. Plus, it's a challenge to develop a new way of working—to not just provide answers but to help her arrive at her own answers."

Some of our greatest learning has come from our roles as trainers. Facilitating training groups for therapists over the last 12 years, we have been challenged to examine our own points of view, look at our blind spots, and develop in ways we never could have predicted. You may be interested in putting together a training group of your own, running a consultation group, or teaching some postgraduate courses. Just as your own mentors provided the necessary teaching and support to help you develop in your early years, by providing the same for younger therapists you are able to develop more fully in the middle years.

The Ripple Effect

Another source of satisfaction during the prime phase is recognizing that your work with individual patients often produces wide ripples. Many are the families that have benefited from "therapy by osmosis." Often, too, we find ourselves treating someone—a teacher, a doctor, a judge—who has a wide sphere of influence. If these people find their compassion and self-awareness increased through therapy, they have the potential to make a significant impact on the world.

Leadership

Prime phase therapists also provide leadership to professional and community organizations. Among our interviewees, one is chairman of the board of Jewish Family Services, another is active in her Quaker Meeting, and another was a founder of the Psychotherapy Institute—a postgraduate training program in Berkeley, California. This sort of activity provides therapists with an opportunity for generativity. At the same time, it raises one's profile in the community and allows for marketing through truly enlightened self-interest.

FINANCIAL PLANNING ISSUES IN THE PRIME PHASE

The prime phase typically covers the ages from the mid-40s to retirement age. Earning power is at its peak, and this phase represents the last chance to put money away before retirement. The stakes in the retirement savings arena are never higher than they are in the prime phase. In all likelihood, if you are to receive an inheritance on the death of a parent, it will come during this phase. If you have a shortfall in your retirement savings, it becomes vitally important in the prime phase to address the shortfall so that your retirement will not be jeopardized.

Paying for disability income insurance is certainly an important goal in your 40s and 50s, but as you get closer to age 65—when most disability policies stop payment—it is often sensible to shift resources from a disability policy into long-term care insurance. There may be some years in your mid- to late 50s when you will want both, but eventually the long-term care coverage becomes more important. You should have enough in your retirement fund by your late 50s that income replacement becomes less of an issue.

If you are expecting an inheritance, it is important that you discuss finances with your parents. Although this can be a sensitive area to discuss with your older parent, it is important that you have some idea what to expect with regard to your inheritance so that you can plan accordingly. It may be useful to meet with your parents' financial planner and/or attorney to get a good picture of their finances. One issue that may be appropriate to bring up with older parents is long-term care coverage. This coverage can help to preserve their estate and your inheritance should they need long-term care at some point. Remember that long-term care coverage is purchased mostly for the purpose of estate preservation, so if preserving your parents' estate is vital to your financial well-being in retirement, talking with your parents about purchasing such coverage, even if such a conversation is uncomfortable, may be well worth it. Most long-term care policies now offer coverage for home care and assisted living, so that the coverage may be viewed as insurance to stay out of a nursing home rather than coverage for a nursing home.

As with all the other phases, health insurance is of paramount concern. Unless you are very wealthy, you really cannot afford to "go bare" with regard to health insurance in the prime phase. As you age, of course, your chances for illness increase, and you have less time to recover from devastating financial loss due to illness than earlier in your career. Health insurance is simply a must. Do not go without it!

ASSET ALLOCATION IN THE PRIME PHASE

As discussed, the prime phase covers a long period of life—from the mid-40s to retirement age, which for many therapists is well into their 70s. Therefore, we cannot make a sweeping statement about appropriate asset allocation during this time. The closer you get to retirement, the more conservative your asset allocation should be. Some planners suggest that you subtract your age from 100 to come up with an appropriate percentage of stocks to hold in your portfolio to complement the fixed-income securities holdings. So, for example, at age 30 your portfolio should be comprised of 70% stocks and 30% bonds and cash. When you are 55, your portfolio should be 45% in stocks and 55% in bonds and cash. At age 70 you would be 30% in stocks and 70% in bonds and cash. The point is that the closer you are to retirement, the more weight you should give to fixed securities, because you have less time to make up for losses in the market and probably want decreased volatility.

Therapists in the first half of the prime phase may want to consider a moderate asset allocation such as the one presented in Figure 4.1. Older therapists may wish to consider a moderately conservative asset allocation such as the example in Figure 4.2.

One mistake we have seen prime phase therapists make is to try to make up for lost time by being overly aggressive in their investing. As you get older, and thus closer to needing your retirement dollars, it generally makes sense to become more conservative in the asset mix of your retirement account. Our advice to prime phase

☐ Money Market 10%	■ Investment Grade Bond 15%
■ High Yield Bond 10%	■ Government Bond 5%
☐ Large Cap Value 10%	■ Large Cap Growth 10%
■ Mid Cap Value 10%	■ Mid Cap Growth 10%
■ Small Cap Growth 5%	☐ Small Cap Value 5%
■ International 5%	■ Real Estate 5%

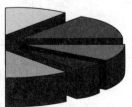

FIGURE 4.1. Moderate Model Portfolio.
(This model is provided for illustrative purposes only. Please consult an investment advisor before purchasing.)

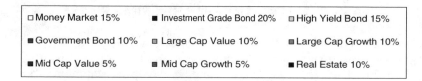

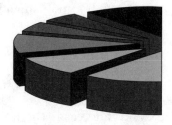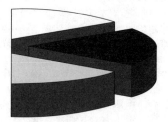

FIGURE 4.2. Moderately Conservative Model Portfolio.
(This model is provided for illustrative purposes only. Please consult an investment advisor before purchasing.)

therapists whose retirement funds are not fully sufficient is to work creatively to find ways to increase regular investments into the retirement fund rather than to invest in ways that are inappropriately risky. In other words, in the prime phase it is generally better to fund aggressively than to skew your asset allocation aggressively.

ESTATE PLANNING IN THE PRIME PHASE

In the prime phase, it becomes increasingly important to address estate planning issues. Among the many important considerations are the financial well-being of one partner should the other predecease him or her; the passing of assets to the next generation; advanced medical directives; and wills. As you move into middle age and beyond, you come increasingly face-to-face with your mortality and thus with estate planning issues.

FACING LIFELONG PATTERNS IN THE PRIME PHASE

Therapists know all too well that characterological patterns can be incredibly resistant to insight, awareness, and change. Dysfunctional financial behavior often causes slow damage to the financial standing of the individual, and by middle age, that slow damage has had time to create a seriously worrisome financial picture. Therapists who find themselves in this position may be well advised to seek out professional psychological and financial help. We have found that many therapists who have thoroughly looked at other of their life issues have not delved very deeply into their financial issues. They have left this dimension of their lives a closed book. In the prime phase, it is clearly not in your interest to avoid vital financial issues. As you face these issues you may well find that the journey of self-discovery is as valuable as the destination of achieving financial stability and well-being.

CHAPTER 5

Elder Phase

What is it about older therapists that is so appealing? Although their bodies inevitably show signs of age, their spirits often maintain a vibrant sense of curiosity and liveliness that many in their 20s might envy. To embark on a career in psychotherapy is to enter into a life-long journey of self-exploration—an ever-deepening appreciation of one's own humanity and the strengths and vulnerabilities of human-kind. Therapists in their elder years have a hard-won wisdom. They have walked with their clients "through the valley of the shadow of death" and arrived at a place where they can truly appreciate life in all its complexity.

AGE AND WISDOM

One of the great rewards of psychotherapy as a profession is the fact that age is an advantage rather than a handicap. Daisy's interns often say to her, "I just can't speak with any authority. People tell me I'm too young." It is very satisfying for Daisy to have reached a position in midlife where she can speak with authority, and even more satisfying to know that as she ages her authority will only increase. Because psychotherapy is a field that values wisdom and integration, the position of elder therapist can be rewarding indeed.

The integration of skill, life experience, and spirituality—however one might define it—finds complete expression in the elder phase.

In looking back on their careers, elder therapists often recognize their own longing for wisdom as a catalyst in their choice of profession:

> "I considered the law, but that was too dry for me. I needed something that dealt with human beings in a very complicated way—that would really help me understand the human condition."

> "Therapy is about a philosophy of life. What we do is work to help people find meaning—not just solve problems, but develop their creativity and begin to live a life that is meaningful to them."

I MIGHT SLOW DOWN, BUT I DON'T WANT TO STOP

A part of wisdom is an increased ability to recognize one's own limitations. It is not possible—nor even desirable—to be all things to all people. Carl Whitaker, one of the great innovators in family therapy, puts it this way: "Over time you have less and less delusion of grandeur and more and more awareness of the process in which you are invested. As you become less enslaved by your role, you have a greater enjoyment of it and experience an ever-growing inner peace of your own."[1]

Aging, of course, brings its own inevitable physical limitations, and the wise elder therapist respects these:

> "I'm 80 years old. When I was about 75, I realized that I needed to let my practice slow down, but I didn't want to give it up and I still don't. Right now I'm in my practice about 10 hours a week—2 of which involve a group I'm leading for the Psychotherapy Institute."

Despite the body's aging, however—even despite struggles with chronic pain or illness—many therapists find their work a source of continued vitality and excitement. One of our interviewees who struggles with fibromyalgia spoke about her feeling that her work is a necessity for her: "I love what I do. It's energizing for me, it keeps my mind going, and offers me connection to the therapist community. My whole life is enhanced by my work."

Therapists also keep their youthful spirit alive through cherishing the rebel, the iconoclast in themselves, and encouraging it in others. From the days of Sigmund Freud, psychotherapy has challenged the status quo. In the words of one of our interviewees:

---

[1] Whitaker, Carl. (1989). *Midnight musings of a family therapist.* New York: Norton.

"There is a piece in me that rebels against conservative rules. Helping people be more of who they really are and let go of trying to be who they think they ought to be is how I keep the rebel in me alive. There's a lot of possibility for freedom in this world. There are certain constraints, I mean I don't kid myself about that, but in terms of how you do the work, there is tremendous freedom, and you get to be on the side of the underdog."

LIVING WITH AMBIGUITY AND INCOMPLETION

We read a comic strip the other day in which one teenager is saying to another: "I thought for sure by the time I was 16 I'd have it all figured out!" It's easy to chuckle at the innocence of that, but many of us live with the expectation that at some point in our lives—maybe 60 or 70 (surely by 80!)—we will have things figured out and feel a sense of completion. The elder phase therapists we spoke with certainly have a sense of satisfaction as they look back on their lives and careers, but not necessarily a sense of completion. According to one therapist, "One of the developmental issues for me in this phase is coming to terms with the fact that everything is going to be incomplete. We don't complete our lives; they are always a work in progress."

One of the challenges for the elder therapist is coming to terms with the unavoidable regrets and incompletions in life and allowing oneself to appreciate the richness of the present moment. It is this sense of balance and wisdom that allows the elder therapist to serve as an invaluable resource to younger members of the community. Many of us in the psychotherapy field come from families in which role models were problematic or absent altogether. It can be both comforting and inspirational to see those on the road ahead of us following that road with courage and grace.

DEALING WITH ISSUES OF MORTALITY

Death is an inescapable fact of life, and during the elder phase this becomes an increasingly personal realization. For some elder phase therapists, a recognition of personal mortality is nothing new:

"My whole practice has been informed by awareness of the fragility of life. I came very close to dying a few years in a row. So I got it, that I don't have forever and that there are things that I need to continue to integrate while there's still time. I'm interested in the questions of What is wisdom? What is transcendence?"

Awareness of mortality frequently leads to life review: "I'm going back to my roots ... looking at what I received in childhood—the good and the bad—and how I have made use of what I received and what I missed."

Perhaps above all, awareness of mortality shapes the way the elder therapist lives his or her life in the present: "How do you live with yourself and others knowing that, you won't be here forever? I'm paying attention to how I can play more, how to give back, how to love people fully and yet be able to let them go."

By the time they have reached the elder phase, most therapists have developed a view of life with a larger perspective—whether traditionally religious, spiritual in a mystical sense, or simply a sense of connection to humanity and the greater whole—that allows them to move through their later years with a sense of confidence and equanimity.

FINANCIAL PLANNING IN THE ELDER PHASE

Retirement Age

Of course, a key issue in retirement planning is the age at which you plan to retire. Whereas 65 was, at one time, the magic age for retirement, this is no longer the case. Some therapists retire early, whereas others enjoy working well beyond age 65. Table 5.1 details the fact that age 65 is being phased out, in favor of age 67, as the full retirement age by the Social Security Administration. For people born in 1937 or earlier, the full retirement age for Social Security remains at 65. For people born in subsequent years, the retirement age gradually rises. For people born in 1960 or later, the full retirement age is 67. Social Security recipients have the option of retiring at 62; however, their benefits are decreased accordingly. In Table 5.1 you will note that taking benefits at age 62 continues to be an option, but with reduced payments.

LIFE EXPECTANCY

The main financial issue surrounding life expectancy is that you not outlive your financial resources. It goes without saying that there is no sure way to know your life expectancy; but because all therapists take social statistics in grad school, you know that such things can be estimated in terms of statistical probability. Visit our website, *http://www.insightfinancialgroup.com,* and choose "Useful Links"

TABLE 5.1
Social Security Chart of Retirement Ages with Reductions for Early Retirement

Year of Birth[a]	Full Retirement Age	Age 62 Reduction Months	Monthly % Reduction	Total % Reduction
1937 or earlier	65	36	.555	20.00
1938	65 and 2 months	38	.548	20.83
1939	65 and 4 months	40	.541	21.67
1940	65 and 6 months	42	.535	22.50
1941	65 and 8 months	44	.530	23.33
1942	65 and 10 months	46	.525	24.17
1943–1954	66	48	.520	25.00
1955	66 and 2 months	50	.516	25.84
1956	66 and 4 months	52	.512	26.66
1957	66 and 6 months	54	.509	27.50
1958	66 and 8 months	56	.505	28.33
1959	66 and 10 months	58	.502	29.17
1960 and later	67	60	.500	30.00

[a] Persons born on January 1 of any year should refer to the previous year.
Source: Social Security Administration. http://www.ssa.gov/retirechartred.htm.

from the side menu bar. Hit the link to the "Life Expectancy Calculator"; there you will be able to obtain a statistical estimate of your expected life span. Once you have estimated your life span, you are ready to estimate the amount of money you need so that you will not outlive your financial resources.

ESTIMATING RETIREMENT RESOURCES NEEDED

Estimating the amount of money you need to support yourself in retirement is a complicated calculation that must account for many factors including inflation, rate of return on investments, life expectancy, and so forth. To help you make this calculation, we have posted a calculator on the Insight Financial Group website. Go to *http://www.insightfinancialgroup.com* and select the "Calculators" link from the menu bar across the top of the page. Next, select the "Retirement" link on the side bar menu and then "Retirement Saving."

To give you an idea of the kind of feedback this tool will provide, we input the following information into the retirement saving calculator:

> You are a single, 60-year-old person with an annual income of $100,000 who plans to live on $75,000 per year when you retire. Retirement savings are $400,000. Inflation is 4%. The desired retirement age is 67 years old. The savings are calculated to last for 20 years. The pre-retirement investment return is 10% per year, whereas the post-retirement income is 8% per year. Social Security benefits are figured into the calculation.

The calculator provides the following estimate based on the data input:

> To provide the inflation-adjusted retirement income you desire, you will need to save 9.2% of your yearly income. This year, for example, the amount would be $9,201, or $767 a month. If you wait just one year to start saving for retirement you will need to save 11.5% of your annual income, which amounts to $11,501 in the first year.

If you first work with the life expectancy calculator and then with the retirement saving calculator, you will have some rational numbers to work with regarding the feasibility of taking your retirement.

DEALING WITH A SHORTFALL IN RETIREMENT FUNDS

Many therapists in the elder phase see patients part time. Two primary reasons include: (1) the continuing need for income to supplement retirement savings, Social Security, and other pensions, and (2) continued excitement for and commitment to the work. If as an elder phase therapist you find that you need to supplement your income with continued clinical work, but you want to stop working, then you should consider consulting with a financial planner to see if he or she might be able to devise a retirement plan. There may be creative ways to solve shortfall problems in the retirement plan.

Ideas for elder therapists who are facing a shortfall of funds include:

Look into a HUD reverse mortgage on your home.
Take out cash values in life insurance policies.
Reduce living expenses by simplifying.
Consider retirement to foreign soil.

HUD Reverse Mortgage

If you are 62 or older and have paid off or have only a small balance remaining on your mortgage, you may want to consider a HUD reverse mortgage (a reverse mortgage program backed by the U.S. Department of Housing and Urban Development). This program gives participants several options for receiving the equity they have built up in their homes. You can receive payments:

In a lump sum (lump sum)
On a monthly basis for a fixed term (term)
On a monthly basis for as long as you live in the home (tenure)
At your discretion with a line of credit (line of credit)

Prospective HUD reverse mortgage applicants are required to receive consumer education and counseling from a HUD-FHA (Federal Housing Administration) approved counselor. The HUD-FHA counselor's job is to help consumers determine if a HUD reverse mortgage is right for them.

A reverse mortgage is different from a home equity loan. A home equity loan requires monthly repayment, whereas the reverse mortgage does not require repayment as long as you live in the home. The lender recovers their principal, plus accrued interest, when you either sell the home or die. Any remaining equity in the home goes either to you, in the event that you sell the home, or to your estate, in the event of your death. If the proceeds of the sale of your home are insufficient to pay the amount owed on the loan, HUD will pay the lender the shortfall. All borrowers pay into a HUD-administered insurance program that creates the pool of money for this contingency.

On a HUD reverse mortgage, the maximum size of the loan is determined by your age, current interest rates, and the value of your home. The older you are at the time of the loan, the higher the percentage of the home's value you may borrow. HUD's website provides hypothetical examples of the percent of home value available at a 9% interest rate (Table 5.2; *http://www.hud.gov:80/*

buying/reverse.cfm). These percentages will vary, so the information is provided to give a ballpark idea of the home value available for a HUD reverse mortgage. The amount that may be borrowed is capped by the FHA mortgage limit for the participant's geographical region. It currently varies from $81,548 to $160,950, depending on housing costs in the participant's locality.

TABLE 5.2
Percentage of Home Value Available for Reverse Mortgage with HUD
Program

Age	Percentage of Home Value Available
Age 65	26%
Age 75	39%
Age 85	56%

Check out the following organizations for more information on reverse mortgages:

U.S. Department of Housing and Urban Development
http://www/hud.gov:80/buying/reverse.cfm
(202) 708-1112

AARP
http://aarp.org
Under "Main Topic Areas," use the "Money and Work" link, then go to "Reverse Mortgages," then "Basics." This website contains thorough and unbiased information.

http://seniorjobbank.org
This website provides extensive information on reverse mortgages.

http://www.simpleliving.com

Using Living Benefits from a Permanent Life Insurance Policy

It is not uncommon for therapists to maintain permanent life insurance while their heirs are still dependent. In some cases, by the time therapists reach the elder phase, their priority shifts from protecting dependents who are now well on their way, to providing for themselves. In such cases it may make sense to explore using living benefits from a permanent life insurance policy.

Surrender for Cash

A permanent life insurance policy may be surrendered for cash. If you have a permanent life insurance policy, you can readily access the surrender value as long as you are willing to accept the tax consequences. The value of the policy minus your current basis in the policy is taxable.

Loans on the Policy

An alternative to surrendering one's policy is to take a loan against the cash value in the policy. Insurance policy loans work very differently from commercial loans. Policy loans will be continued even if no payments are made as long as there is enough cash in the policy to pay the interest. The policy stays in force as long as outstanding loans on the policy are less than the cash value. Many policyholders take loans on their policies with no intention of paying back the loan in their lifetime. Instead, the death benefit to their heirs will be reduced by the outstanding loan amount at the time of the insured's death. Moreover, exceptionally favorable tax treatment exists for life insurance loans. As long as the policy stays in force, there is *no current income tax* due on a policy loan.

Trading your Policy for an Annuity Contract

You may exchange your permanent life insurance policy for an annuity contract tax free as long as there are no outstanding loans on the life insurance policy. You may take the surrender value or maturity of a permanent life insurance policy in the form of an annuity, and defer taxation. Annuity payments may provide elder phase therapists with a guaranteed lifetime of income, or payments over a specific period of time. Annuities are generally difficult for creditors to access and therefore may be worth considering if an elder phase therapist has outstanding debts.

Living Simply

Many elder therapists have lived their lives helping others and have not, for whatever set of reasons, put enough away for retirement to continue with their previously maintained standard of living. If you find yourself in this position, it is important that you work with it creatively. Perhaps you will discover hidden gifts in your set of circumstances as you work with the issues. One shift that such a set of circumstances might lead you to is to work consciously and creatively with simplifying your lifestyle, so that you do not need so much money to live abundantly.

Many therapists are tuned in to the fact that money does not buy happiness. It can be challenging, however, to not let fear take over if you are older and facing a financial shortfall. To work with these issues, elder phase therapists may want to reach out to others who are working with similar issues. You may find such support in a faith community, or with others who have values similar to your own. Two excellent resources for people who want and need to simplify are discussed below:

> Simple Living is a company headed by Janet Luhrs. She directs the website (*http://www.simpleliving.com*), is the author of several thoughtful books, and puts out a journal on the spirituality and joys of living simply. She provides tools and philosophical inquiry into the enjoyment of life in a slower, more attuned mode. Simple Living has become a movement among people who wish to get off the merry-go-round of American materialism. Even if you have all the financial resources you could wish for, you may find much of value in Janet Luhrs' approach.

> *Your Money or Your Life* is a book by Joe Dominguez and Vicki Robin that has become a bible to many people who want to simplify their lives and live according to ecologically and spiritually sound principles. Dominguez and Robin have developed a nine-step system for achieving a life that is "outwardly simple and inwardly rich."

> *Choosing simplicity, often difficult in a consumer culture, means readying oneself for a life that is truer to one's gifts, passions and sense of purpose. ... we have used the term "frugality" to describe this elegant fit between our real needs and we enjoyably and ethically fill those needs.*[2]

Retirement to Foreign Soil

The key to foreign retirement is the strength of the dollar compared to the strength of the local currency. A Social Security pension that is marginal in the United States may afford a very appealing lifestyle in

---

[2] Dominguez, Joe, & Robin, Vicki. (1999). *Your money or your life* (p. xvii). New York: Penguin USA.

another country. A solid resource for foreign retirement is *http:// www.escapeartist.com*, a website devoted to providing realistic information to people who want to retire or move to foreign countries. It has specific information about favorite destinations for U.S. retirees: Argentina, Belize, Canada, Costa Rica, Czech Republic, Ecuador, France, Great Britain, Greece, Ireland, Italy, Mexico, Portugal, Spain, and Thailand.

Three useful books are *The World's Top Retirement Havens*,[3] edited by Margaret J. Goldstein, *Your Guide to Retiring to Mexico, Costa Rica and Beyond: Finding the Good Life on a Fixed Income*,[4] by Shelly Emling, and *The Grown Up's Guide to Retiring Abroad*,[5] by Rosanne Knorr. All are available at *http://www.amazon.com*. There are communities of American retirees living abroad who love their lives outside of the U.S. This option is clearly not for everybody, but if you find the idea intriguing, perhaps some further research will be of interest.

ASSET ALLOCATION IN THE ELDER PHASE

Asset allocation is of critical importance in all phases of a career in private practice. As one gets older, one should generally be more conservative with asset allocation. Therefore, in the elder phase, asset allocation will generally be conservative. A conservative portfolio has a relatively larger position of bonds and money market funds, with a relatively smaller position in stocks. Some exposure to stocks is usually recommended, even in retirement, to allow the portfolio to grow faster than inflation.

A conservative portfolio might have 20% in the money market, 20% in investment-quality bonds, 20% in government bonds, 20% in high-yield (junk) bonds, 10% in large cap value, and 10% in large cap growth (Figure 5.1). The stock positions in the portfolio are a protection against inflation risk; that is, the risk that inflation will grow faster than your portfolio.

REQUIRED DISTRIBUTIONS IN THE ELDER PHASE

If you have a retirement plan such as an IRA, 403(b), SEP, SIMPLE, or 457 plan, you will generally need to start making withdrawals

---

[3] Goldstein, Margaret J. (Ed.). (1999). *The world's top retirement havens.* Berkeley, CA: Publishers' Group West.
[4] Emling, Shelly. (1996). *Your guide to retiring to Mexico, Costa Rica and beyond: Finding the good life on a fixed income.* New York: Avery Penguin Putnam.
[5] Knorr, Rosanne. (2001). *The grown up's guide to retiring abroad.* Berkeley, CA: Ten Speed Press.

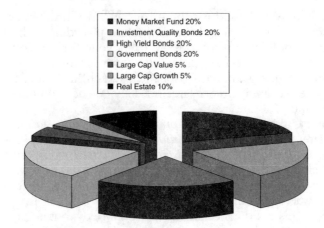

Money Market Fund 20%
Investment Quality Bonds 20%
High Yield Bonds 20%
Government Bonds 20%
Large Cap Value 5%
Large Cap Growth 5%
Real Estate 10%

FIGURE 5.1.   Conservative Model Portfolio.
(This model is provided for illustrative purposes only. Please consult an investment advisor before purchasing.)

from your plan at age 70½. The reason is quite straightforward: the federal government puts a limit on the amount of time it will defer taxes on retirement money. This money is tax deferred, not tax free. Each year after age 70½, you must take a minimum amount out of your retirement plan. This money can then go to fund your living expenses, or, if you do not need it for living expenses, can be reinvested. If you qualify, it can sometimes make sense to move your distributions into a Roth IRA, which goes in as after-tax money but subsequently grows tax free.

Many elder clinicians have 403(b) plans from working in school districts and for other qualifying employers. If you have 403(b) retirement dollars that were contributed prior to 1987, you may be able to delay distribution of those dollars until you are 75 years old. You should discuss these issues with your financial advisor to be certain as to your obligations with regard to making distributions on your 403(b). Another exception for the 403(b) is that if you continue to work past age 70, you can defer the beginning date of your required distributions until the April 1 following the year in which you retire. If you have already rolled your 403(b) into an IRA, then you must follow the 70½ age rule for beginning distributions.

Generally speaking, these distributions will be treated as ordinary income by the IRS. If you have money in your qualified plan payable to a beneficiary when you die, that money will be included in your taxable estate. The money going to your beneficiary will be taxed as ordinary income, but the taxes may be reduced by estate taxes paid on the retirement money. This type of taxation to your beneficiary is known as "income in respect to a descendent."

THE FORM OF YOUR RETIREMENT DISTRIBUTIONS

It is often sensible to have a portion of one's distributions annuitized, while another portion is withdrawn as needed. For example, let's say that Ann Howard, MSW, is 75 years old and has $250,000 in an IRA and $150,000 in a 403(b) from employment with a school district. She has additional assets to help support her retirement. She may want to put her IRA into an annuity contract that will guarantee her income for life while keeping her 403(b) funds in investments that she can draw on as needed. This approach gives her the peace of mind that comes with a lifetime annuity on her IRA along with the flexibility of the investments in her 403(b) plan.

If you are wealthier, or if you have other sources of annuitized income such as a defined benefit plan from your own work or from a spouse, then you may choose to not annuitize your retirement dollars and keep the plan as flexible as possible.

ESTATE PLANNING ISSUES FOR HIGHER NET WORTH THERAPISTS IN THE ELDER PHASE

If your assets are sufficient such that you do not worry that you will outlive your assets, but instead, how much you will leave to your heirs, then some important issues must be considered with regard to your retirement accounts. The estate planning problem with retirement accounts for high-net-worth individuals is that the undistributed value in the retirement plan may be taxed after death as part of the estate. If the plan is then distributed to the beneficiary, it is taxable again to the beneficiary as ordinary income. The effect of these two taxes can take quite a toll on the assets you want to pass on.

One solution to this problem is to stretch the payments of the IRA to include the lifetime of the beneficiary, thereby retaining the IRA's tax-deferred status over several lifetimes. If, for example, your spouse does not need the income from your IRA on your death, you could make your child the beneficiary of your IRA. The IRA's tax-deferred status stays intact and minimum distributions are then calculated according to your child's life expectancy. If, for example, your child is 30 at the time of your death, his or her life expectancy is 52.2 more years, so the IRA's tax deferral could be maintained for an additional 52 years while making minimal distributions each year. If you qualify, you may convert your traditional IRA to a Roth IRA and then stretch the Roth out over more than one lifetime, thereby allowing the minimum distributions to be taken tax free. However, conversion to a Roth is complicated for wealthier clients by the earnings cap for Roth contributions. If the IRA is used to help pay estate taxes, it may not be stretched out in the ways described above.

Another estate planning solution to taxation of the retirement plan after the death of the retiree is to set up an irrevocable life insurance trust. The life insurance death benefit will not be taxable to the beneficiary. Required distributions from the plan can be used to fund the payment of the premium on the life insurance. The life insurance proceeds can generate money for paying estate taxes as well as providing a tax-free wealth transfer to the beneficiaries of the trust. The irrevocable life insurance trust can be a valuable estate planning tool to ensure that you meet your goals for paying your estate expenses and passing on wealth to the next generation.

Yet another way to reduce taxation of your retirement is to gift the maximum allowable $11,000 to family members without incurring gift or estate taxes. You can use your minimum distributions to fund these gifts, and thereby pass the money on to the next generation in a tax-advantaged way. You can give $22,000 to each member of a married couple in any given year if they "split" the gift between husband and wife. Therefore, if you have one child who is married, you can give them a total of $44,000 in a given year without tax consequences. You can gift a child through a 2503(c) trust set up for the benefit of the child. A uniform gift to minors account or uniform transfer to minors account may also be used to make a tax-free gift to a child.

HEALTH INSURANCE IN THE ELDER PHASE

Medicare

Throughout your career you have paid taxes in one way or another that go into the Medicare system. As a private practitioner who pays self-employment taxes, you pay a 2.9% tax for Medicare. We point this out to remind you that Medicare is a benefit you have been paying for your entire career, and if you are age 65, in all likelihood, you are eligible to receive Medicare benefits. Medicare Part A is available to most older Americans at no cost. Medicare Part B was available in 2003 for a premium of $58.70 per month. You should contact Medicare about 3 months before your 65th birthday. You can call them directly at 1-800-633-4227 or you can find them online at *http://www.medicare.gov*. Links to Social Security and Medicare can be found on *http://www.insightfinancialgroup.com* in the "Useful Links" section.

Medicare Part A is hospital insurance. Various deductibles and limitations apply to Medicare Part A. Table 5.3 summarizes deductible and coinsurance coverage provisions for Medicare Part A.

TABLE 5.3
Summary of Deductibles and Coinsurance for Medicare Part A

	Deductibles	Coinsurance
Inpatient hospital	$840 for first 60 days	$210 for 61st–90th day $420 for 91st–150th day for each "lifetime reserve" day used
Skilled nursing facility	No deductible for first 20 days	$105 per day coinsurance (21st–100th day)
Home health care	No deductible (durable medical equipment is subject to $100 deductible)	20% for durable medical equipment
Blood	Cost for the first 3 pints of blood used	

An important note about skilled nursing coverage under Medicare is that custodial care is not provided unless skilled nursing or rehabilitative services are also being provided. Skilled nursing care is provided only when the patient has been hospitalized for at least 3 days. Within 30 days of the 3-day hospital stay, the physician must certify that the patient needs skilled nursing. Again, this is for skilled nursing or rehabilitation, not for custodial care. Skilled services refers to those provided at a separate facility from the hospital with at least one full-time registered nurse, the supervision of a physician, and a physician on call for emergencies.

Home health care can be provided under Medicare after a hospital or skilled nursing facility stay. Home health care benefits under Medicare will pay for the cost of part-time home health aides, medical social services, occupational therapy, medical supplies, and equipment. Medicare does not pay for assistance with housecleaning, meal preparation, dressing, shopping, or bathing. Medicare Part B may cover additional visits or visits without a prior hospital stay. Such Part B home health care must be set up by a physician and require skilled nursing, physical therapy, or speech therapy.

Medigap Insurance

You can see from the discussion above about Medicare that there are a good many deductibles and co-payments involved with the Medicare program (please see Table 5.4). For this reason, many

TABLE 5.4
MEDICARE PART B SUMMARY

Premium	Deductible	Coinsurance	Blood
$58.70 per month in 2003	$100 annually	Most services reimbursed at 80% of Medicare allowable fee	Deductible consists of the cost of first 3 pints

older Americans are choosing Medicare supplemental insurance, known in the industry as Medigap insurance. As the name implies, Medigap insurance is designed to fill in gaps in Medicare coverage. Medigap insurance has been standardized by the National Association of Insurance Commissioners (NAIC): in most states there are 10 plans available, labeled A through J, with increasingly more comprehensive coverage. All individuals age 65 or older may buy any supplemental policy, regardless of health status or preexisting conditions, during the 6-month period after initial enrollment in Medicare Part B.

Insurers cannot exclude coverage of preexisting conditions for more than 6 months. Therefore, it may well be in your interest to purchase such coverage during the period when the insurance companies are obligated to accept your application.

If you have chosen a managed care option for your Medicare coverage, then some special rules apply for Medigap coverage. We have provided a link to the official Medicare site on our website, *http://www.insightfinancialgroup.com*. The Medicare site contains comprehensive information on the rules for guaranteed issue of Medigap coverage. We recommend you examine this information closely, because Medigap coverage can be valuable.

The following information was taken from the official Medicare website in August of 2003.[6] At the time of this writing, the U.S. Congress is working on Medicare coverage issues, the outcome of which may affect the information provided here.

Table 5.5 lists standardized Medigap plans for all states and Washington, DC, except Minnesota, Wisconsin, and Massachusetts. Every company offering Medigap insurance must offer Plan A. In addition, companies may include some, all, or none of the other plans.

---

[6] *http://www.medicare.gov/mgcompare/Search/StandardizedPlans/TenStandardPlans.asp.*

TABLE 5.5
Medigap Plans

Optional Riders	Plans									
	A	B	C	D	E	F[a]	G	H	I	J[a]
Basic benefits	Y	Y	Y	Y	Y	Y	Y	Y	Y	Y
Medicare Part A: inpatient hospital deductible		Y	Y	Y	Y	Y	Y	Y	Y	Y
Medicare Part A: skilled nursing facility coinsurance			Y	Y	Y	Y	Y	Y	Y	Y
Medicare Part B: deductible			Y			Y				Y
Foreign travel emergency			Y	Y	Y		Y	Y	Y	Y
At-home recovery				Y			Y		Y	Y
Medicare Part B: excess charges						100%	80%		100%	100%
Preventive care					Y					Y
Prescription drugs								Basic Y coverage	Basic Y coverage	Extended Y coverage

[a] Plans F and J also have a high-deductible option. If you choose this option, you must pay $1,620 out of pocket per year before the plans pay anything. Insurance policies with a high-deductible option generally cost less than those with lower deductibles. Your out-of-pocket costs for services may be higher if you need to see your doctor or go to the hospital.

Basic benefits included in all plans are:

Inpatient hospital care: Covers the cost of Part A coinsurance and the cost of 365 extra days of hospital care during your lifetime after Medicare coverage ends.

Medical costs: Covers the Part B coinsurance (generally 20% of Medicare-approved payment amount) or co-payment amount, which may vary according to the service.

Blood: Covers the first 3 pints of blood each year.

Disability and Long-Term Care Coverage

In the elder phase, you likely will want to put dollars that previously went to disability insurance into long-term care coverage. We discuss long-term care coverage and disability insurance in Chapter 20, but for the present discussion we will mention that most disability policies stop paying benefits when the insured reaches age 65; so as you approach 65, you should review the actual protection you are receiving from your policy. On the other hand, long-term care coverage usually makes more sense as you age. You may want to pass on the risk of devastating long-term care costs to an insurance company. We often suggest long-term care coverage to our clients in their mid-50s, but we frequently have recommended policies to clients in their 60s and 70s. When considering long-term care insurance, you should discuss it with your financial planner, whose interests are aligned with yours and who is interested not in selling a policy but in advocating for your overall financial well-being. There are many circumstances under which long-term care insurance may not be a necessary expense, particularly if the therapist has either a high net worth or a low net worth. Long-term care insurance makes the most sense for people who are neither rich nor poor (the wealthy may self-insure, whereas low-income seniors may get Medicaid coverage) and who want to save their assets for their heirs.

CONCLUSION

In summary, elder phase therapists are a treasure of experience and wisdom. The psychotherapy field is especially suited to people who wish to continue to work into their elder years. From the financial planning perspective, many issues specific to retirement must be considered. Asset allocation should generally be conservative and income producing; there needs to be a focus on appropriate health and long-term care insurance; and estate planning issues come increasingly to the foreground.

Psychological and Therapeutic Considerations

CHAPTER 6

The Other Side of the Coin: An Overabundance of Money

Money is the most transformational substance in our society. It is seductive, alluring, fascinating and perceived as greatly desirable. It is the American dream.[1]

As we have looked at the phases of the therapist life cycle, we have discussed ways to use one's private practice to provide financial support for oneself and one's family. But what if this is not an issue for you? For a fair number of therapists, the need to make money is not high on their agenda. They may be inheritors—either part of a generational line of family wealth or offspring of parents who worked and saved to be able to pass on a sizeable inheritance to their children. Alternatively, they may have a spouse or partner

---

[1] O'Neill, Jessie. (1996). *The golden ghetto: The psychology of affluence.* Center City, MN: Hazelden Information Education.

who brings in more than enough income to support the family. Why, then, struggle to build a career?

THE ARCHETYPAL JOURNEY OF INDIVIDUATION

As therapists, we understand better than most the power of the archetype. One of the most powerful of these archetypes is the hero or heroine's journey. Countless myths and fairy tales as well as biographies and autobiographies describe the difficulty and the importance of this journey. If the prince had no need to hack his way through the briars to claim his bride, if the princess had no need to open her heart to the beast in order to find the prince within, there could be no story. So it is with our lives. Without struggle, risk, and failure, success becomes meaningless. Jessie O'Neill, author of *The Golden Ghetto*, a therapist and an inheritor herself, has noted, "In America, the archetypal journey of individuation involves making one's own way financially."[2] If financial security is a given, one must carve out another path to self-development. Without the spur of "needing the money" it can be tempting to treat a therapy practice as an avocation—dabbling with a few hand-picked clients rather than doing the work necessary to build a substantial practice. Alternatively, therapists of independent means may tend to treat their practices as "good works," taking a great many pro bono clients and paying no attention to the financial bottom line. Each of these avenues carries its own dangers.

HOW MUCH YOU MAKE = HOW MUCH YOU ARE WORTH

It may be unfortunate, but it is nonetheless a fact of society that people are judged to some extent by how successful they are financially. Because this attitude is so pervasive, most therapists have internalized it. If you offer your services for very little, you can begin to question, "Is what I have to offer really valuable? Would people want it if they had to pay the going rate?" Self-doubt creeps in, and you find it difficult to honor what you do and to command the respect of others.

---

[2] O'Neill, Jessie. (2003). Personal communication.

NO, I'M REALLY NOT MOTHER TERESA

Therapists talk to their clients a good deal about setting limits, taking care of themselves, and avoiding the stance of either "victim" or "rescuer." This important advice applies to therapists as well. No matter how dedicated you are to your profession, no matter how committed to service, no matter how comfortable financially, you must be fairly reimbursed for what you offer. To fail to demand this does a disservice not only to yourself but to your clients. It is difficult for clients to value what they do not pay for; furthermore, it is hard for clients to achieve self-respect when the therapist sends the message that the client cannot manage self-support. When there is an equitable exchange between client and therapist the therapy is built on a stronger foundation than if the therapist devalues his or her services by charging an artificially low fee.

TAKING YOURSELF SERIOUSLY

We have a psychotherapist friend—an heir to a sizeable fortune—who once told us, "I got really bored sitting in a little room all day, so I told all my clients I was taking 6 months off." Because he was charging his clients very little, they were in no position to protest. However, what sort of statement was he making about his own professionalism, commitment to his clients, and, indeed, his understanding of the therapeutic process? To grow in your profession, deepen in your knowledge, and develop your level of skill, it is vital that your practice be a business, not a hobby.

CONCLUSION

Like many things in life, unearned money can be a double-edged sword. It can buy opportunity, a sense of security, and freedom to pursue one's goals without economic concern. On the other hand, if not used with consciousness and deliberation, it can hinder individuation and a sense of personal accomplishment. If you do not need the money your practice generates, then your motivation to create a serious practice must come from within. Seriousness of purpose—as evidenced by involvement in one's professional community, setting professional fees, constancy, and commitment—is vital for succeeding in the journey of individuation that will allow the psychotherapist of independent means the satisfaction of a career well-realized.

CHAPTER 7

The Psychological Dimension

Money—is it the root of all evil or life's highest good? Perhaps it is actually neither of these, but something much more. It is certain that we cannot live without money and equally certain that it carries multiple layers of meaning, some conscious and some unconscious.

It has been said that most people would much rather reveal their sexual secrets than their financial ones. Why is this? The very question, "How much are you worth?" carries a double meaning. Whereas its surface meaning may concern monetary net worth or the bottom line of one's financial statement, at a deeper level the question can resonate with one's insecurities, vulnerabilities, and fears of being "not quite enough." Are you successful "enough"? Are you measuring up to your peers? To your parents' expectations?

Your attitudes toward money are deeply ingrained and have their roots in your earliest history. Your family of origin sent many messages, both tacit and overt, about the meaning of money, its proper place in your life, appropriate ways to use it and talk about it, etc. Because they are often so deeply buried, issues about money can be among the most difficult to bring to consciousness. Daisy remembers thinking, as she was involved in intensive therapy in her 30s, "If I work to develop myself in every other area, I think it would be okay to just leave money alone." The naiveté of this idea leaves Daisy speechless now. However, it is our experience that this kind of attitude about money on the part of therapists is not too uncommon. Looking at your attitudes toward and wounds around money can be painful and frightening. Nevertheless, it is a vital piece of building a solid financial foundation.

Achieving a level of comfort with money attitudes is equally important for your work with patients. If you shy away from the topic, you deprive the people you work with a safe space to explore a significant area of their lives. On both a personal and a clinical level, you ignore money issues at your peril.

MONEY: WHAT IS IT REALLY?

As with many of life's fundamental issues, money is both real and symbolic. Although the answer to "What is money?" may seem obvious, the reality is that there are many answers. On a physical level, money is the "greenback dollar." On a social level, money is an agreement between and among people to honor a particular medium of exchange. On a spiritual level, money can be said to be energy made visible. This discussion concentrates on the emotional meaning of money—something that can vary widely from one individual to the next.

AN OBJECT RELATIONS PERSPECTIVE

What was the meaning of money in your family of origin? Was there never enough of it, so that it took on the aura of the frustrating, unattainable object? Was there too much available, making it into an exciting, overstimulating object? Did your parents treat money as a weapon? As a pacifier? As a substitute for other kinds of nurturing? Almost everyone has feelings of guilt, shame, and anxiety around money. Based on your experience in your family of origin, you have developed a particular representation of the self as a financial person, a representation of money as an object, and an affect state linking the two.[1]

Maybe your father (like Daisy's) was a controller who used money as a way of maintaining his power over family members. His need to be "the one with the knowledge" required the rest of the family to assume an ignorant and helpless role in relation to money. Daisy grew into adulthood feeling as if she were totally powerless in money matters. Her feelings toward her father had been transferred

---

[1] Kernberg, Otto. (1992). *Aggression*. New Haven, CT: Yale University Press.

to money itself. Indeed, just trying to balance a checkbook could send her to bed with a migraine. Needless to say, her feelings of powerlessness were neither realistic nor helpful to her as an adult. However, they were so firmly embedded in her unconscious that it took years of work to see them for what they were. Any efforts to deal with financial issues aroused such negative feelings about herself that she would begin to feel tremendous anxiety and then defend against that anxiety (i.e., the migraine).

Contrast this with the experience of a college friend whose father was a high-stakes gambler. Her father constantly carried the family through wildly fluctuating cycles of "boom and bust." Her mother was passive and co-dependent, either unable or unwilling to confront her father about his lack of responsibility. At an early age, my friend took on the mantle of "the responsible one." She pinched pennies, squirreled away money, and never told anyone the full truth about how much was available. Today, she is a physician making a very comfortable living. However, the old habits still hold. She has a separate account that she is unwilling to discuss with her husband, and she stashes cash in various hiding places around her home and office. She is unable to decathect from her relationship to money as something unpredictable and elusive.

The following exercise can be useful in beginning to uncover your underlying feelings about having or not having money. Take 30 minutes to sit quietly with a journal or notebook. Ask yourself these questions:

What is my earliest memory concerning money?
What painful memories do I have concerning money? What is the emotion involved?
What pleasant memories do I have around money? What is the emotion involved?
What do I remember my mother telling me about money?
How about my father?
What seemed to be the general feeling in the family when the subject of money came up?

Half an hour may seem like a very short time to work with this material, and indeed it is enough only to make a beginning. However, once you dip your toe in the water, chances are good that memories will continue to surface and you may find yourself developing a new understanding of how you relate to money and how this impacts your life in the present.

CHAPTER 8

Characterological Defenses Around Money Wounds

No one in this culture grows up without some form of wounding around money issues. Money, and the excess or deficiency thereof, is such a powerful force in our society, and yet there continues to be so little understanding of and dialogue about its power. The result is that people develop defenses that prevent them from dealing with money in a healthy, life-affirming way. The following section provides an opportunity for you to reflect on the way you, your clients, and your family members deal with money and financial issues. Remember that—as Peter likes to say to anxious trainees—"Everybody's got to have their defenses." A clearer understanding of where you are now is the first step on the road to where you would like to be.

NARCISSISTIC DEFENSE

For people with narcissistic wounds around money, money can function as an externalized way of dealing with precarious self-esteem regulation. Money represents the inflated self. This can manifest in two ways. For the narcissist who identifies with the inflated self, money is a means of winning the admiration and approval of others through the projection of a "larger-than-life" image and thus becomes a manifestation of the false self. This can be expressed through overspending, excessive credit card debt, or the "large hat—no cattle" syndrome in which the appearance of success is maintained at the expense of true financial well-being. For the person with grandiose narcissistic defenses, driving a Honda Civic would produce a sense of shame that would trigger unbearable anxiety. Much better to overextend credit and buy a Mercedes. As the individual becomes increasingly overextended, the feelings of worthlessness (deflation) increase, and these feelings must be defended against with ever more frantic overspending.

In contrast, people who are defending from a deflated narcissistic position may pride themselves on how well they are able to "do without." In this case, driving a Honda Civic would also be a source of shame. It is much more ego-syntonic to buy a 15-year-old clunker that they hold together with baling wire. Narcissistic characters may live far above or far below their means. In either case, money is used more to silence the inner voice ("You'll never really measure up" or "Who do you think you are, anyway?") than to serve the individual's true best interests. Future needs (e.g., retirement planning) are ignored in favor of easing feelings of anxiety and shame in the present.

Whereas both the grandiose and the deflated narcissistic defenses focus on avoiding shame, the malignant narcissistic defense carries this avoidance to a whole new level! In the person of this character type, anger has become rage and anxiety has become terror. There is a deep-seated conviction that others cannot be trusted, and therefore one has to maintain power and control in any way one can. Such individuals believe they live in a hostile world that is waiting to take away whatever is not well protected and where there is no justice except for what power provides. Money represents parental power over them in childhood and their power over others in the present. Any vulnerability spells tremendous danger, and so they work tirelessly to make themselves financially impregnable. Money is not a means to enjoying luxuries or attaining freedom, but quite simply a way of amassing power in the interests of an ever-elusive sense of safety. As one patient told me, "I keep thinking that the next million will do it, but somehow it's never quite enough."

The internal conflict for those with malignant narcissistic character is between their belief in their own "larger-than-life" qualities (reinforced by the mother) and their "lower-than-dirt" qualities (attacked by the father). Feeling both entitled and under attack, such people use money as a way to control and intimidate others. Intimacy and even empathy are experiences they cannot afford. To fend off feelings of worthlessness, they must work tirelessly to achieve more and ever more. As they move toward midlife, they may well feel isolated and depressed, having insulated themselves so successfully that their human connections have atrophied.

ORAL DEFENSE

Stephen Johnson describes people with the oral character as living in the land of "paradise lost."[1] People with this sort of defense had an experience of being cherished and nurtured and then abruptly lost it. Perhaps a younger sibling was born too soon. Perhaps their mother became ill or depressed or absented herself in some way. Such individuals carry this sense of having been let down or abandoned into adulthood and develop a sort of chronic, unappeasable neediness. You may have had the experience of counseling such a patient and feeling that nothing you do can possibly be enough.

Because the needs of people with an oral character are so painful, and acknowledging them seems hopeless and overwhelming, they defend against those feelings with a sort of counterdependency: "I can take care of everyone. I really need nothing for myself." Unable to meet or even acknowledge their own needs in the interpersonal sphere, these people will often turn to self-soothing through spending. Fearing that their needs for love and intimacy are doomed to disappointment, they use the accumulation of material goods as a substitute. For example, after an argument with her husband ("He never listens to what I want!"), such a woman may well visit the mall and max out her credit cards. This, of course, will lead to a feeling of guilt over her "selfishness," so she will spend even more money buying gifts to "take care" of the other. As with the narcissistic character, people with the oral character may spend more than they can afford—not in an effort to impress others, but rather an increasingly frantic effort to soothe their own sense of deprivation.

SYMBIOTIC (BORDERLINE) DEFENSE

The central issue for people with a symbiotic defense structure is an abiding fear of abandonment. James Masterson has written eloquently of the anxiety that arises in this character type when they move toward self-activation.[2] In an effort to avoid this anxiety, those

---

[1] Johnson, Stephen M. (1994). *Character styles.* New York: W.W. Norton.

with a symbiotic character can fall into the trap of allowing themselves to be defined by the other. Differentiation can seemingly result only in abandonment. They often find themselves in serious financial difficulties due to their inability to confront the financial behaviors of those close to them. If they have a circle of friends who can afford to spend freely on entertainment and travel, they will follow their lead, ignoring the reality of their own more modest means or their need to provide for their future.

The trouble is magnified when a person with the symbiotic character has a partner who is financially irresponsible. I (Daisy) once worked with a patient who had worked hard and lived frugally in order to put aside a substantial sum for retirement. When she was in her 50s, she turned over her entire retirement account to her husband to invest in a "hot stock tip." Within 2 years, he had lost 2/3 of the money, as well as a substantial amount belonging to my patient's elderly mother! Needless to say, my patient was enraged. But it was her own symbiotic defense that had sabotaged her. Unwilling to "stand apart" from her husband and risk his abandonment, she had turned a blind eye to his financial dealings—never questioning, or even inquiring about, his decisions.

The symbiotic defense results in an avoidance of confrontation and often an effort to control through manipulation. Rather than look squarely at their own thoughts and feelings, needs and desires, such people will expect the other to "read their mind" and respond to their obliquely expressed wishes. This allows them to maintain the illusion of merger ("It's amazing how we think alike!") and sidestep the difficult and threatening work of understanding and expressing themselves as individuals.

MASOCHISTIC DEFENSE

The person with a masochistic defense struggles with a core feeling of being controlled and victimized. Money has come to represent the controlling parent who withheld the nurturing needed for the child to survive and develop. Raised in a family that was both controlling and withholding, those with a masochistic character develop a bitter resentment of the world, which "just doesn't treat them right." As children they felt (and indeed were) helpless in the face of more powerful adults and so learned to turn this resentment inward. As adults, they may take a certain perverse pride in their own financial suffering, as it demonstrates how poorly they continue to be

---

[2] Masterson, James. (1990). *The search for the real self.* New York: Touchstone Books.

treated. The masochistic defense leads to self-defeating behavior around financial matters. Such people may consistently pay their bills late, racking up late fees and damaging their credit. They may delay routine maintenance on their home until minor repairs become major expenses. They may take jobs that are well beneath their abilities and complain bitterly about being underpaid.

One of us sees a patient who is an extremely capable nurse who is well able to get an advanced degree or move into management. However, she stays in her staff position, all the while protesting that, "It just isn't fair. Floor nurses should get paid better." Because of the secondary gains (proving conclusively that it's all "their" fault), letting go of the masochistic defense can be difficult. It means shifting one's self-image and one's worldview. Failure to do so, however, can only result in the masochistic character becoming stuck in a box that grows ever smaller through the life cycle.

SCHIZOID DEFENSE

Having been neglected, abandoned, or hated by their parents in early childhood, people with a schizoid defense carry a feeling that they deserve none of what money can offer. Their defense is to withdraw from both themselves and others. In the extreme, this can become a dissociated state. Individuals with the schizoid character typically have trouble accessing their life force. To reach out for anything—food, affection, or material goods—does not feel possible. Indeed, these people are often convinced at a very deep level that they do not have a right to take up space or exist at all.

A schizoid defense does not necessarily stem from material deprivation in early life. Peter has treated several people with schizoid characters who grew up with considerable wealth. Despite their comfortable childhood environment, these patients were emotionally destitute because their self-absorbed, absentee parents left the job of childrearing to hired caretakers. As adults, people with a schizoid defense may have trouble holding a job equal to their abilities. They may live in a style so simple as to be almost spartan, denying themselves comfort and sometimes even the basic necessities. The schizoid defense allows only the most arid of lives; and as these people grow older the world appears to be an increasingly frightening, overwhelming place. To begin to move out of this pattern, they need patient support and a great deal of courage.

REPETITION OR HEALING?

Therapists are only too familiar with the repetitive impulse. Driven by a powerful, unconscious urge to "make it come out different," most people replay old patterns from their childhood. The woman with an alcoholic father somehow winds up marrying one alcoholic man after another. The man with a cold and distant mother finds himself drawn only to women who cannot return his affection. The same impulse plays itself out in people's financial lives. My mother grew up during the Great Depression and was hard pressed to throw anything away. Today, I (Daisy) still catch myself saving string and rubber bands far beyond the bounds of common sense.

However, the repetitive impulse is not the only force at work in our unconscious. Equally powerful is the inclination toward growth and healing. Indeed, without this inclination psychotherapy would be a fruitless endeavor. When it comes to working with financial issues, two aspects are equally important. First, you must develop an understanding of your defenses and the wounds that underlie them. As you begin to work with and resolve your emotional issues, you free yourself to learn to deal effectively with your finances on a practical level. Allowing yourself to be ruled by the repetitive impulse can be very dangerous to your financial well-being. To avoid this, you must be willing to tolerate a fair amount of anxiety as you explore both the internal and the external dimensions of your financial picture. It is in taming this anxiety that we can begin to work creatively with money.

Once you have gained insight into money's symbolic meaning in your emotional life, you become more empowered to move toward financial mastery. You learn the "rules of the game"—how money works and how you can make it work for you. As you gain mastery, your old wounds around money become less debilitating and a positive cycle is set in motion.

The key here is maintaining a stance of patience and self-acceptance. Few people have had good role models or helpful mentors around money matters. Almost everyone struggles with feelings of shame or inadequacy: "Certainly (at my age, with my education, with my years of experience) I 'should' know more than I do." There may be a sense that "I can't possibly get there from here." However, as Gestalt therapists maintain, true change occurs only through first accepting what is. The greater your willingness to learn about yourself without attacking yourself, the greater your potential for moving forward.

CHAPTER 9

What Is Financial Well-Being?

I don't want to end up simply having visited this world.[1]

Is it true that "the one who dies with the most toys wins"? Does financial success equal being able to buy whatever you want whenever you want? Most therapists have worked with enough miserably unhappy wealthy people to know that the following adage is correct: "Money does not buy happiness." True financial well-being ultimately depends on being able to answer "yes" (at least most of the time!) to two questions:

Are you making conscious choices?
Is your life in balance?

Making conscious choices involves defining your values, your goals, and your priorities and living a lifestyle that supports them. One of our daughters is a yoga instructor who lives on a very minimal income. Whereas her friends from college are buying

---

[1] Oliver, Mary. (1993). When death comes. In *New and selected poems*. Boston: Beacon Press.

condos and new cars, she lives in a studio apartment and drives a 1989 compact. However, her life is rich in relationships and in a conviction that she is following her spiritual path and making a significant contribution to her community. Certainly, her priorities may shift over the years, but hopefully she will continue to consciously choose a lifestyle that reflects her core values.

At the other end of the spectrum, we have a friend who has decided to work at her maximum capacity, putting away 2/3 of her income, for the next 5 years in order to be able to retire at 55. She is sacrificing present comfort and leisure for the promise of a life that she can shape entirely as she chooses. She has consciously set her priorities and is living in a way that reflects her values.

Living a life in balance means developing an orientation to money that is respectful without being overanxious. A respectful attitude toward money allows us to appreciate it as the power that it is. Money can be said to be energy made tangible. We give our time in exchange for it and it provides a necessary foundation for our lives. If we act out around money (through overspending, mismanagement, willful ignorance, etc.), we demonstrate a dangerous lack of respect. On the other hand, too much anxiety around our treatment of money can be equally disastrous. If we save compulsively, without ever spending freely; if we feel compelled to earn more and more because "it's never enough," then money takes on the role of a tyrant in our lives. Both disrespect and overanxiety prevent us from working creatively with money. Balance allows us to make use of our money to create a life that is whole, in which all the pieces—work, spending, relationships, and values—fit together.

MONEY IN THE FAMILY SYSTEM

Psychological Individuation—Intertwined with Financial Individuation

Financial autonomy is a powerful symbol of adulthood. Nothing signifies individuation more than making one's own way financially, and conversely, nothing keeps families enmeshed quite like money entanglements. As we have discussed, the ways people deal with money frequently represent unresolved issues from childhood. As one moves forward on the lifelong journey of individuation, the resolution of the psychological issues is interwoven with learning how to make one's financial life function effectively.

"Pseudo" Financial Individuation

Success at making money does not, in and of itself, demonstrate that one is successfully individuating. Indeed, the drive to make huge sums of money may be more reflective of the person's succumbing to family-of-origin pressures than of having the necessary integration to follow his or her own path. People often try to resolve emotional issues through financial means. For example, Daisy works with a patient whose father constantly belittled his dreams of becoming a writer. Wealth was the only goal worth pursuing in the father's eyes, and there was no such thing as enough. Today, this man is incredibly successful financially. He has learned to manipulate the economic system most effectively. At midlife, however, with his relationships in shambles, he is finally face to face with the fact that his life has been much more about proving something to his father than about pursuing his own path. A somewhat less extreme example is a colleague with training and interest in Jungian analysis. He, too, comes from a family that values wealth over self-expression. He was able to withstand family pressure and pursue psychological training, but now does psychological evaluations almost exclusively, "because it just pays so much better" than problems whose nature is more emotional. Clearly, wealth and success are no substitute for resolution of the psychological issues of childhood.

At the same time, psychological integration alone is not sufficient. We have a close friend who is, in many ways, one of the most emotionally and spiritually developed people we know. She has a very busy practice and has worked in her own therapy and her spiritual practice toward self-knowledge and integration. However, she has paid little or no attention to the financial realities of life. Her pro bono cases often outnumber her paying clients and she has managed to put away almost nothing toward her retirement. As she enters her 60s, she is faced with the prospect of working to a much older age than she would choose. If she should suffer a debilitating illness, her only choice would be to become dependent on her adult children.

True individuation entails assuming the mantle of adulthood in all areas. We must accept responsibility for ourselves and our lives both emotionally and financially. In doing so, we have the potential to free ourselves from enmeshment—with our families of origin, our partners, or our own children.

FAMILY RULES AROUND MONEY

We teach a community education class in Sacramento, California, called "Seven Steps to Financial Well-Being." In that class we ask people to tell their family stories about money. As they talk we are listening for examples of their family rules around money. As family therapists know, rules may be either overt (explicitly stated) or covert (never spoken aloud, but everyone shares an understanding). In listening to these family stories over the years, it has become clear to us that rules about money most often fall into the covert category. When something goes unspoken (the elephant in the living room) it tends to assume enormous psychological power. Covert rules become embedded in the psyche, and it can be very difficult to even begin to articulate them, let alone think about changing them.

Because the couple forms the foundation of the family, understanding how couples communicate about money can be the beginning of understanding how family rules are made. Increased understanding can free the couple and the family to consider what rules they are living by and to make conscious decisions about rules that support the values they want to uphold. In the following chapter we explore couples and money.

CHAPTER 10

The Couple's Money Dance

Once you become a member of a committed couple, your financial life is no longer yours alone. How successful you will be in living consciously depends, in part, on your partner and the effectiveness of the communication that the two of you establish. Certainly, a saver and a spender who never communicate about money have a partnership in serious trouble. However, trouble can also arise in more subtle forms. In this chapter we take a look at a model that provides ways for a couple to deepen their communication and more effectively address the emotional, interpersonal, and practical dimensions of their financial life together.

MONEY—THE QUINTESSENTIAL INTERPERSONAL ISSUE

Money's very purpose is to serve as a medium of exchange between people. This purpose makes it, perhaps, the quintessential interpersonal issue. Inevitably, then, money reflects both the conscious side and shadow side of human relations. On the conscious side, money can represent generosity, individuation, self-esteem, self-activation, and the ability to care for oneself and one's family. On the shadow, or unconscious, side, money can represent social injustice, feelings of deprivation, entitlement, enmeshment, lust for power, and a myriad of unresolved family-of-origin issues. Both the conscious and unconscious sides become manifest in marriage and other intimate relationships. Only as you are able to bring the shadow side into awareness and communicate about it with your partner will you be able to shape your financial life successfully.

Freud taught long ago that the id, ego, and superego comprise a dynamic system that is ever changing. This applies to money issues no less than to other areas of life. No one can deal with money solely from the ego, or conscious, part of their being. The stakes are too high, anxiety is too great, family history is too compelling, social class issues are too powerful, and primitive feelings of greed, entitlement, and deprivation are too strong for anyone to have a simple, one-dimensional relationship with money.

Whereas individuals may strive for as much financial self-awareness as they can muster, for couples, it is communication that allows them to work productively with the unconscious material. We are not proposing some platonic ideal of perfection for couples in their communication about finances. Rather, we are suggesting that couples can move toward increasing their conscious awareness, insight, and communication in forming an effective financial partnership. Deepening financial communication can help couples function together in such a way that money supports their life goals and enhances their relationship.

FOUR LEVELS OF COMMUNICATION

Level 1: Rigid financial communication
Level 2: Concrete financial communication
Level 3: Emotionally informed financial communication
Level 4: Flexible and effective financial communication

CASE STUDY: BARBARA AND DAVE

Barbara and Dave are a married couple in their early 40s with three young children. Barbara is a psychologist in private practice and Dave is a self-employed carpenter. Their combined annual income is about $160,000, with Barbara making substantially more than Dave. Barbara and Dave fought about money frequently, but had not addressed the underlying emotional issues until they started couple's therapy. Barbara felt that Dave overspent on himself. Dave felt that Barbara was controlling and selfish about money. Their arguments about money felt endless and fruitless to them.

Barbara and Dave spent several years in couple's therapy. Because money was a volatile and complicated issue for them, much of their time was spent working on communication around financial matters. As their work progressed, Barbara and Dave moved through the four levels of communication, away from stereotyped roles and rigid communication toward intimate communication about feelings.

Dave's History

Dave had been very much neglected as a child by parents who lived a "high life" and did not attend to his needs. Dave's father, a heavy drinker, was a lobbyist who spent his high-flying clients' money lavishly on legislators and other influential people but did not support Dave in his endeavors, such as athletics and science. Dave felt himself to be a castoff, a bum. Although quite intelligent, Dave never went to college. He carried a "wad of cash" in his pocket, which made him feel good and which he spent rather lavishly, giving financial gifts and bonuses frequently to guys working in his carpentry crew. The wad of cash made Dave feel powerful, was something of an identification with his free-spending father, and served as a transitional object that he could touch and feel, reassuring him that he was not a "loser."

Barbara's History

Barbara was raised by a perfectionist mother while her father was largely absent. Her parents divorced when she was 8 and fought for years over her custody more as a way to stay engaged and enraged at each other than out of a desire to parent her. She specializes in custody evaluations and her professional mission is to help children who are caught in divorcing families. She sees herself very much as the child's advocate. Her self-image was that of the girl who could not do things quite well enough to please her critical mother. Her mother had a perfectionistic approach to finances: she insisted that everything should be highly organized, controlled, and well planned out. Although Barbara rebelled against this financial perfectionism (which was part of her attraction to Dave), she had also internalized much of it. So, when Dave walked around with a wad of cash in his pocket and spent it, she felt highly critical of him for behaving in such an uncontrolled, imperfect manner.

Difficulties in the Relationship

When Dave overspent, Barbara felt the internalized criticism of her mother for his wastefulness along with the feeling that she was being neglected by Dave as she was by her absent father. She would lash out at Dave with verbal tirades. When she would rage, all he could hear was that she wanted the financial resources for herself. He felt she was neglecting his needs and that she was a "controlling bitch." They fought about his spending habits and her controlling perfectionism. Until they were able to address the underlying emotional issues, they were caught in a repetitive, frustrating, destructive conflict.

RIGID FINANCIAL COMMUNICATION

When a couple is caught in rigid communication, they often live as if they are simply two individuals sharing the same house, but with separate financial lives. Another scenario is that one person takes control and the other person does not feel the need to be involved in the finances. Whatever shape the rigidity takes, rigid communication assumes that the financial issues are simple and that an inflexible, noncommunicative structure will suffice to take care of them in a life partnership. Our experience with couples is that this rarely remains the case for very long. Life has a way of complicating the best-laid plans to keep things simple. Even couples with prenuptial agreements frequently find that finances have a way of becoming commingled and complicated.

Couples using rigid communication are acting on the unspoken assumption that the financial life of a couple can be kept uncomplicated and untouched by the emotional issues that affect the relationship. Not only is this vision of an uncomplicated financial life almost always illusory, it ignores the potential of working with the financial issues to foster intimacy. When the couple realizes that their financial lives are indeed intertwined, they can begin a process of communicating about their financial needs, responsibilities, and difficulties.

Barbara and Dave using Rigid Financial Communication

Barbara and Dave married in their late 30s. Both were established in their work when they married. In the first few years Barbara took control of the family finances. After all, she was organized and he was not. It seemed the obvious and simple way to approach the family finances. Soon, however, certain patterns of behavior on both of their parts began to annoy and anger the other. She disapproved of his "wad of cash" and wasteful spending, and he found her to be controlling and judgmental. When Barbara became pregnant with their first child, the arguments got worse, and rigid communication gave way to concrete communication.

CONCRETE FINANCIAL COMMUNICATION

At this level of financial communication, the couple is dealing openly with the external, pragmatic financial issues that face a couple or family. This level of communication is an improvement on rigid communication because it does allow for give and take around the practical issues. However, in concrete communication the underlying emotional issues and assumptions are not directly addressed openly. Because of this, issues tend to get acted out in ways that are indirect and possibly destructive.

Dave and Barbara using Concrete Financial Communication

Dave and Barbara fought constantly. She complained bitterly about his spending habits while he felt that she just wanted control for its own sake. Unaware of any underlying emotional issues, they engaged in bitter arguments of accusations without any movement toward understanding or resolution. When the arguments seemed to threaten the viability of their relationship, they came in for couple's therapy.

EMOTIONALLY INFORMED FINANCIAL COMMUNICATION

At this level, the couple has developed some insight into their emotional issues with money. They have begun to understand how their feelings about money derive from their history, as well as develop some understanding and empathy for the family-of-origin issues that affect their partner's attitudes toward and behaviors around money. At this level, communication is often far less rancorous than it was at the level of concrete financial communication. Communication at this level requires the capacity to speak about and listen to the underlying issues. Compassion will often emerge in the couple as the issues are articulated at the emotional level.

Dave and Barbara using Emotionally Informed Financial
Communication

In the therapy sessions, Dave and Barbara learned about each
other's history with money in their families of origin. They
came to understand where the other was coming from emotionally. For example, Barbara learned that carrying the wad
of cash was very reassuring for Dave. Dave learned that just
carrying the cash around was enough to make him feel good,
and he felt less need to actually spend it. Dave also learned
that Barbara's need to keep financial matters under control is
more than just a "power trip." As Barbara came to better
understand her anxiety around loss of control, she became
less apt to lose her temper with Dave. He, in turn, learned
that Barbara's mother would shame her when things were not
"perfect" and thus he developed a sense of understanding
and compassion for her. This allowed him to be patient with
her anxiety over his more casual approach to money.

FLEXIBLE AND EFFECTIVE FINANCIAL COMMUNICATION

This optimal level of financial communication is achieved when the
couple has developed an understanding of each other's emotional
issues with money. The couple is now able to deal effectively with
the practical financial concerns while also addressing their emotional
issues. They are able to plan together, laugh at their foibles, make
decisions, and deal with mistakes without undue recrimination.
Admittedly, no couple can maintain this level all the time; but once
a couple has learned to function in this way, they begin to build a
foundation of trust and goodwill that will serve them well during the
difficult passages that all couples inevitably face.

Dave and Barbara using Flexible and Effective Financial
Communication

Dave and Barbara struggled diligently in therapy for several
years and learned a lot about themselves and each other.
Glimpses of flexible, effective financial communication
could be seen when they were buying a new house.
Although they fought about the old issues, they were rather
quickly able to rise out of the old rancor and deal with some
anxiety-provoking issues with a good deal of awareness and
capacity for self-reflection. They bought a house that met
their needs quite nicely and did so with a good deal of

cooperation and good humor. When Barbara started complaining that the house was not quite good enough and that the deal was less than perfect, Dave suggested to her that her old perfectionism was at work, and she was able to laugh at her own proclivities while moving forward with a deal that was in her self-interest.

CHAPTER 11

Complementary Work: Referring to and Working with a Financial Planner

So far the focus of this book has been on examining how money and our responses to money impact our lives. In this chapter we would like to explore three very specific ways in which money impacts a therapist's clinical work and how the clinical work impacts financial decisions.

Do you remember taking your licensing exam? I think all therapists remember that stage of their careers and the anxiety that accompanied it. In Daisy's experience, one of the principal things the examiners were interested in was her ability to make appropriate referrals—to a physician, a psychiatrist, 12-step groups, and so forth. For many clients, and for yourself, referral to a financial planner might be most helpful. If you can find a financial planner who understands the emotional dimension of financial work, you might talk with him or her about cross-referring. Working with a psychotherapist on the emotional issues and a financial planner on the practical issues can provide your clients with the powerful tools they need to get their finances in order.

The therapeutic task is not so much to change the meaning and associations your clients have to money as to help bring these feelings, thoughts, and associations to conscious awareness. When brought to awareness, clients' feelings about money can help them move forward, empowering action with conscious motivation in their economic life, rather than to act out unconscious material. The task of the financial planner, then, is to help clients translate this newly developed consciousness into practical steps designed to create financial security and empowerment.

EXAMPLE: SARAH

Sarah, a 60-year-old clinical social worker, is one of our financial planning clients. She grew up in an upper middle class Jewish family in Marin County, California, where her father was an attorney and her mother was a homemaker. Her financial issues centered around the fact that her father was authoritarian and controlling about money. Her mother was kept on a tight allowance for family expenses. Money was never discussed but was nevertheless used as a weapon of paternal power and control. Her father lavished money on her brother's educational expenses for law school but was tight fisted with Sarah's educational expenses. He did not encourage her social work career, viewing social work and psychotherapy as frivolous compared with the practice of law.

Sarah had been self-supporting since completing her MSW. She had lived on a private practice income (supplemented with some agency-based work) while raising her son as a single mother. She frequently felt overwhelmed and anxious about her financial life but did not receive financial help from her parents because she found asking for money to be shameful and humiliating. When her father died 2 years ago (her mother had died 9 years earlier) her inheritance was sizable. Although she had been looking forward to the financial independence her inheritance would bring, she nevertheless felt considerable anxiety about dealing with it.

Because the account was in a self-help online brokerage that her father had managed, she was receiving no professional investment advice before she connected with us. She had became immobilized about doing anything with her inheritance, which sat unattended in stock securities, some of which had held ground while others had lost ground during a recent market decline. When she came for financial consultation, she was feeling scared because of the decline in value in her stock portfolio. She was afraid to take action to change the portfolio but was also afraid *not* to take action. In crafting an investment strategy, we designed a mix of securities and bonds that fit her time horizon and risk tolerance. Concurrently, we discussed the emotional issues that the inheritance brought up for her.

We referred her to a therapist with a psychodynamic orientation. In a rather short amount of time, she gained insight into the sources of her anxiety and was much better able to contain the anxiety in order to work with her portfolio in a rational way. She became aware that her father had humiliated her and had damaged her sense of self as an empowered agent in her financial life. She also became aware of her identification with her mother, who also was subject to her father's authoritarian style. She further worked through some difficult issues with her brother around family history and the inheritance.

In facing her fears, Sarah became able to separate her emotional responses from the investment decisions she needed to make in her own self-interest. It was the insight into her own history and growing mastery of her anxiety that gave her the emotional containment she needed to manage her inheritance effectively.

In dealing with money, it is important to honor the feelings and then to act with rational, enlightened self-interest. Honoring and sorting through the feelings can be a difficult and anxiety-provoking journey. When you commit yourself to doing the hard work of self-discovery, you are laying important groundwork for your financial success.

HOW TO CHOOSE A HIGHLY QUALIFIED FINANCIAL PLANNER

For most therapists in private practice, it makes good sense to work with a financial planner, because running one's own business necessitates a good many financial decisions, many of which may benefit from professional input. Probably the best way to find a reputable financial planner is to ask people you respect in your personal and professional network if they are working with a financial planner with whom they are happy, and then interview him or her. If you choose to work with a financial planner, the following can help you determine if he or she is highly qualified.

Look for someone with advanced training and qualifications. The ChFC and CFP are the two most widely accepted professional designations for financial planners. The ChFC (chartered financial consultant) designation is administered by the American College in Bryn Mawr, Pennsylvania. The CFP (certified financial planner) certification is administered by the CFP Board of Standards in Denver, Colorado. ChFCs and CFPs have taken a comprehensive curriculum in financial planning and have met specific experience, continuing education, and ethical requirements. Some CPAs earn a financial planning designation called the PFS (personal financial specialist), which consists of a comprehensive financial planning curriculum on top of the usual CPA requirements. Other qualified financial planners hold an MBA or law degree.

HOW FINANCIAL PLANNERS ARE PAID

Financial planners are paid in one of three ways (often in combination): (1) a commission, (2) a fee based on assets under management, or (3) a fee for service, such as a yearly or hourly fee. At our firm, we prefer to work with fees based on assets under management, because we feel that approach aligns our financial interests with our clients and provides a sound financial framework for providing professional services. Too many financial planning clients have no idea how their financial planner is paid. Your financial planner's method of getting paid should be made clear to you. He or she should be willing to openly and honestly discuss this with you.

DIFFERENTIATING BETWEEN FINANCIAL PLANNERS AND STOCK BROKERS

Most financial planners are not "stock pickers," nor should they be. Stock brokers or money managers play an extremely important role in your financial plan, but the role of your financial planner should be to find you highly qualified money managers for each asset class in which you are invested. If your financial planner is taking the time he or she should to consult with you and other clients, there is not time to research investments as thoroughly as a dedicated money manager should. Commonly recognized money managers run large mutual funds and other instruments where many investors' money is pooled. The money manager earns his or her fee by taking a very small percentage of a very large pool of money, so that the cost to the individual investor is kept low. Steer clear of mutual fund companies who have been involved in scandal. There are plenty of reputable, well-managed mutual fund companies that have proven to be honest stewards of their clients' money. Your financial planner should be able to direct you to such reputable funds. Another alternative is individually managed accounts that utilize money managers for each asset class in an environment where individual securities are bought and sold on behalf of the client.

Be wary of financial salesmen who call you frequently with stock tips. This may be a sign that they are making transactions to generate commissions that are in their self-interest but not necessarily in yours. This form of unethical conduct is called "churning" in the industry. Also be wary of a stock tip generated by the Wall Street firm that is both performing investment banking services for a given corporation and then sending its sales force out to sell the company's stock. If you have been reading the papers lately, you know that this type of client abuse has been all too common at some of the major brokerage houses in recent years. Although the brokerage firms have pledged to stop such abuses, it is best for you, the consumer, to be informed that these unethical practices have occurred in the recent past and could well occur again in the future. If you receive frequent calls about hot stock tips from a financial salesman who is managing your money, it may be time to start looking for a professional financial planner who will take a holistic view of your financial well-being and not try to ply you with offers that are not in your best interest.

CONCLUSION

Look for a financial planner who will meet with you regularly, who is willing to take the time to teach and listen, and who has good interpersonal skills. Dealing with the financial dimension of life causes many people a high degree of anxiety. Therefore, the ideal financial planner will have the technical facility to give state-of-the-art financial advice along with a capacity for helping clients deal with their emotional responses so as to make sound financial choices. Ask for references and take the time to call them. Other clients can tell you a lot about your prospective financial planner's interpersonal skills, technical skills, organization, and professional demeanor. Finding a qualified financial planner that you are compatible with is an important step on your path to mastering the financial dimension of your life and your practice. Take time to carefully choose the financial planning professional who feels right for you.

CHAPTER 12

Money as Transference Object in Therapy

For many patients, the fact of having to pay for a therapist's time and attention is bound to evoke early emotional wounds. Money evokes feelings about the self, feelings about money as the object and yokes them affectively. For example, the masochistic defense binds a sense of the self as victim and the money-object as victimizer, and the affect that binds them is resentment. When these issues are acted out with money, the money itself comes to represent the control of a domineering parent, and self-defeating or passive-aggressive financial behavior comes to represent the feeling of resentment. It is no wonder then that the act of paying for therapy may well become fertile ground for acting out. The masochist may, for example, act out in passive-aggressive ways by not paying the bill, forgetting the checkbook, bouncing checks, and so forth.

Payment for therapy represents the needs of the therapist in the therapeutic relationship and thereby frequently evokes ambivalent feelings on the part of the patient. In our earlier discussion about finding your niche, we discussed the inherent tension between the patient's needs in therapy and the therapist's needs. Patients need to work on their life issues, whereas therapists need to earn a living by providing their expertise and doing work that they find rewarding. This relationship is by no means equal—the therapist has a great deal more power than the patient. Payment for therapy—representing, as it does, the reality of the needs of the therapist—is apt to evoke ambivalent feelings in the patient. Therapy, by its very nature, evokes to varying degrees the child part of the patient, who relates to the therapist as a child does to a parent. However, in the original situation, the child does not need to pay for parenting (at least not with money!). The fact that he or she must now pay for the therapy with money may bring up many of the feelings connected to the deficits in the original experience of being parented.

If payment for therapy represents the therapist's needs in the relationship, then the therapist should be clear, both in his or her own mind and with the patient, that those needs are legitimate. Therapists have a legitimate need to be fairly paid for their services. It is vital that therapists be aware of their own money issues so that patients' financial acting out does not evoke retaliatory or compensatory acting out on the part of the therapist. For example, a borderline patient might fail to pay her therapy bill as an expression of the transference wish that the therapist selflessly mother her. The therapist should not reward this kind of acting out with an overly accommodating stance about prompt payment of the bill. Instead, the issue needs to be discussed in its deeper dimensions while a limit is set for the bill payment. The therapist may open up a dialogue and offer meaningful interpretations about the feelings that the requirement for payment evokes in the patient. This dialogue is essential to sorting through both the emotional and the financial issues. Again, therapists must be highly aware of their own money issues in order to maintain their sense of clarity and appropriate boundaries.

In every business, situations arise that require a balance to be carried. We are not suggesting that therapists have inflexible boundaries around the payment of the bill. What we are suggesting instead is that therapists be clear about their own motivations when they find that the money boundary seems to be slipping with a given patient (or in their practice in general). It is important to bring these issues to clinical consultation or even personal therapy so that the therapist can sort through the transference and countertransference issues involved.

A Therapist's Money Guide

Filling in the Knowledge Gap

We would like to begin this chapter with a case study. Although Dr. Friedlander is a composite of numerous clients, we hope that taking a look at her struggles and successes will provide a human perspective for this financial planning discussion.

CASE STUDY: A BRILLIANT CLINICIAN WITH UNDERDEVELOPED FINANCIAL SKILLS

Dr. Rachel Friedlander is a 48-year-old clinical psychologist practicing in Bethesda, Maryland. She is divorced and lives with her 16-year-old daughter, Sarah. Dr. Friedlander has worked diligently to build a highly successful psychotherapy practice. She attended Georgetown University for her undergraduate degree, received her PhD from the University of Michigan, and followed up with postdoctoral training at the Baltimore-Washington Institute for Psychoanalysis. She is a talented and successful clinician. She has earned a respected place in her professional community, with many of her referrals coming from fellow therapists. She grosses well over $100,000 per year and lives comfortably. Most of her income has gone toward providing for herself and her daughter. Her ex-husband pays child support, but she will not receive income from his federal government pension at retirement. She maintains a SEP-IRA that she has funded sporadically. She is anticipating approximately $200,000 in inheritance if her parents do not eat up their own assets in retirement. She has accumulated a little less than $100,000 in her SEP-IRA.

Dr. Friedlander's retirement savings are far below where they will ultimately need to be to fund a comfortable retirement. Moreover, at age 48, she has less time than she once had to make up the difference. As Dr. Friedlander moves closer to retirement she is becoming increasingly concerned about what the future holds. She would like to be able to retire in her mid-60s but is not sure that is a realistic possibility. To make her vision of a financially secure retirement a reality, she will have to develop some new skills—begin to view her practice from a more business-like perspective. She will need to reorient herself to the reality that fully funding her retirement is a vitally important life goal.

Dr. Friedlander's dilemma is similar to that of many therapists in private practice: she is a highly skilled and successful clinician, but her financial planning and business skills are significantly less developed than her other professional skills. It is for Dr. Friedlander and her peers that this book is intended.

THE FINANCIAL KNOWLEDGE GAP

The goal in this section is to fill in the knowledge gap that many therapists have about the business and financial planning aspects of private practice. Whereas all professional therapists have extensive clinical education and training, few have any training in running the business and financial end of their private practice. With little or no financial training, private practitioners frequently take a "seat of the pants" approach to financial planning, picking up bits and pieces of information along the way from various sources such as "money" magazines and financial shows on radio or TV. However, just as a professional therapist does not learn to practice psychotherapy by reading self-help books, learning to deal effectively with one's finances requires more than putting together bits and pieces of (often conflicting) information.

IN THE UNITED STATES, A "SEAT OF THE PANTS" APPROACH JUST WON'T DO

A lack of serious attention to the financial dimension might be adaptive if we were Swedish therapists living in a Democratic-Socialist society rather than U.S. citizens living in the individualistic social reality of modern American capitalism. In Sweden, we would have healthcare provided by the state, and cradle-to-grave social services—childcare, housing, and college tuition—would all be highly subsidized. In the United States, however, we are expected to fend for ourselves. In particular, private practitioners and entrepreneurs have chosen a high degree of freedom coupled with a high degree of responsibility for their financial security.

It is true, of course, that at retirement age most therapists will be eligible for Social Security. However, if one does the calculations and looks at the actual amount one will actually receive, it will quickly become apparent that Social Security is merely a supplement to a personal retirement plan—not a substitute. For a detailed explanation of Social Security benefits see "Social Security and the Private Practitioner" in Chapter 23.

FOUNDATIONS OF PUTTING YOUR FINANCIAL HOUSE IN ORDER

You must put your own financial house in order from the bottom to the top. If you do not do this for yourself, who else will? From the perspective of a psychotherapy practice, putting one's finances in order begins with effective and accurate bookkeeping. Getting the bookkeeping level properly organized is foundational to higher order thinking and action in the financial dimension of a practice. Therefore, getting one's bookkeeping in good shape is vital.

Have you been to your dentist's or family doctor's office lately? Have you noticed their clerical staff, who takes care of things such as insurance billing, scheduling, ordering of supplies, and computer upkeep? Most therapists in private practice do not have that kind of clerical support. They typically rely on themselves, or sometimes a spouse, to deal with the administrative side of their practice. Between clients, paperwork, consultations, conferences, and so forth, there is a temptation to procrastinate about bookkeeping chores. Yet this clerical or bookkeeping level of practice management is a vital prerequisite to addressing the broader issues of financial life planning. The bookkeeping level addresses the nuts and bolts of generating income, whereas the financial planning level deals with allocating that income into a financial, legal, and tax structure that supports the therapist's long-term needs and goals. Both levels must be addressed and mastered for the financial dimension of a private practice to work successfully.

BOOKKEEPING RESOURCES

One support for mastering this level is bookkeeping software. To help you get started, we have provided a thorough discussion of QuickBooks® in Addendum III. One of the nice things about using a bookkeeping software package such as QuickBooks® is that it helps private practitioners organize their books into appropriate categories. For therapists who are not computer savvy, several very effective "one-write" bookkeeping systems, which were quite popular before the PC age, are still available. Although providing the nuts and bolts of one-write accounting is beyond the scope of this book, you can find all the one-write resources needed through Safeguard, the venerable producer of noncomputerized bookkeeping forms. Safeguard can be found on the web at *http://www.gosafeguard.com* or toll free at 800-523-2422. Once the private practitioner's bookkeeping is more organized, either by hand or by computer, the more conceptual issues around business and retirement planning are far easier to deal with.

TREATING YOUR PRACTICE AS A BUSINESS

Sound bookkeeping allows the private practitioner to think like a businessperson about the practice. Good bookkeeping allows the practitioner to know how much money the practice is generating and from what sources. Once the practitioner understands the expenses better, he or she is better able to see the big picture of income and outflow in the practice. This is important because being self-employed is expensive, and one needs to be in charge of cash flow so that one can deal intelligently with the many expenses involved in private practice.

WITH THE FREEDOM OF PRIVATE PRACTICE COMES A RESPONSIBILITY TO YOURSELF

Most private practitioners we know cherish their freedom. Therapists love working for themselves and doing work that they find deeply meaningful. However, one price you pay for this freedom is that you frequently work outside the formal benefits structure of employment. All those things that an employer would provide for you, you must provide for yourself. You must act as both employer and employee when you are in private practice. What does this mean in practical terms? It means that your financial self-care must be proactive. Proactive financial self-care refers to being a good employer to yourself. In the next chapter we will look at five of the most common financial planning mistakes therapists make. One thing all of these mistakes have in common is a failure to treat the practice as a business, to meet the responsibilities of the employer role.

CHAPTER 14

Common Financial Mistakes of Private Practitioners

This chapter presents five common financial mistakes made by therapists in private practice. Notice that they all derive from failing to think about the financial dimension from a good employer's perspective. A good employer would provide a sound retirement package from the business's revenue stream—not spend all the business's revenues on salary. A good employer would make prudent investment decisions for the retirement plan, obtain adequate insurance, and set up a business structure that minimizes taxation. These considerations are simply fundamental to doing business in a professional way. Let's look at how therapists often neglect such fundamentals and how such mistakes can be addressed.

The five most common financial mistakes of private practitioners include

Treating all income as money you can freely spend
Underfunding your retirement plan
Inappropriately allocating assets in your retirement plan
Failing to obtain adequate insurance
Creating excessive tax liability

Let us examine these mistakes one by one and consider appropriate solutions for each.

MISTAKE #1: TREATING ALL INCOME AS MONEY YOU CAN FREELY SPEND

Solution

Put yourself on a salary.

As you begin thinking of your practice as a business, the danger of this mistake becomes clear. Obviously, no business owner could afford to spend all his or her income on salaries. Overhead, salaries, and benefits must all come out of the business revenue. Anything left over after all expenses are paid is profit for the business.

The private practitioner's biggest expense is his or her salary. A good rule of thumb is that your salary should be about 60% of your target revenue. A percentage of that salary (depending on your tax bracket) will need to be set aside for taxes. About 15% percent of your target revenue should be earmarked for overhead expenses such as rent, continuing education, consultation, furnishings, liability insurance, and so forth. That leaves about 25% of target revenue for funding a benefits package, which includes health insurance, disability insurance, and a retirement plan. Under most circumstances, these benefits, retirement costs, and overhead costs will reduce your tax liability.

Because your revenues minus your expenses equal your profits (revenues – expenses = profits), there are two basic ways to increase your profits:

TABLE 14.1
Example: Current Revenues and Expenses for Mary Smith's Private Practice

CURRENT REVENUES	
Total client fees: approx. 20 clients per week, an average fee of $100 per session, and approx. 2 weeks per year of vacation	$100,000
CURRENT EXPENSES	
Salary (taxes come out of this)	($60,000)
Overhead expenses	($15,000)
Benefits package	($25,000)
PROFITS	
Total profits	$0

Note: All figures are approximations.

Increase your revenues. Consider the following possibilities: raising
  your fees, seeing more patients, adding groups to your practice,
  taking on consulting clients, bringing in passive income from
  rental property, and so forth.

Reduce your expenses. This can be accomplished in a myriad of ways:
  shop for a cheaper liability policy (I recently saved several hun-
  dred dollars per year by switching carriers), reduce your rent
  (perhaps by sharing your office), reduce your continuing education expenses, and so forth.

Thinking creatively about your business means constantly review-
ing how well your business is working, looking for new ways to
increase your revenues and reduce your expenses. As you allow
your unconscious—your creativity—to inform your thinking, you
will be able to shape your practice in ways uniquely suited to you.
The result will be a business that is not only more satisfying but also
more profitable.

Mary Smith (Table 14.1) is an example of a therapist who decided
to increase her profits by both methods: increasing her revenues and
decreasing her expenses. She first considered ways to generate more
revenue. Mary enjoys group work, so it seemed like a natural step
for her to start two new therapy groups. With two weekly groups of
seven members each, she can gross an additional $490 per week (at
$35 per person per session). If the groups meet 50 weeks out of the
year, she will bring in an additional $24,500 per year. Mary's efforts
to reduce her expenses result in less dramatic, but still rewarding,
improvements. She decides to sublet her office on Saturdays and
Wednesday evenings. (Having added two groups to her practice,
she is only too pleased to have this time at home!) This reduces her
rental expenses by $150 per month, or $1,800 per year.

TABLE 14.2
Example: Target Revenues and Expenses for Mary Smith

TARGET REVENUES	
Individual client fees: approx. 20 clients per week, an average fee of $100 per session, and approx. 2 weeks per year of vacation	$100,000
Additional revenues (adding two therapy groups)	$24,500
TARGET EXPENSES	
Salary (taxes come out of this)	($60,000)
Overhead expenses	($15,000)
Expense reduction (subletting the office)	$1,800
Benefits package	($25,000)
PROFITS	
Total profits	$26,300

Note: All figures are approximations.

Let us see how Mary's strategies have improved her bottom line (Table 14.2). Now Mary has a profit. This brings her to a choice point with important implications for her financial well-being—present and future. Has she always wanted a more appealing office? Does she need to increase her advertising to boost her practice? Is she long overdue for a vacation? Mary has innumerable opportunities to spend her profits. Before she decides how to spend that money, however, she should consider an important (albeit unsexy) priority—more fully funding her retirement plan.

MISTAKE #2: UNDERFUNDING YOUR RETIREMENT PLAN

Solution

- Develop a realistic projection of your retirement needs.
- Implement a tax-advantaged retirement plan designed to meet your future needs.
- Set realistic funding goals that take into account both your current and future needs.

Choosing a Plan

Before you can fund a retirement plan, you must have one in place. A wide variety of retirement plans are available, each with its advantages and limitations. Each has its own set of rules for tax-advantaged investing. Widely used plans are the SEP-IRA, the individual 401(k), and the Keogh profit-sharing plan. Annuities can also play a useful role in your retirement planning. Choosing the plan that best fits your situation is a complex and important decision. Throughout this book (especially Chapter 15) you will find the tools you need to choose the most appropriate plan for you. Most therapists in private practice would also be well advised to consult with a financial planner and tax advisor before making this important decision.

Taking Care of Your Future Self

No matter what sort of retirement plan you choose, it cannot serve you well unless you fund it at the appropriate level. A good financial advisor can provide crucial advice and support. We once heard Phil Jackson, the legendary basketball coach, say that when the team is behind in crucial situations he simply points out what needs to be done to win the game. In the same spirit, your financial advisor's job is to point out what you need to do to "win the game" of retirement: that is, adequately fund your retirement plan. This role of the advisor is seldom a popular one. Deferred gratification is no one's favorite pastime. However, your financial advisor can be an advocate for you in your elder years, helping you keep in mind the long-term goals you have set. A comfortable retirement at the time you choose to stop working is something you owe yourself.

Dealing with the Nitty Gritty

A qualified financial advisor can help you work out a mathematical projection that will determine the level at which you will need to fund your retirement account. In brief, the projection should include

Amount you expect to need to live comfortably in retirement
Projected return on your investments
Projected inflation rates
Your current level of funding
Your expected retirement date
Social Security and other retirement benefits (your or your spouse's pension plan, anticipated inheritance, and so forth)
Other sources of income, if any
Expected healthcare expenses

A useful way to develop such a projection is to work backward from retirement. First, estimate at what age you plan on retiring. Second, estimate your expenses in retirement and make some actuarial assumptions about your estimated life span. These steps will allow you to estimate the ongoing level of funding required to ensure that you will have a retirement income sufficient to your needs for as long as you reasonably expect to live. Our website (*http://www.insightfinancialgroup.com*) provides a calculator that can give you a ballpark idea of how much you need for retirement and how much you need to put away now in order to get there.

When making your projection, there may be other factors, unique to your situation, that you should also take into account. You may be expecting an inheritance later in life. You may have a partner who is also contributing to your retirement plan. You may have worked for an employer who provided a retirement plan that will kick in later on. You may have other sources of revenue, aside from your therapy practice, such as another business or rental property. Your retirement plan should account for all these individual factors.

Your gender also affects your retirement plan. If you are a woman, you face gender-specific challenges in financial planning:

Statistically, women tend to live longer than men. Thus, the amount needed to fully fund a woman's retirement will, in general, need to be higher than the amount needed to fund the retirement of a man of the same age and lifestyle.

Women tend to be family caretakers. If a family member is ill, the woman often becomes the caregiver. This can result in increased expenses while concurrently reducing the woman's ability to earn.

Divorce is another life event that tends to take a higher toll on women, often contributing to the phenomenon that sociologists have called "the feminization of poverty." All too often, women wind up with a net reduction in lifestyle and income following divorce, whereas men's income and lifestyle tend to improve after divorce.[1]

Once you have considered the variables of your situation and determined what you need to invest now to fully fund a reasonable retirement, your job is to do your best to ensure that your practice supports that level of funding. This may feel overwhelming at first. However, once you recognize the importance of properly preparing for retirement and begin to "hold the image" of taking care of yourself in this way, you will find yourself thinking creatively about ways to increase income or reduce costs.

MISTAKE #3: INAPPROPRIATELY ALLOCATING ASSETS IN YOUR RETIREMENT PLAN

Solution

Calibrate asset allocation to your needs, goals, and time frame for retirement.

This solution sounds so obvious! However, we have worked with many therapists for whom misallocation of assets is a major problem. Most commonly, the issue is one of overly aggressive investing. Sometimes this is a result of poor advice received from unprofessional stockbrokers who allow their self-interest to take precedence over the interests of their client. Misallocation can also be the result of do-it-yourself investing with insufficient information. Without thorough research it is impossible to make wise, informed choices. Anxiety, overexcitement, or greed can also lead to a hyper-aggressive approach in an attempt to make "a quick killing." As recent

---

[1] Feinberg, Rene, & Knox, Kathleen E. (Eds.). (1990). *The feminization of poverty in the United States: A selected, annotated bibliography of the issues, 1978–1989.* New York: Garland.

stock market reversals demonstrate, hyper-aggressiveness can lead to dismaying results.

Many psychotherapists in private practice have learned this lesson in a most painful way. During the "tech bubble" boom market of the late 1990s, what seemed to be an exciting ride that would never end did indeed end with a bang—leaving many therapists who were aggressively invested with a sense of fear and disappointment.

A Portfolio Out of Balance (A Composite Example)

John Jefferies, LCSW, and Jennifer Jefferies, PhD, had lost more than 50% of the value in their retirement accounts over the last 2 years. John had been in full-time private practice for many years and Jennifer had recently left her position with a private psychiatric hospital to open her own practice. Needless to say, they were nervous about the future. At this point, they acknowledged the need to meet with a financial planner. During the technology stock boom, John had invested very aggressively (Jennifer had left the investing decisions to John), wanting to benefit from the rising tide in stock prices. When the stock prices started to fall, they figured that it would not be long before they would come back up. They had been waiting for the tide to turn for some time and were feeling burned and angry when they came for their first financial planning appointment. They had not put new money into the market for over a year and were keeping their money in a money market account that was earning very low returns.

John and Jennifer knew very well the misstep they had taken in the 1990s. They had invested far too aggressively, creating a great deal of volatility in their portfolio. They had learned a painful lesson and intended to invest more moderately in the future. However, that did not help them in deciding how to move forward. Should they hang on to their tech-heavy, growth-type investments in the hope that those stock prices would return to higher levels, or should they reinvest more conservatively? Having been burned so badly, they were hesitant to rely solely on their own judgment.

Their consultation with a financial planner was the first time they had sought professional advice. Their financial planner's answer to the question of whether to hang on to the volatile portfolio or cut their losses was that they should do some of both. What did that look like?

John and Jennifer's financial planner recommended that they take some time to analyze where they are in their lives. He asked them to take a look at when they want to retire or at least cut back on work. He also asked them to look at their other financial responsibilities. Further, he asked them to explore how much risk they were willing to tolerate in the market at this juncture in their lives. After exploring these issues, they decided on a moderate asset allocation. This entailed a mix of various categories of stocks, bonds, and cash. Next they had to get from a hyper-aggressive portfolio to a moderate one. They analyzed the stock portion of the portfolio and kept some of the stronger growth-oriented investments while harvesting the losses in others. ("Harvesting losses" refers to reporting securities losses to the IRS in order to take advantage of capital losses, thereby offsetting capital gains.[2])

They then reinvested in a mix of securities—stocks, bonds, and cash—that provided an appropriate allocation of assets for the Jefferies at their current life stage. They also put money into several investments (e.g., real estate) outside the stock market, providing further diversification. Now that John and Jennifer had achieved the moderate asset allocation more appropriate to their needs, they were in a better position to deal with a sometimes-volatile stock market. They had reduced their exposure to stock market volatility with bonds, cash, and other investments not directly related to the stock market. On the other hand, they maintained a portion of the portfolio in stocks to position themselves for growth in a rising stock market.

The Importance of Proper Asset Allocation

Proper asset allocation goes to the heart of modern portfolio theory (see our discussion in Chapter 16) and is a core strategy for successful investing in both bullish and bearish markets. Attempting to time the market (i.e., attempting to buy stocks high and sell them low) has proven to be a perilous strategy for many investors. No one can accurately predict the future. Missing the 10 best trading days since 1992 would have cost an investor 43% of their average return; in other words, an average return of 6% as opposed to 10.6%.[3] Because the best trading days are recognized only in hindsight, generally the best strategy is to stay invested in the stock market rather than trying to outguess it.

Diversification is a strategy that reduces volatility while allowing for growth. Although diversification does not guarantee a profit or protection from a loss, it does allow the long-term investor to avoid many of the pitfalls the hyper-aggressive investor falls into. To illustrate. a recent publication from Fidelity Investments notes that from "1926 to 2001 a diversified mix of stocks, bonds and T-Bills would have returned 8.35% per year vs. 10.7% for the

---

[2] It is not intended that any part of this book provide specific tax advice. Please consult with a tax professional about the tax consequences of any actions you may take.
[3] Fidelity Investments Institutional Services Company 316470.001. "How to Stay the Course in Volatile Times."

S&P 500.[4] The diversified portfolio would have incurred only half the risk of the S&P 500 portfolio. The worst monthly return for the S&P 500 would have been –29.7% (–36.7% for small caps), whereas the worst monthly return for the diversified portfolio would have been –16%."[5]

Proper asset allocation entails proactive planning, a disciplined investment strategy, and the willingness to hang in there over the long haul.

MISTAKE #4: LACK OF ADEQUATE INSURANCE

Solution

Make a realistic assessment of your insurance needs.

All businesses need insurance, and yours is no exception. The purpose of insurance is the transfer of risk. Rather than assuming an intolerable risk (catastrophic medical expenses, for instance), the practitioner transfers that risk to an insurance company.

Health Insurance

Unless you have sufficient assets to cover your own catastrophic medical expenses, you will need health insurance. This may be taken care of through your spouse's employer if that is allowed by his or her health plan. Failing this, you will need to find a plan (perhaps through a professional organization) that provides the needed coverage.

How Much? What Type? How much and what sort of insurance you want are very much a factor of your lifestyle, personal preferences, and risk tolerance. To determine what best fits you, ask yourself the following questions:

- Do I make frequent office visits to my MD?
- Do I use a lot of prescription drugs?
- Is choice of doctor important to me, or am I okay with whomever the HMO assigns?
- Are mental health services something I use or anticipate using?

---

[4] The S&P 500 is an unmanaged index considered to be representative of the stock market in general. An investor may not invest directly in an index.

[5] Fidelity Investments Institutional Services Company 316470.001. "How to Stay the Course in Volatile Times."

- Do I prefer alternative health practitioners not covered by standard insurance?
- How much could I afford to spend in the event of a major medical problem?
- Which is more important to me: total coverage for every possible eventuality or paying lower premiums?

The trade-off here is between higher premium payments and comprehensiveness of coverage. Another issue to keep in mind is the importance of obtaining coverage while your health is good. Once a serious or chronic problem develops, it may become well nigh impossible to find the kind of individual coverage needed.

Disability Insurance

Disability insurance provides income replacement in the event of debilitating illness or injury. This type of insurance may be unpleasant to think about. After all, no one wants to consider the possibility that they might be disabled to an extent that would make self-support impossible. However, denial or procrastination can result in disaster. Your financial planner can help you sort through a number of options in disability insurance and business overhead coverage. A good rule of thumb is to plan on spending 3–5% of your gross revenue for this coverage. Disability insurance does not come cheap, but ensuring that you will have a consistent income flow, even in the case of disability, is an important consideration for almost all therapists.

Liability Insurance

Responsible practitioners carry professional liability insurance from internship onward. However, it may pay to make rate comparisons, because rates can vary dramatically among carriers. Most liability insurance carriers provide continuous insurance; in other words, year 2 of your coverage covers you for acts committed during years 1 and 2; year 3 covers you for years 1, 2, and 3, and so forth. For this reason, premiums will probably increase each year until a "cap" has been reached. It pays to check both the initial premium charged and the cap when you compare policies. As with health insurance, it is important to purchase enough coverage to feel well protected.

Life Insurance

Life insurance is a complex topic. We discuss it as an investment vehicle in Chapter 15 and will take an in-depth look at the entire subject of life insurance in Chapter 20. At this point, remember only that there are two main types of life insurance: term insurance, which provides coverage for a specific period of time, and permanent life insurance, which provides a death benefit as well as tax-deferred growth on cash values in the account. You will be better prepared to answer the questions of how much and which kind is right for you after reading the pertinent chapters. Your financial planner can be a valuable aid in helping you determine which, if any, policy best fits your needs.

MISTAKE #5: CREATING EXCESSIVE TAX LIABILITY

Solution

Engage in year-round tax planning.

By this point, you may be gnashing your teeth as you consider all the expenses involved in being your own employer. Do not despair! There is a silver lining. As a self-employed person, practically all of your business-related expenses can be tax deductible.[6] Make an appointment with your tax advisor. Do not wait until March, when tax season will make it impossible for you to have his or her full attention. Tell your advisor that you would like help organizing your records, keeping track of business expenses, and calculating your estimated quarterly taxes. If you are not paying estimated taxes now, you might be surprised (and dismayed) to see what the IRS charges you in penalties and interest each year. This is another area about which your tax advisor will be glad to enlighten you.

Taking advantage of all potential deductions is important. However, private practitioners can realize their greatest tax savings by making use of one or more tax-advantaged investment plans. By investing in a plan that allows you to defer paying taxes—either on the money invested or on the money accrued—you can reduce your tax liability while you build toward a financially secure future.

PAUSE TO REFLECT

This might be a good place to stop for a moment and tune in to how you are feeling. Has the discussion left you feeling excited? anxious? confused? If you are like most people, the answer is probably "all of the above." Achieving financial mastery is not an overnight event,

---

[6] It is not intended that this book provide specific tax advice. Consult with a tax professional.

any more than achieving clinical mastery. If you are feeling a bit overwhelmed, consider a "bite-size" approach:

Decide which issue to work with first. This could be the one that feels most pressing or the one with which you already feel somewhat comfortable.
Talk with the appropriate professional (i.e., financial planner, tax advisor, insurance agent).
Take one concrete step—buy the insurance policy, begin making estimated tax payments, set up a retirement account, and so forth.
Give yourself time to assimilate and take satisfaction in the first step before looking forward to the next one.

A solid financial footing increases the structural integrity of a psychotherapy practice. By dealing with the financial dimension, you are not only providing for the comfort and security of yourself and your family, you are also building a container that will allow you to work with your patients in a way that is deeply supportive and healing.

Whatever you can do or dream you can, begin it. Boldness has genius, power and magic in it.

Goethe

PROFITABILITY WORKSHEETS

Use the worksheets in this section to begin the process of thinking about revenues, expenses, and profitability in your practice. As you work with these issues in your practice, you will develop a more businesslike approach that will help you improve your bottom line.

Revenues – Expenses = Profits (or Losses)

Figure target revenues and expenses using Table 14.3. Projecting these figures gives you something to shoot for. If you are exceeding your targets, then you are doing well and heading for a profit for the year. If you are falling short, then you may need to either boost revenues or reduce expenses. Good businesspeople constantly ask themselves three questions: How can I increase revenues? How can I reduce expenses? and How can I reduce my tax liability?

TABLE 14.3
Target Revenues Worksheet (Psychotherapy: Individuals and Couples)

Approx. No. of Clients per Month	Ave. Fee per Session	Ave. Monthly Revenue from Individuals and Couples
A	B $	(A*B) $

Other Sources of Revenue
(e.g., groups, consulting, teaching, interns)

Source of Revenue 1 Description	Source of Revenue 2 Description	Source of Revenue 3 Description	
Approx. Monthly Income $	Approx. Monthly Income $	Approx. Monthly Income $	Total Monthly Revenues $

Projected Monthly Expenses

COMPENSATION	
Your monthly salary	$
BENEFITS	
Health insurance	$
Disability insurance	$
Retirement investing	$
TAXES	
Federal taxes	$
State taxes	$
Local taxes	$
GENERAL BUSINESS EXPENSES	
Liability insurance	$
Rent	$
Furnishings	$
Cont. ed., consultation	$

PROJECTED PROFIT OR LOSS

Projected Revenues	Projected (Expenses)	Profit or Loss
$	($)	=

Use the worksheet in Table 14.4 to enter your actual revenues and expenses. By comparing these with the projected figures in Table 14.3, you will be able to set goals and then measure performance against those goals. This is the first step in finding creative solutions to profitability problems.

TABLE 14.4
Actual Revenues Worksheet (Psychotherapy: Individuals and Couples)

Approx. No. of Clients per Month	Ave. Fee per Session	Ave. Monthly Revenue from Individuals and Couples
A	B $	(A*B) $

Other Sources of Revenue
(e.g., groups, consulting, teaching, interns)

Source of Revenue 1 Description	Source of Revenue 2 Description	Source of Revenue 3 Description	
Approx. Monthly Income $	Approx. Monthly Income $	Approx. Monthly Income $	Total Monthly Revenues $

Actual Monthly Expenses

COMPENSATION	
Your monthly salary	$
BENEFITS	
Health insurance	$
Disability insurance	$
Retirement investing	$
TAXES	
Federal taxes	$
State taxes	$
Local taxes	$
GENERAL BUSINESS EXPENSES	
Liability insurance	$
Rent	$
Furnishings	$
Cont. ed., consultation	$

PROFIT OR LOSS

Actual Revenues	Actual (Expenses)	Profit or Loss
$	($)	=

CHAPTER 15

A Therapist's Guide through the Maze of Tax-Advantaged Investing Plans

In this chapter we explore selected retirement vehicles in greater depth. First, we look at employment-based retirement vehicles: the 401(k) for individuals and the Keogh profit-sharing plan. Next we consider IRAs: the SEP-IRA, the traditional IRA, and the Roth IRA. Then we examine insurance-based vehicles: variable universal life insurance and variable annuities. Finally, we consider two tax-advantaged education savings plans: the education IRA and 529 plans.

A comprehensive discussion of retirement vehicles is beyond the scope of this book, as they constitute a complicated area of tax and employment law. Instead, we have tried to sift out the information that you, as a private practitioner, need to make informed choices as to the retirement plan you might choose. We strongly recommend you seek professional advice in putting together your retirement plan. Please bear in mind that practitioners with employees must follow strict guidelines for funding the qualified plans and SEP-IRA.

These plans can be significantly less complicated for someone in a solo practice.

EMPLOYMENT-BASED VEHICLES: QUALIFIED PLANS

"Qualified plans" *qualify* for tax-favored status by the IRS and are available only to employers who open such accounts for the benefit of their employees. If you are a therapist in solo practice, you are considered your own employer and can therefore participate in certain qualified plans. In this chapter we discuss two qualified plan vehicles: the 401(k) and the Keogh profit-sharing plan.

401(k) for Individuals

Until recently, many therapists in private practice have felt that 401(k) plans were not a good fit for their retirement investing needs. Before the passage of the Economic Growth and Tax Relief Reconciliation Act of 2001 (EGTRRA), it did not make sense for the self-employed to establish 401(k) plans. Small business owners could sometimes save just as much through a Keogh, SEP, or SIMPLE IRA, without the costly setup and maintenance fees, complex rules, and burdensome administration associated with 401(k) plans. But as of January 1, 2002, therapists in solo private practice can establish 401(k) plans that in some cases allow them to put away more than the amount allowed by other tax-deferred plans. Here is an example of how this new, simplified retirement option may work for you:

> Mary Smith is an LCSW in private practice and has self-employment income of $100,000. By establishing a solo 401(k), she can put away as much as $31,000 in 2002, or $32,000 if age 50 or older. This total amount is tax deductible and all earnings grow tax deferred until withdrawn.

For Mary, the maximum deductible contributions allowed under other plans in 2002 would be less than those allowed in the 401(k). The new 401(k) for individuals allows private practitioners to contribute both as the employer and the employee. If you practice as a sole proprietor, the employer contribution is based on your schedule C net income and is capped at 25% of compensation. It is not subject to federal income tax or Social Security (FICA) taxes.

The salary deferral contributions are excluded from federal income tax but are subject to FICA. The maximum salary deferral amount for 2002 is 100% of pay, up to $11,000 or $12,000 if you are age 50 or older. Your practice receives a tax deduction for both employer and salary deferral contributions. Employer contributions plus salary deferral contributions cannot exceed $40,000 ($41,000 if age 50 or older) or 100% of compensation.

The new individual 401(k) has many benefits beyond its generous contribution limits. You decide each year whether to contribute and how much to contribute. Unlike traditional 401(k) plans, no complicated discrimination tests or administrative requirements exist. Among the few administrative requirements is an IRS Form 5500 filing, but only after plan assets exceed $100,000. You may be able to take loans tax free and penalty free under the same guidelines available to large, corporate 401(k) plans. Retirement assets from other plans can be consolidated into the new 401(k). This new planning opportunity is available to private practitioners who employ only owners and their spouses, including C corporations, S corporations, partnerships, and sole proprietorships. It is not suitable for practices with employees or those that plan to hire additional employees in the future.

Part of the price private practitioners pay for their freedom is that most must attend to their own retirement planning. If you have to fund your own retirement, then you should be putting a significant percentage of your earnings into your retirement. The new 401(k) provides a terrific opportunity for you to save on taxes today by preparing for tomorrow.

Profit-Sharing Plan

The profit-sharing plan (sometimes known as a "Keogh" profit-sharing plan) is another popular retirement vehicle for the psychotherapist in private practice. As a qualified plan, the profit-sharing plan can be established only by an employer. A solo practice therapist who sets up a profit-sharing plan is considered both the employer and the employee. The title "profit-sharing plan" can be a bit confusing for the solo practitioner. The title comes from the fact that the plan is designed to allow employers to share profits with their employees in a tax-favored environment. Again, as a sole proprietor, you are employer and employee, so in effect, you (the employer) are sharing profits with yourself (the employee). The Keogh is funded with pre-tax dollars. As such funding, it will help reduce your tax liability. Funding limits on the profit-sharing plan have been increased with the new tax law. You can now put up to 25% of self-employment income in a profit-sharing plan, up from the 2001 limit of 15%. At income levels of around $100,000 you can put away more with the individual 401(k), but the Keogh profit-sharing plan is still a fine choice for many solo practitioners.

INDIVIDUAL RETIREMENT VEHICLES

SEP-IRA

The simplified employee pension (SEP)-IRA has been a popular pre-tax retirement vehicle for solo practitioners for many years. The SEP-IRA is something of a hybrid between an employment-based plan and an individual plan. It shares characteristics of both. It is an individual retirement arrangement for an employer to use for employees (you are the employer and employee if you are in solo practice). Employer contributions are placed into the individual IRA of the employee. The amount a sole proprietor can contribute is a percentage of schedule C net income. With the new 2001 tax law, its funding provisions have been significantly increased. As a sole proprietor in private practice, the amount that you can put into your SEP is up to 25% of your net schedule C income, with a yearly limit of $40,000. The SEP does not allow you to borrow against money in the account, as the 401(k) may. Not being able to borrow against your retirement may in fact be an argument for the SEP as opposed to the 401(k), because you may not want that temptation. The SEP-IRA is usually funded with securities such as stocks, bonds, and mutual funds. One can also utilize a variable or fixed annuity in a SEP-IRA.[1] SEP-IRAs have generous funding limits and can reduce your taxable income. It is probably the most popular retirement vehicle among private practitioners today, and although its funding and borrowing provisions are more restrictive than the new 401(k) for individuals with income of about $100,000, it is still an option well worth consideration.

Traditional IRA and Roth IRA

Traditional and Roth IRAs represent two different approaches to individual tax-advantaged investing. With the traditional IRA, contributions are tax deductible and taxes are collected when distributions are made. With the Roth IRA, contributions are made in after-tax dollars but distributions are nontaxable. With the new tax law, both Roth and traditional IRA contributions have been increased to $3,000 for the years 2002–2004. The limits increase again (to $4,000) in years 2005–2007. In 2008 and after, the limit will be $5,000 and will

---

[1] Because SEP-IRAs and other tax-qualified retirement plans are already tax-deferred, and there are no additional tax benefits when purchasing an annuity. Other benefits such as lifetime income payments and protection of principal through death benefits may make such a purchase suitable for some investors.

be raised in $500 increments with inflation. Certain qualifications apply to the tax advantages on both the traditional and Roth IRA, so please consult with a tax professional before investing.

If you are a practitioner who has an employment-based retirement plan such as a 401(k) or 403(b) that you are funding in the current year [say, for example, you are a psychiatrist who splits time between a hospital-based practice and private practice, and you participate in the hospital's 403(b) plan], then you probably cannot invest in a traditional IRA. However, the Roth IRA may still be available to you. The Roth has many advantages. Although it is funded with after-tax money, the fact that the gains are not taxable, even when they are withdrawn in retirement, makes the Roth a unique tax-advantaged vehicle. If you meet the IRS's guidelines for investing in a Roth IRA, it may be well worth your consideration.

"CATCH UP" CONTRIBUTIONS TO IRAS

If you are age 50 or older and meet the law's adjusted gross income limits for making IRA contributions, then you may invest an additional $500 per year in your Roth or traditional IRA. The IRS refers to these increased IRA contribution levels for older people as "catch up provisions." In 2006, individuals who have attained age 50 will be able to invest $1000 per year in addition to their regular IRA contribution.

CURRENT INFORMATION ON IRS FUNDING LIMITS AND INCOME RESTRICTIONS

The IRS limits the amount retirement savers can put into any tax-advantaged plan. These restrictions relate to how much income one can earn while maintaining eligibility, along with maximum amounts one can put into such plans. We post the most current information on these issues on our website (*http://www.insightfinancialgroup.com*). From the home page, click "Tax Center" on the top menu bar. There you will find updated information on eligibility and restrictions on tax-advantaged investing plans.

INSURANCE-BASED VEHICLES

Variable Universal Life Insurance

The common wisdom about life insurance used to be "buy term and invest the rest"; the idea being that one should buy low-cost term insurance and invest the difference between the cost of the term insurance and the cost of higher priced whole life insurance. There are instances when this wisdom may still hold true. Life insurance can be used for a variety of purposes, and we will take an in-depth look at the various types of life insurance and the purposes best served by each in Chapter 20. Here, however, we examine a type of life insurance that is well designed for both investment and death benefit purposes: variable universal life insurance.[2] Here is how it works.

The policy allows you to invest in separate accounts that consist of a variety of underlying investments such as various classes of stocks and bonds. Many of these accounts are managed by well-known money management firms. Investments can range from very conservative bond and money market investments to very aggressive growth investments. This product is known as "variable" life insurance because the value in the separate accounts will vary with the market. Part of the premium you pay goes to cover the cost of the life insurance death benefit, part of it goes to paying various expenses, and part of it goes to fund the separate accounts. The contract is treated by the IRS as a life insurance policy as long as it is funded within certain parameters, about which your investment advisor and insurance company will inform you. You pay the premiums with after-tax dollars, but the money grows tax deferred within the separate accounts. You may borrow against the cash value in the separate accounts and will not be taxed on the loan. However, any loans not repaid will reduce the cash value and death benefit. The death benefit is treated as life insurance and therefore will generally pass directly to your heirs without having to go through probate and is generally not taxable to the beneficiary.

The variable universal life insurance concept allows investors to both save for retirement and create an estate for their family in the event of their death with the life insurance death benefit. It allows

---

[2] Variable life insurance policies are not short-term investments and are offered by prospectus only. An investment in a variable life product involves investment risk, including the possible loss of principal. Investment return and principal value will fluctuate, so your shares when redeemed may be worth more or less than original cost. Read the prospectus carefully before investing or sending money. An investment in the securities underlying the policy is not guaranteed or endorsed by any bank, is not a deposit or obligation of any bank, and is not federally insured by any government agency.

investors with dependents to create an instant estate via the death benefit and to fund a retirement nest egg through tax-deferred growth in the separate accounts. Of course, the separate accounts can lose value just as any market-based investment can. Variable universal life insurance can serve as the centerpiece of retirement and estate planning for the therapist in private practice, but it is most appropriate for investors who really need the life insurance aspect of the policy. If you have dependents or a spouse who will need significant resources in the event of your death, and you also want to put money away that can grow tax deferred, then variable universal life may be worth investigating.

Variable Annuities

A variable annuity is a contract with an insurance company. As with variable universal life insurance, variable annuity investments are made in separate accounts that are frequently managed by leading money management firms. Also, like variable universal life insurance, the variable annuity is usually funded with after-tax dollars (although annuities can be used in a tax-deferred vehicle such as a SEP-IRA and funded with pre-tax dollars). In the variable annuity (as in variable universal life insurance) the separate account investments grow tax deferred. You pay tax on the growth in the investment when money is taken out at retirement.

Although the variable annuity has some features in common with variable universal life insurance, it is not life insurance. Death benefits do not transfer to the next generation with the same favorable rules that apply to life insurance.[3] Its one unique feature, however, is that it is the only vehicle that can offer the retiree a guaranteed lifetime income. The guaranteed lifetime feature of annuities along with the tax deferral of growth in the separate accounts can make the variable annuity an attractive, integral part of the private practitioner's retirement plan. The life of an annuity has two distinct phases. The first phase is the funding phase. This phase occurs when the private practitioner is working and putting money into the

---

[3] Variable annuities are sold by prospectus only. Investors should read the prospectus carefully before investing. Annuities are long-term investments designed for retirement purposes. Withdrawals of taxable amounts are subject to income tax and, if taken prior to age 59½, a 10% federal tax penalty may apply. Early withdrawals may be subject to withdrawal charges. An investment in the securities underlying a variable annuity involves investment risk, including possible loss of principal. The contract, when redeemed, may be worth more or less than the original investment. The purchase of a variable annuity is not required for, and is not a term of, the provision of any banking service or activity. Guarantees are backed by the claims-paying ability of the issuer.

annuity. The second phase occurs when he or she retires and "annuitizes" the contract. When the contract is annuitized, payments are made from the insurance company to the annuitant according to the terms of the annuitization. Commonly, the annuity is set up to pay until the death of the annuitant. Sometimes the contract stipulates that it will pay for a certain number of years to the annuitant's beneficiary, even if the annuitant dies prematurely during the annuitization period.

TAX-ADVANTAGED EDUCATION SAVING PLANS

If you have children or grandchildren, you are undoubtedly aware of the high cost of a college education. The bad news is that college is very expensive and is becoming more so with each passing year. The good news is that the Economic Growth and Tax Relief Reconciliation Act of 2001 has significantly enhanced existing programs that provide for federally tax-advantaged college savings.

Education IRAs

You may make a nondeductible contribution to an education IRA for a designated beneficiary. That money will grow free of federal taxes on capital gains and distributions. If distributions are used for qualified educational expenses, they are not taxed as income. Beginning in tax year 2002, the new law increased the maximum annual contribution from $500 to $2000 per beneficiary. Under the old law, qualified expenses were limited to post-secondary educational expenses, but under the new law some expenses such as uniforms, computers, and room and board expenses are allowable for students enrolled in private K–12 schools. The new law allows corporations and nonprofit organizations to make contributions. It also eliminates the 6% penalty tax on contributions to an education IRA made in the same years that contributions are made to a 529 plan. Although clearly the new tax law has made many enhancements to the education IRA, as always, we suggest that investors speak with a professional tax advisor and financial planning professional before investing.

529 Plans

529 plans are funded with after-tax dollars and are allowed to grow, federally tax deferred, until the funds are used for qualified

higher education expenses. Under the new law, when distributions are used for qualified expenses they are not taxed as income. This represents a substantial benefit for college savings. The new law allows for tuition credits or other amounts to be transferred tax free from one 529 plan to another for the same beneficiary. Additionally, the new law allows institutions of higher learning to create 529 plans for prepaid tuition to that institution. One can make a yearly contribution of up to $11,000 into a 529 plan and may contribute up to $55,000 in a given year as long as there are no further contributions for the following 5 years. As with the education IRA, there are many advantages to the 529 plans, and as always, we suggest that you seek professional tax and investment advice before investing.

Many new opportunities exist for therapists to help their children and grandchildren pay for higher education expenses. Planning early is important, so that you are prepared when the time comes to pay the high cost of tuition, room and board, and other expenses.

CONCLUSION

This chapter provides a brief overview of therapists' many options to save on taxes and prepare for three important financial concerns: retirement, protection for dependent survivors, and college funding. Which vehicles you use will depend on your individual circumstances. An investment professional can help you tailor a plan to your needs. Many roads lead to Rome, and there is no one correct way to set up your investment plan. When choosing your tax-advantaged vehicles, bear these issues in mind:

Reducing your tax burden through tax-advantaged investing while preparing for your retirement usually makes a lot of sense.

Keep your plan flexible, so that in good years you can put in more money and in less profitable years you are free to put in less.

Direct your investment choices with an asset allocation mix that is right for you.

You can address the needs of your dependent survivors in the case of your death with life insurance.

Once you have designed an investment plan that fits your needs and circumstances, the next step is to implement your plan. You will need to build the funding of your retirement plan into the financial structure of your practice. You can then settle into a routine of funding your retirement in a consistent and disciplined way.

CHAPTER 16

A Therapist's Guide to Fundamental Investing Concepts

DOLLAR COST AVERAGING: A PRESCRIPTION FOR THE FLUCTUATING MARKET BLUES

Most everyone loves a strong bull market, but bear markets are an inevitable part of the cycle, and investors must learn to deal with the bad times along with the good. The stock market is in constant motion, responding to an ever-changing set of conditions. Economic and political factors such as interest rates, taxation policies, and the business cycle all influence the stock market along with international political factors and intangibles such as the psychology of investors.

I advise against trying to "time the market"; that is, waiting to invest until you feel market conditions are ideal. Instead, you might want to consider a time-tested approach known as "dollar cost averaging." With dollar cost averaging, you invest a given dollar amount each month into your portfolio of securities regardless of current stock market conditions.

To illustrate, suppose you invest $1,000 a month in a given security within your individual 401(k). This means you automatically buy more shares when the price is low and fewer when the share price is high. Because you accumulate more shares for your money when the market is down, your average cost per share will be less than the average market price per share in fluctuating markets. Dollar cost averaging involves continuous investment in securities regardless of fluctuation in price levels.[1]

If you can continue to invest regularly through changing market conditions, dollar cost averaging can be an effective way to accumulate assets. It makes sense to make the *accumulation* of securities a goal, because it gives you an advantage in a market downturn—your automatic investment is going to buy you more shares when the price of shares is down. Those same shares will be more valuable when the market has its next upswing!

Like people's emotional lives, the stock market has sometimes unpredictable cycles—periods during which they are generally up and periods during which they are generally down, with variations on a daily basis. Psychotherapists are trained to help their clients develop resilience to weather life's inevitable ups and downs. To be a successful investor, you must develop resilience to deal with the inevitable ups and downs of the marketplace. Just as anger, sadness, loneliness, and so forth are as much a normal part of life as feelings of joy and satisfaction, so, too, are bear markets as normal and inevitable as bull markets. Moreover, in the stock market, as in a functional person's life, the good has historically outweighed the bad.

A quick review of the S&P 500, a broad index of the stock market, reveals that, overall, stocks as an asset class have historically had a positive trend. To illustrate the overall long-term trend in stocks, we have looked up the same date at 10-year intervals starting in 1953 (accounting for the date falling on a weekend) and noted the closing value of the S&P 500 on each of those dates (Table 16.1). You can see that the closing quote shows a consistent, long-term, positive general trend in stock prices. Remembering the stock market's long history of upward movement can give you the confidence you need to invest wisely in your future.

---

[1] Keep in mind that for dollar cost averaging to work you must be prepared to commit the financial resources and have the resolve to make the contributions on each appointed date. Regular investing does not ensure a profit and does not protect against loss in declining markets. Investors should consider their ability to invest continuously during periods of fluctuating price levels.

TABLE 16.1
S&P 500 Selected Dates

Date	Closing Quote
9-8-1953	23.61
9-6-1963	72.84
9-7-1973	104.76
9-7-1983	167.96
9-7-1993	458.52
9-8-2003	1031.64

Source: MSN MoneyCentral. *http://moneycental.msn.com.*

ASSET ALLOCATION

Asset allocation is the investment strategy of diversifying your investments among a variety of investment classes. Broad categories of investment classes include stocks, bonds, and cash. Within these three categories are a great many subcategories. Table 16.2 presents the items included in a typical asset allocation model.

The essential idea behind asset allocation is to align your investment portfolio with your investment goals while avoiding two traps:

Trying to time the market.
Putting all your eggs into one basket.

Your financial advisor should be well versed in asset allocation strategies designed to meet your goals. He or she can help you design and implement a rational strategy.

TABLE 16.2
Asset Classes

Stocks	Bonds	Cash	Specialty
Value stocks	Government bonds	Money markets	Real estate
Growth stocks	Corporate bonds	CDs	
Foreign stock	Government agency bonds	Bank accounts	
Large cap stocks	Junk bonds		
Mid-cap stocks	Municipal bonds		
Small cap stocks			

STEADY AS YOU GO: COMBINING DOLLAR COST AVERAGING WITH ASSET ALLOCATION

A strategy therapists commonly use in their retirement plans is that of combining dollar cost averaging with an asset allocation strategy. This combination can be used in any qualified or individual retirement plan. As we have discussed, dollar cost averaging involves investing the same amount of money on a regular basis (usually monthly) into a given investment. Combining dollar cost averaging with asset allocation involves investing a fixed amount of money each month into a variety of investments that comprise a particular asset allocation mix. For example, Mary Smith, LCSW, invests $1,500 per month into her individual 401(k) plan. She has established an asset allocation model with her financial advisor that includes 70% into a mix of equities-based securities, 20% into bonds, and 10% into cash equivalents. Each month, $1,050 goes into her equities securities, $300 into her bond securities, and $150 into her money market fund.

The whole process can be automated with scheduled bank deductions that go toward the purchase of the securities in the asset allocation model. The regularity of investing helps put the investor in a more proactive and disciplined frame of mind.

Fluctuations in the market can be compared to fluctuations in weather conditions. Just as you would not close down your office during cold weather or cancel a client because it looked like it might rain, so is it important not to allow changes in the market "weather" to dictate your investment activity. Dollar cost averaging plus asset allocation provides a disciplined, consistent way to structure your investing on your path toward establishing a sound financial footing.

MODERN PORTFOLIO THEORY

In the 1950s economist Harry Markowitz wrote about optimizing a portfolio through diversification. Markowitz looked beyond the picking of individual stocks and considered the issue of creating overall portfolios that are efficient in terms of generating maximum return for a given degree of risk. Markowitz's innovative approach to stock market investing won him the Nobel Prize in economics. His approach is known as modern portfolio theory. This theory has been highly influential among investment professionals and is a widely respected approach to investing.

Markowitz noted that certain stocks have an inverse correlation to each other in terms of price. For a simplified, hypothetical example, let us say that low fuel prices are good for the airlines and bad for the oil companies. Conversely, high fuel prices are bad for the airlines and good for oil companies. If the stock prices of ABC Oil Company and XYZ Airlines reflect these issues, than the prices of these stocks may exhibit a history of low correlation with each other. A correlation coefficient of 1 means that the prices of two securities move in lock step. A correlation coefficient of 0 means that two securities move totally independently of each other. A correlation coefficient of −1 means that two securities move simultaneously in opposite directions. You would attain better diversification if you invested in ABC Oil and XYZ Airlines than if you invested in ABC Oil and DEF Oil. Diversification lends stability to a portfolio.

Markowitz and his colleagues quantified a series of observations about risk, return, correlation coefficients, and portfolio efficiency. The process of establishing an efficient portfolio involves asset allocation among individual securities or asset classes that are chosen in part for diversification purposes. An efficient portfolio maximizes total return for a given risk level.

Although a discussion about the correlation coefficients of various asset classes may not be scintillating, it is important for you to consider your overall portfolio and its asset allocation in making your investment decisions. It is very difficult for even the most experienced professional to consistently pick winning individual stocks. It is even harder for people outside of Wall Street to pick winners. If you orient yourself to proper asset allocation based on modern portfolio theory, you do not need to "pick a winner." Instead, you can put together an asset allocation, based on your risk tolerance and life circumstances, that makes sense and that comprises an efficient portfolio. Your financial planning professional should be able to help you assemble a portfolio that is appropriate for your needs.

TIME VALUE OF MONEY AND TAX-DEFERRED INVESTING

Anyone would prefer to receive $10,000 today than $10,000 a year from now. There are two basic reasons for this. The first is that the sooner one has one's money in hand, the sooner one has an opportunity to make money with that money. The second reason is that inflation decreases the value of your money, so that $10,000 a year from now will in all likelihood buy you fewer goods and services than it does today. A familiar illustration of the time value of money is the savings bond. When you buy a $5,000 series EE savings bond, you pay half the face value for the bond, or $2,500. Interest accrues monthly on the bond at a variable rate until it reaches the face value. If interest rates are high, then the bond will mature earlier. If interest rates are low, it will take more time for the bond to mature. If you were to buy a $5,000 series EE savings bond for $2,500 that earned an average rate of 5%, it would take that bond 14½ years to mature. The U.S. government has priced the *time value* of having possession of your $2,500 for 14½ years at $2,500.

How does the time value of money relate to your financial life? Let us look at the issue of tax-deferred savings versus taxable savings. With tax-deferred savings, you have the opportunity to hang on to more of your money, because you are deferring the payment of taxes on capital gains and dividends that you would pay with a taxable account. The fact that you can defer payment of taxes allows for the possibility of amplifying the time value of your retirement money and represents the chief advantage of tax-deferred investing for retirement.

Consider the case of Joseph Sanders, MD, a psychiatrist in private practice who earns $150,000 per year and pays federal income taxes at the rate of 35%. Dr. Sanders has just completed a course of treatment with a patient suffering from depression. He bills her insurer and receives a payment of $7,500. Because Dr. Sanders is taxed at the rate of 35%, he must pay $2,625 of his fee in taxes, leaving him with $4,875. If he were to invest that money in a portfolio of securities for 1 year and achieve a gain of 10%, he would add $487.50 of gain to his $4,875, giving him $5,362.50. However, when he sells that security after 1 year, his gain is taxed at the long-term capital gains rate of 15% (if he sells before 1 year, his capital gains are taxed at his income tax rate of 35%). This reduces his gain by $73.12, leaving him with $5265 saved after 1 year.

On the other hand, if Dr. Sanders puts that $7,500 into his qualified retirement plan, then he could avoid all of the taxes discussed

TABLE 16.3
Taxable vs. Tax Deferred on $7,500 in Income (1 Year)

	Taxable Account	Tax-Deferred Account
Amount of insurance payment	$7,500	$7,500
Subtract 35% for taxable account	$2,625	No taxes due
After-tax amount saved	$4,875	$7,500
Earn 10% interest	$487.50	$750
Subtotal	$5,362.50	$8,250
Deduct long-term capital gains rate of 15% after 1 year when security is sold	$73.12	No taxes due on interest earned
Total after 1 year	$5289.38	$8,250

above. If he were achieving a 10% return, after 1 year he would have made $750 in interest and the $7,500 would now be worth $8250. This is quite a contrast with the $5289.38 (Table 16.3).

Now consider the time value of Dr. Sanders' investment in his tax-deferred account. Again, bear in mind that he is not paying taxes on capital gains or dividends on his investments, thereby amplifying the effect of compounding. Let us assume that Dr. Sanders is 40 years old at the time he receives the initial $7,500 payment, that he holds the money until age 65, and that his average annual rate of return is 10%.

TABLE 16.4
Tax-Deferred Accumulation on a $7500 Payment over 25 Years

Years	Tax-Deferred Accumulation
Initial payment	$7,500
Amount saved after 1 year on a payment of $7,500 (from Table 16.4)	$8250
Year 2	$9075
Year 3	$9983
Year 4	$10,981
Year 5	$12,079
Year 6	$13,287
Year 7	$14,615
Year 8	$16,077
Year 9	$17,685
Year 10	$19,453
Year 11	$21,398
Year 12	$23,538
Year 13	$25,892
Year 14	$28,481
Year 15	$31,329
Year 16	$34,462
Year 17	$37,909
Year 18	$41,699
Year 19	$45,869
Year 20	$50,456
Year 21	$55,502
Year 22	$61,052
Year 23	$67,157
Year 24	$73,873
Year 25	$81,260

Note: Assumptions: 10% annual return, 25 years of savings, tax rate of 36%. This example is for illustrative purposes only. Rates of return are hypothetical and are not representative of any one investment. Individual investors' results may vary. Please note: Investments with higher rates of return are associated with higher volatility and degrees of risk.

When taxation is deferred, the time value of money is higher, because gains in the tax-deferred account will be taxed only when the account owner withdraws the money in retirement. In the meantime, the power of compounding is not reduced by taxation. Table 16.4 illustrates how investors can put the time value of money to work for themselves very effectively when they combine the effect of compounding with the deferral of taxation. This explains the popularity of tax-qualified retirement accounts among therapists in private practice. It also provides a strong argument for starting a savings program as early as possible, so that you have time to put the time value of money to work for you.

CHAPTER 17

Common Investments for Therapists

STOCKS

Stocks are classified as equity instruments because they provide the stockholder with ownership or equity in a corporation. Common stocks are the most widely held type of equity security. As an investor, you can own common stocks directly or through a variety of instruments such as mutual funds or separate accounts in variable annuities and variable universal life insurance. Common stocks are initially issued by the corporation in a stock offering for investors; this offering raises money for the corporation. Thereafter, common stocks are traded in the various stock markets from one investor to another.

Corporations are owned by their stockholders. The stockowners elect a board of directors, who in turn appoint upper management. Many common stocks pay dividends out of the corporation's profits, but corporations are under no legal obligation to pay dividends to common stockholders. Some stocks pay low or no dividends but are attractive to investors because the company has growth potential that will hopefully be reflected in rising stock prices. A typical dividend-paying stock might be a well-established utility company that is not likely to grow a great deal but has healthy profits from which to pay dividends to stockholders. A typical growth stock that does not pay dividends might be a relatively new high-tech firm that has the potential to grow. Such a firm may well use its profits to invest in its future growth rather than to pay profits to shareholders.

Stock investing inherently involves risk. Investments in stocks are not guaranteed to grow in value, or even to have any future value whatever. If you bought stock in the XYZ Internet Firm at the height of the tech bubble and the firm subsequently failed (as many did), the stock value may well have gone to zero, leaving you with worthless equity in a nonexistent company. On the other hand, many intelligent and prudent people are heavily invested in common stocks. The reason many investors assume the risks of stock ownership is the possibility of financial rewards. From 1926 to 2001 the S&P 500, a standard index of leading stocks, showed an average return of 10.7%.[1] Historically, stocks have provided returns higher than inflation, and many investors value stocks as a fundamental component of their investment portfolio.

BONDS

Bonds are debt securities or IOUs issued by governments, government agencies, and corporations. They are usually purchased at face value. The bond issuer pays the bondholder regular interest payments until the bond matures. At that time, the bond issuer pays back the face value of the bond. Bonds are initially purchased by investors from representatives of the issuing entity. They can then be sold to other investors on the secondary market. Bond prices on the secondary market fluctuate inversely with interest rates. When interest rates go up, bond prices on the secondary market decline; when interest rates go down, bond prices on the secondary market rise. Overall, bond prices will fluctuate less than stock prices (although a bond could become worthless if the issuing entity goes bankrupt). Investors typically purchase bonds for their income potential and to diversify their investment portfolio. As a general rule, more conservative portfolios will have a higher percentage of bonds relative to stocks in the asset allocation. More aggressive portfolios will have a higher percentage of stocks.

Bonds issued by corporations usually have a $1,000 face or par value. An intermediate-term bond has a maturity of 2–10 years and is usually called a "note." Long-term bonds have maturities greater

---

[1] Fidelity Investments Institutional Services Company 316470.001. "How to Stay the Course in Volatile Times."

than 10 years. Corporate bonds have a periodic interest payment rate called the "coupon rate." Interest is paid twice a year to the owner of the bond. Corporate bonds mature at a specified date, at which time the issuer pays the owner the face value of the bond. Corporate bonds are rated by independent rating companies for the financial strength of the issuer. Moody's, Standard & Poor's, Fitch, and Duff & Phelps are the major bond rating companies. Bonds with strong ratings are considered "investment grade." Bonds with lower ratings are known as "junk bonds" and of course are riskier than investment-grade bonds. Investors will take on more risk if they can achieve a higher reward, so the more risk inherent in a bond, the higher the coupon rate that will be offered.

Bonds issued by municipalities are called "munis." Munis pay interest that is federally tax free, so they have lower coupon rates than other bonds, and the interest may be subject to the alternative minimum tax. You should avoid buying munis within a tax-deferred retirement account because taxes are already deferred in these accounts. You are better off with higher yielding taxable bonds in your retirement account.

The federal government is a major issuer of bonds. The U.S. Department of the Treasury issues Treasury bills (T-bills) that have a maturity of less than 1 year, notes that mature in 1–10 years, and bonds that reach maturity in more than 10 years. Federally issued bonds pay less than bonds issued by corporations, because the default risk on a federally issued bond is considered to be negligible. Because T-bills are short-term securities that mature in 1 year or less, they do not pay interest semi-annually. Instead, the investor buys T-bills for a price less than their face value. When the T-bills mature, the U.S. government pays their face value. The interest paid is the difference between the purchase price of the T-bill and what the U.S. government pays out at maturity. For example, if you bought a $10,000 26-week Treasury bill for $9,800 and held it until maturity, your interest would be $200. Treasury notes and bonds, being longer term, pay a fixed rate of interest every 6 months until they mature, at which time the U.S. government pays their face value. The difference between a Treasury note and a Treasury bond is the length of time until maturity. You can usually buy notes and bonds for a price close to their face value. Government securities are guaranteed by the full faith and credit of the U.S. government as to timely repayment of principal and interest if held to maturity.

The U.S. government sells two kinds of Treasury notes: fixed-principal and inflation-indexed. Both pay interest twice a year, but the principal value of inflation-indexed securities is adjusted to reflect inflation as measured by the Consumer Price Index. The U.S. Treasury calculates the semi-annual interest payments and maturity payment based on the inflation-adjusted principal value of the inflation-indexed note. Inflation-indexed securities have the advantage of removing the risk that inflation will outpace the coupon rate of the bond.

As with the purchasing of stocks, many investors leave the purchasing of bonds to professional money managers. Bond mutual funds are often a convenient and prudent way for the average investor to get involved in the bond market. We discuss mutual funds in more detail below.

CASH INSTRUMENTS

Savings Accounts and Bank CDs

Depository institutions such as banks, savings and loan institutions, and credit unions offer savings accounts that are insured up to a maximum of $100,000 by the Federal Deposit Insurance Corporation (FDIC). Such institutions also offer certificates of deposit (CDs). CD maturities range from 30 days to 10 years. Like bank savings accounts, bank CDs are insured by the FDIC for up to $100,000.

Money Market Funds

The money market consists of very short-term debt securities issued by the federal government, banks, corporations, and other financial institutions. Money market funds use the interest payments they receive on such securities to provide interest payments to their investors. Money market funds attempt to maintain a stable price of $1.00 per share. The money market is very liquid. Most money market funds provide checking features, with no sales charge for early withdrawal of funds.[2] Money market instruments such as Treasury bills, commercial paper, and large bank CDs are considered very secure. Investors participate in the money market for stability of their principal and liquidity. Money market instruments are often referred to as cash.

---

[2] An investment in a money market fund is not insured or guaranteed by the Federal Deposit Insurance Corporation or any other government agency. Although a money market mutual fund seeks to preserve the value of your investment at $1 per share, it is possible to lose money by investing in these funds. CDs are FDIC insured up to $100,000 as to timely payment of principal and interest if held to maturity.

Mutual Funds

A mutual fund pools the resources of many investors into a professionally managed portfolio of securities.[3] Each share represents a proportional ownership of the mutual fund's portfolio. Funds may invest in a variety of securities, but most invest in stocks and/or bonds. Mutual funds are commonly held by large and small investors alike. They allow investors to share the cost of stock transactions with other investors and allow smaller investors access to professional money management and diversified holdings. Mutual funds offer instant diversification, in that one share of a mutual fund represents your proportional ownership in all of the stocks underlying a particular fund. Further diversification occurs when the investor participates in a variety of mutual funds, each focusing on a different asset class.

Mutual funds are a fundamental tool for investing in today's financial marketplace and are commonly held by therapists. They may be an appropriate investment vehicle for therapists who do not have the time, expertise, or inclination to pick their own stocks. There are a great many mutual funds to choose from. Many are very specialized, focusing on a specific type of investment or asset class. This specialization allows you and your financial advisor to create a well-diversified portfolio.

In our earlier discussion of asset allocation, we mentioned a variety of asset classes that typically comprise the elements of a diversified portfolio of securities. In Table 17.1, we provide a brief definition of major asset classes that are commonly held in mutual funds.

REAL ESTATE

Although real estate can be a profitable investment, it is not suitable for all investors. Many therapists would be better advised to invest in real estate-related securities as part of a well-diversified portfolio rather than to buy property directly. Without the ability to invest a fairly significant amount of capital, and without disposable income to devote to the "care and feeding" of property in the early stages, investing in real estate is not a wise option. Before making a real estate investment, consider the following issues:

---

[3] Mutual funds are an investment that fluctuates with market conditions, so they do involve risk. Investment return and principal value will fluctuate so that, when redeemed, an investor's shares may be worth more or less than original cost. Mutual funds are sold by prospectus only. Please read the prospectus carefully before investing or sending money.

TABLE 17.1
Major Asset Classes Defined

STOCK FUNDS	
Value funds	Stocks that are considered a good buy primarily because analysis of the stock indicates that it is underpriced in relation to the earnings and overall health of the issuing corporation.
Growth funds	Stocks of corporations that are poised to grow. Typically, growth funds will invest in corporations with higher risk and higher potential for growth, with dividend payments being a secondary consideration.
Foreign stock funds	Stocks of non-U.S. corporations diversify a portfolio to temper the risk of macro-economic factors affecting the entire U.S. stock market.
Large cap funds	These funds invest in companies with large capitalization, many of which are household names such as GE, GM, IBM, Coca Cola, and so forth. These funds provide the stability of highly established corporations in a portfolio. Such funds are likely to pay more in dividends than do growth funds.
Mid-cap funds	These funds invest in companies with medium capitalization. They tend to be more volatile than large cap funds.
Small cap funds	These funds invest in companies with relatively small capitalization. They tend to be more volatile than large or mid-cap funds.
BOND FUNDS	
Government bond funds	These funds provide investors with a variety of issues of the U.S. Treasury. They are considered conservative investments that provide stability to a portfolio. The interest from U.S. government bonds is not subject to state and local taxes.
Corporate bond funds	These funds generally focus on high-quality, investment-grade corporate bonds. Make sure to read the prospectus, because some corporate bond funds invest in below-investment-grade securities (junk bonds), which are of course more risky than investment-grade securities.
Junk bond funds	These funds focus on high-paying bonds of entities with below-investment grade ratings. Such funds can play a useful role in a given portfolio but should not be confused with more secure bond funds of higher rated bonds. These funds are sometimes called high-yield bond funds.
Government agency funds	These funds focus on debt securities from government agencies such as mortgage giants FNMA "Fannie Mae" and GNMA "Ginnie Mae."

	They usually bear a slightly higher interest rate than government funds and are a popular choice for investors seeking relatively secure investments.
Municipal bond funds	These funds are comprised of municipal bonds issued by entities such as states, cities, and counties. They are usually exempt from federal income taxes. They are not appropriate investments in a tax-deferred account.
SPECIALTY Real estate funds	These funds invest in real estate-related securities such as real estate investment trusts and companies in the real estate and construction businesses.
CASH Money market funds	These funds are the most conservative element in a mutual fund portfolio. Comprised of secure, short-term securities, money market funds attempt to keep the value of a single share at $1.00. Most mutual fund companies and brokerage houses allow investors to write checks against their money market funds, because they are highly liquid.

Investment in real estate inevitably entails risk. You will need to take out a substantial loan as well as make a down payment. The capital you invest will be "illiquid"; that is, not easily converted to cash. When looking for property to buy, many investors look for a "desperate seller." This is something you do not want to be. You must be able to hold the property until market conditions are favorable and you are able to find a qualified buyer willing to pay an acceptable price.

There will inevitably be a vacancy factor—the period between when one tenant moves out and the time you are able to find another suitable tenant. Real estate investors typically calculate the vacancy factor as 5% of their total rents. In a "down" market, it could climb as high as 10% or more, putting a significant dent in your cash flow.

You will need funds for emergencies, maintenance, taxes, covering the vacancy factor, and so forth. A wise real estate investor maintains a "slush fund" for unexpected expenses. You should plan to put a percentage of each month's rental income (typically 3–5%) into this fund.

Real estate investments require regular supervision and attention. If you do not live nearby, or for some reason are unable to provide this attention yourself, the property must pay enough of a return to cover hiring a property manager.

Investment property can be quite time consuming. The property must be kept clean and in good repair, rents collected, tenants kept satisfied, and proper bookkeeping maintained. These tasks require time and a certain degree of skill. Unless you can afford the services of a property manager, bear in mind that each hour spent on property management is an hour you are not managing your practice.

A good credit rating is vital to obtain favorable mortgage rates and loan terms.

We do not mean to discourage anyone from considering real estate investments. Certainly, many fortunes have been made in real estate. We simply want to be clear that real estate investing requires four things:

Sufficient capital
The time and skill necessary to manage and maintain the property
A willingness to tolerate a fair amount of risk
The ability to be comfortable with the prospect of having your money tied up for an indefinite period of time

If you have these attributes and investing in real estate appeals to you, it may be an excellent alternative for you. Regardless, you will want to maintain a diversity of other investments to provide yourself with a balanced portfolio.

Buying the Building in Which You Practice

If, having considered the issues listed above, you feel ready to make the leap into real estate investing, you might want to consider buying a building to house your practice. Many therapists (including your authors) find owning the building they practice in to be good both as an income-producing investment and as a practice-building venture.

Owning the building in which you practice and renting space to other professionals can have a number of benefits:

Rather than spending money each month on renting an office, you will be building capital.

Your tenants will (at least theoretically!) cover your mortgage, providing you with rent-free office space.

You will have the freedom to shape your space to suit your own tastes rather than adapting to a landlord's.

You will have control over the people with whom you share your space. You will have the authority to screen and select tenants.

Because you will be at your office on a regular basis, supervision and maintenance of the property can be more easily accomplished.

Your investment should decrease your tax liability.[4]

Becoming a landlord is another way to become known in your professional community.

If you own a well-kept and well-run office building and lease space to fellow therapists, your name will become increasingly familiar to others in the community. Gaining respect as a landlord can be a form of indirect marketing for your practice, just as becoming more established in your practice can make a building you own more appealing to other therapists seeking office space. The downside of renting to colleagues is that you may be tempted to be less than businesslike in your dealings with them. If you find yourself offering people "special deals" or overlooking past due rent because they are friends, you will quickly discover that your investment has become a liability. In our experience, most therapists are cooperative, responsible tenants. You must do your part by being clear about expectations and living up to your part of the bargain (i.e., providing a well-maintained space with a pleasant, professional atmosphere).

Buying a professional building need not be a grandiose undertaking. Many therapists work in older homes that have been converted for professional use. This type of arrangement can be quite congenial for the therapist as landlord, in that owning this type of building has much in common with owning one's own home and may be less intimidating, and more financially feasible than buying a building that was originally designed for commercial use. An older home often has the kind of comfortable feeling that can be quite appealing to therapists and clients alike.

---

[4] This is not intended as specific tax advice. Please consult your professional tax advisor for information suited to your individual situation.

Real Estate-Related Securities

If investing directly in real estate is not for you, you might consider the possibility of participating in the real estate market indirectly through real estate stocks or other real estate-related securities. Several types of indirect real estate investments may be suitable for you.

REITs

A real estate investment trust (REIT) is a company that owns, operates, and in some cases finances commercial real estate such as apartment buildings, shopping malls, warehouses, or hotels. REITs were created by an act of Congress in 1960. There are three kinds of REITs: equity REITs invest in commercial property; mortgage REITs make construction and mortgage loans; and hybrid REITs do both. The majority of REITS are equity REITs. In creating the legal structure for REITs, Congress's purpose was to make available to the small investor the many financial benefits that accrue to the well-capitalized commercial real estate investor. The financial resources of many small investors are pooled, and the combined capital is put in commercial real estate ownership and financing. REITs are required by law to pay 90% of their taxable income each year to their shareholders.

As a shareholder in an REIT you are paid a dividend. At the time of this writing, REIT dividends can reach 8–9% per year (this may well have changed by the time you read this, so do your research). REIT dividends are partly taxable (part of the dividend is a return of capital, which is not taxable). So, a good place to own an REIT is inside your retirement account, where the taxation will be deferred. Illiquidity has traditionally been the bane of real estate investors. However, with an REIT that is publicly traded on a major stock exchange, you can turn your investment into cash immediately. A list of stock exchange-traded REITs is available at *http://www.investinreits.com.*

Another attractive feature of REITs is that they have a low correlation to other stocks and bonds, so they can help diversify your portfolio. Whether stocks go up or down, REIT prices tend to act independently, giving your portfolio balance. A report from Ibbotson Associates, a leader in asset allocation strategies "show(s) that, given their low correlation (to the price of stocks) real estate stocks are an important and effective source of diversification."[5] Some

---

[5] "REITs' Low Correlation to Other Stocks and Bonds Is Key Factor for Portfolio Diversification." National Association of Real Estate Investment Trusts. 29 May 2001.

financial advisors recommend that 10–20% of holdings in a diversified portfolio should go to REITs as a counterweight to stocks.[6]

Mutual Funds that Hold REITs

Buying into an REIT is not unlike buying an individual stock. You should do a good deal of research and due diligence before you buy. Of course most therapists have neither the time nor the expertise to do the necessary research. If you have a financial advisor, he or she may guide you in finding an REIT that is reputable and appropriate for you. Otherwise, you might consider investing in a mutual fund that invests in REITs. These funds are professionally managed and offer a diversity of REITs so that your risk is spread out. An online resource for learning about REITs and REIT mutual funds is *http://www.reitnet.com*, which contains a comprehensive list of REIT mutual funds and allows you to sort by various factors such as net asset value and return. REIT mutual funds also offer the advantage of liquidity, allowing you to turn your investment into cash at your convenience.

Limited Partnerships

You may recall that real estate limited partnerships (RELPs) were quite popular as a tax shelter until 1986, when the U.S. Congress changed the rules as part of the Tax Reform Act of 1986. We have worked with many psychiatrists and other mental health professionals who were heavily invested in RELPs, which turned significantly downward after the tax rules changed. RELPs can work successfully if you know well the track record of the general partners and have fully vetted every aspect of the deal. However, for most therapists, who probably lack the resources to fully vet such partnerships, it is usually best to steer clear of these investments. One of the principal problems with RELPs is a lack of liquidity—they are usually difficult to sell and frequently cannot be liquidated until the general partners liquidate the entire limited partnership. Therefore, the limited partner has little control over when he or she can take out principal.

CONCLUSION

As one builds and maintains a financial portfolio, one becomes aware of the importance of owning a diversity of investments. Each

---

[6] "*REITs: Own Real Estate Without the Hassle.*" Mary Rowland. MSN MoneyCentral. 1 Jan. 2003. <*http://moneycentral.msn/vpm/content/P39600.asp?Printer*>.

of the investments discussed in this chapter has unique characteristics. Bonds, stocks, real estate and other investments discussed in this chapter all perform differently from each other. It is our hope that readers will have gained a greater understanding of their investments and a fuller appreciation of the contribution of each investment to a successful and resilient portfolio.

CHAPTER 18

Socially Responsible Investing

Most therapists are, by nature and training, attuned to the social dimension of life. After all, you have chosen work that is deeply human. You care about people. Understanding that money is a powerful energy that can have both positive and negative effects on the world, it may be important for you to align your investment decisions with your values. Socially screened investment options exist for mutual funds, annuities, variable universal life insurance, and individually managed accounts. A good resource for socially responsible investing is *http://www.socialinvest.org;* it is a clearing-house of information on all aspects of such investments. Socially responsible investing involves making a social analysis of the companies in which you invest. Perhaps you do not want your money going to a tobacco-producing company. Perhaps you are concerned about ecological issues and do not want to invest in companies that have a poor environmental record. Perhaps you are concerned with children's issues and do not want your money invested in companies that hire child labor in underdeveloped countries. Perhaps you are tuned into women's issues and want to avoid companies with poor conditions for women. Perhaps you do not want to invest in arms manufacturing. Socially responsible investing is the practice of taking these kinds of issues into account when determining which companies to invest in.

A good deal of research supports the assertion that investors do not need to sacrifice returns with socially responsible investing. Two websites address this issue of return (*http://www.kld.com* and *http://www.sristudies.org*) and are filled with academic studies exploring this issue. Both are well worth visiting if you are seriously considering a socially screened portfolio.

Socially responsible investing can work in a number of ways. The first way is by avoiding companies with poor records for social responsibility. Another way is by advocating for corporate change with shareholder resolutions. This means that the socially responsible money management firm may stay invested in a corporation with practices that it considers less than fully responsible. Shareholder resolutions are then used as a leverage to create dialogue with the company about the practice in question. Common shareholder resolutions deal with environmental and workplace practices of the corporation. If your social concerns are being addressed in your investment portfolio, it may help you feel better about investing, and therefore help you to more actively integrate your financial thinking into your life.

CHAPTER 19

Debt and Credit Issues

Backpackers who want to pack lightly have an apt saying: "take care of the ounces, and the pounds will take care of themselves." So it goes in one's financial life; wasted dollars lead to wasted thousands of dollars, and so on, until it turns into real money. On the other hand, staying conscious and conservative with small expenses can lead to surprisingly significant improvements in the bigger picture. Therapists typically cannot look forward to "a big deal": a sale or transaction that can bail them out. Just by the nature of the profession and the regularity (hopefully) with which you generate income, you are the financial "tortoise" rather than the "hare." Therefore, you must constantly bear in mind the overall trajectory of your financial life. It is important to be conscious of your spending habits while attending to the profitability of your professional practice. If you can do these two things consistently, you will, over time, build a strong financial structure for your life.

Choices you make about debt are particularly important in determining the direction of your financial trajectory. Debt is, by design, easy to get into and difficult to get out of. The credit industry is huge and extremely sophisticated, and they stay in business by making a profit on your debt. It is their right to make legal profits from the uninformed consumer. Accordingly, it is the consumers' responsibility to be informed in order to act in their long-term self-interest.

Let us take a look at some ways in which consumers can use credit wisely, increasing their financial well-being rather than undermining it.

KEEPING ON TOP OF YOUR CREDIT

Your credit report is significant, because it can affect the cost of a number of your business and personal expenses. Whenever you apply for credit of any kind, a good credit rating can result in your being offered more favorable rates and terms. It can even be the deciding factor in whether or not you are able to move forward with a particular transaction. Your credit rating may affect:

- Your office lease terms
- The mortgage rate on your home
- The availability of a home equity loan
- The rate on your car loan
- The availability and desirability of credit cards
- The rates on life and homeowners insurance

So, what is your credit rating? It is actually quite easy to find out. All consumers are given a FICO score, which is a numerical evaluation of their overall credit. This score is the criterion on which most creditors base their lending decisions. Scores range from 300 to 850. A variety of factors go into generating a consumer's FICO score, including one's financial stability, outstanding balances, and past payment history. Consumers can go online to *http:// www.Equifax.com* or *http://www.myFICO.com* to find their FICO score. The report informs consumers about their scores, compares them with national averages, and gives information about how to improve them.

GETTING HELP FOR DEBT AND CREDIT PROBLEMS

Once you have checked your FICO score, you have an idea of how well you are doing in managing debt and credit in your life. At this point, it is important to be honest with yourself. Issues around debt and credit can loom large, and many people experience a good deal of shame if they get into difficulty in these areas. For most people who struggle with credit issues, credit cards present the biggest temptation and the biggest problem. We will look specifically at the question of credit cards below. If you are having difficulty with debt and credit card issues, here are some general guidelines:

- Come clean with your spouse or partner. In Chapter 10, we addressed the importance of open, flexible communication regarding finances. If you are hiding details about your credit history or your financial dealings from your partner, you are creating a recipe for disaster. Have a frank discussion and enlist your partner's aid in working through whatever problems with which you are struggling.
- Consider accessing professional financial help. You may need to talk with an attorney, a tax advisor, a financial planner, or all of the above. Help is available to sort through legal tangles and put you back on course.
- Consider professional psychological help. Chapter 7 and Chapter 8 explored the powerful unconscious forces that underlie the ways people deal with money. Working with your own therapist to come to a better understanding of how these forces influence your financial decisions can be enlightening and liberating.
- Pay careful attention to the discussion of credit cards that follows.

CREDIT CARDS—NINE STEPS TO DEBT REDUCTION

Credit cards can be to personal finance what cigarettes are to your health. Daisy smokes one cigarette a day at most. Many days she goes without any cigarettes at all. The five cigarettes she has per week are (so she assures Peter) not excessively harmful. Peter, in contrast, used to be a two-pack-a-day Camel Filters man. Today, he does not smoke at all, because he knows that moderation is not possible for him. Daisy is able to use tobacco without becoming addicted, whereas Peter is a tobacco addict. There is a corollary in the way in which people use credit cards. For people who can pay off their credit cards each month without carrying a balance, they can be useful and convenient. However, if you are carrying thousands of dollars of credit card debt and making the minimum payments each month, you may consider looking at your use of credit as a form of addiction.

How serious is this addiction? In researching for this chapter, we found some sobering statistics:

- The average American carries a credit card balance of $8,400.[1]
- At a 20% APR for this level of debt, consumers are paying $1,680 per year in interest alone.

---

[1] *"Pay Off Your Credit Card Debt."* Ian McDonald. TheStreet.com. 28 Oct. 2001. <*http://aol.thestreet.com/funds/mutualfundmonday/10003085.html*>.

- Consumers often pay late fees and annual fees in addition to the interest.

Now let us look at what you could do with this money if you were not using it to pay off credit card debt. Beginning at age 40, you could invest that $1,680 into an IRA each year. Assuming a 6% rate of return and retirement at age 65, at retirement time the investor would have more than $102,000 in his or her IRA. When consumers carry credit card debt, they are not only paying out exorbitant interest and fees, they are also paying a lot in lost opportunity. Those with credit card debt lose opportunities to invest in themselves—their retirement, their children's education, along with their professional development and other life goals.

Like the cigarette companies, the credit card companies are simply offering consumers the right as Americans to exercise their freedom to choose. Fair enough. But (also like the cigarette companies) they target young people and manipulate the consumer with sophisticated and misleading marketing. They make money by seducing consumers into overspending and then charge exorbitant interest and fees. To put it bluntly, the credit card companies are not your friends.

Dr. Eric Hollander, a highly respected researcher at the Mt. Sinai School of Medicine in New York, is studying the question of whether to include "compulsive shopping" as an impulse disorder in the upcoming *DSM-V*. In an interview on National Public Radio's (NPR) "Talk of the Nation,"[2] Dr. Hollander stated that many people think of compulsive shopping as a trivial problem. We think of it in terms of the normal pleasure in making a satisfying purchase. Compulsive shopping, however, can be compared to compulsive overeating. Making purchases, like eating, is a normal and necessary part of daily life. The compulsive shopper, though, makes purchases not out of necessity or even out of real desire but rather out of a need to soothe internal feelings of anxiety or emptiness. Just as the compulsive overeater can feel bloated without ever feeling satisfied, the compulsive shopper can acquire a warehouse full of goods without a sense of enough. Perhaps the saddest irony is the fact that people who shop compulsively often spend down the financial resources that would allow them to seek out the psychotherapy that could help them.

In our view, the credit card industry along with the advertising industry have played on the susceptibility of consumers. The message to buy is ubiquitous—now advertisers are even spreading their messages in schools. Credit card offers start coming in before a

---

[2] Hollander, Eric, MD. Interview with Neal Conan. *Talk of the Nation*. National Public Radio. 6 Jan. 2003.

young person has even graduated from high school. Kicking the credit card habit is a little like quitting junk food: everywhere you turn, you are invited to spend impulsively, just as the innumerable junk food outlets you encounter daily invite you to eat impulsively and without thought.

When Peter was a smoker, he used to think of his familiar Camel Filters as a friend. Now, he recognizes them as an adversary. This kind of cognitive reframing may be useful with regard to credit card use. In modern America, it is just about impossible not to use plastic. But thinking of consumer credit as your adversary rather than your friend will begin to put you in a more realistic frame of mind about your spending. When you use plastic, it is best to have a debit card arrangement, which limits the funds you have available. If you are using credit to obtain airline miles, be sure to pay those balances off each month. It will be a lot cheaper for you to buy your tickets online than it will be to pay 15–20% on revolving credit.

If you have determined that you want to work on your credit card spending, take the following practical steps:

Make a "fearless and searching inventory" of your credit card debt. Study your balances along with the interest and fees you are paying. To help contain the anxiety, it can be helpful to have a trusted friend simply sit with you while you look carefully over your balances.

List the cards by the interest rates they charge, ranking them from lowest to highest.

If you have a credit card with an interest rate of 14% or less, move your balances to that card.

If you do not have a card with a low rate and you have a good credit standing, go to *http://www.cardweb.com* for comparison card shopping. Get a lower interest rate card and transfer your higher interest card balances to that card.

Many cards have low introductory fees. Move the balances to one of these cards and pay aggressively for those first 6 months.

Determine the maximum you can to afford to pay each month in order to pay off your balances. Remember: "No pain, no gain." Make a pledge to yourself to pay off at least 2.5% of the balance each month. If you make only the minimum payments, it will take you a very long time and a great deal in interest payments to get down to a zero balance. How much could you pay each month if you absolutely had to? $500? $750? $1,000?

When paying off credit card debt, pay off your highest interest rate cards first.

Resolve that you will use your credit only for emergencies. If you cannot afford something, then do not buy it. Save money until you can pay for it in cash.

Refinancing your home will usually give you a more favorable interest rate plus possibly some tax benefits. Refinancing or a home equity loan may be good alternatives for paying off credit card debt. But beware: Do not then run up the credit card bills again!

Hang in there! Credit cards are seductive and the ensuing debt can be seriously damaging. Do not give up.

Peter lost count of the number of times he "quit smoking for good." However, he refused to get discouraged and today has been a non-smoker for 15 years! You can get the credit card monkey off your back! Do not give up until you succeed!

HOME MORTGAGE—TERMINABLE AND INTERMINABLE

As we begin this discussion, remember your ultimate goal—a financially secure and low-stress retirement. A cornerstone of such a retirement is a paid-off mortgage. There are just a few obvious points that we would like to make to frame this discussion. Most people, and therapists are generally no exception to this, will have less income in retirement than they had during the heyday of their income-earning years. It is common practice in financial planning to project reduced income and expenses in retirement. Factors leading to reduced expenses in retirement include: the children's education has been paid for, office expenses are reduced or eliminated, and wardrobe expenses are lessened. The most significant factor in reduced expenses in retirement, however, is a paid-off mortgage. Paying off the mortgage is an important goal in most people's retirement planning.

Let us take a look at home mortgages and the pros and cons of refinancing. At the time of this writing, interest rates are at historic lows, and refinancing one's mortgage is currently a popular strategy with homeowners. Although it may make sense to refinance your home when rates go down, there is another side of the story. The amount of equity you have in your home represents an important asset. Whereas it is difficult for many people to save, building equity in one's home is a kind of forced saving, in that one must pay the mortgage or else lose the house. Although many people invest less than they should in their qualified retirement plan, it is not an option to miss payments on the home mortgage.

The issue at hand is that every time you refinance, you start a new mortgage. If interest rates have gone down, then the good news is that your monthly payment should be lower. However, if the overall period of time that you are paying the new lower rates extends your mortgage over many additional years, then you may well be paying more for the new loan over the course of time.

Not All Mortgage Payments Are Created Equal

Amortization is the process of gradually reducing the debt owed on your mortgage. It occurs over the lifetime of a mortgage loan. In the early years of a mortgage, the great majority of your payment goes to paying interest, whereas in the later years, increasing percentages of the payment go to paying down principal. Let's look, for example, at a 30-year, $275,000 loan at a fixed rate of 6%. This 30-year loan has 360 payments. The chart below shows the 1st, 90th, 180th, 270th, and final payments on the loan. Observe how much of the payment goes toward paying interest in the early years of the loan. Even in the 15th year, at the halfway point of the life of the loan, well over half of the total payment amount goes to interest.

If you repeatedly refinance your home, you start at the beginning of the amortization process over and over again, never really gaining on your equity. If, for example, you purchased your home in the year 2000 with a 30-year loan and then refinanced in 2003 with another 30-year loan, you have extended the life of your mortgage payment to 33 years. Do it again in the year 2010 and you will have extended the life of your mortgage to 40 years. If, on the other hand, you stick with your loan over the years, you are gradually paying off more and more principal, thereby increasing your equity in your home. In making a decision about whether to refinance, a balance must be struck between the desirability of reducing the interest rate and the goal of paying off the mortgage in the shortest number of years.

If current rates are sufficiently lower than the rate you are paying on your mortgage, you may well want to consider refinancing. Do

TABLE 19.1
Amortization

Year	Payment Number	Principal Balance	Payment Amount	Interest Paid	Principal Applied	New Balance
1	1	$275,000	$1,649	$1,375	$274	$274,726
7	90	$244,406	$1,649	$1,222	$427	$243,980
15	180	$196,053	$1,649	$980	$668	$195,384
22	270	$120,304	$1,649	$602	$1,047	$119,257
30	360	$1,640	$1,649	$8.20	$1,641	$0

not just look at your reduced monthly payments, however. You should also look at the amount you will be paying over the life of the new loan and compare that number with the amount you will pay over the life of the current loan. Try to avoid the interminable home mortgage. A declining principal balance is what will eventually lead to a home owned free and clear; and a free and clear home is a great thing to have in retirement.

Prepayment of Your Principal

Whether or not you refinance, making prepayments on your principal balance due can often be a good strategy. However, some words of caution apply here as well. First, whenever you refinance, be certain that the loan does not have prepayment penalties. You do not want to have to pay the bank a fee every time you prepay. Second, make certain that the bank will recompute the interest that you owe when you pay off principal early. Some lenders do not recompute the interest owed and simply follow their set amortization schedule, thereby disallowing the main advantage you gain through prepayment: speeding up the amortization of the loan. If the bank is not reducing your interest due, you are in effect loaning your bank interest-free money every time you make a prepayment! If your lender does recompute the interest owed with prepayment, then you can pay off your principal more quickly by making 13 payments over the course of the year (i.e., one extra payment per year). Such a strategy will reduce a 30-year mortgage by at least 8 years. Another approach is to simply designate a fixed amount of money that you add to your monthly payment to go directly to the reduction of principal. Yet another approach is to get an amortization schedule from your lender and pay the amount that is due on the following month's principal payment with this month's payment.

If your lender will not recompute the interest you owe when you pay off principal early, an alternative exists. Instead of making the extra payment to your bank, consider opening an account that is specifically earmarked to invest the money you would have used to pay off your mortgage early. A Roth IRA might work well for this purpose.

Suppose you are 40 years old and just starting a 30-year mortgage. You do not have a prepayment penalty, but when you call the bank you find that the fine print of your loan states that the bank will not recompute the interest you owe if you pay off principal early. Instead, the amortization table applies and the bank simply takes your prepayment as an interest-free loan from you to them. You decide that prepayment is not in your best interest and instead you open an investment account. Let's call this account your mortgage empowerment account. Your mortgage is a 30-year 6% fixed rate on $225,000. Each monthly payment is $1,649. To save the equivalent of approximately 10% of your monthly payment, you invest $165 per month in your mortgage empowerment account. (You have it automatically deducted from your checking account so that you do not miss any payments.) Under certain circumstances, it might make sense to invest your mortgage empowerment account in a Roth IRA. In any event, this money is invested in a mix of stock and bond investments that earn you a hypothetical return of 8% per annum. Skip forward 22 years. Now you are age 62 and would like the freedom to retire, or at least cut back your practice. Your biggest expense is your mortgage payment. You are about to make your 270th mortgage payment and you have a principal balance on your mortgage of $120,304. You take a look at your mortgage empowerment account and find that you have a balance now of $124,914. You can simply pay off the mortgage or follow the following strategy. Up until this point you have been reinvesting your earnings in the mortgage empowerment account and have been investing in a combination of growth and income securities. Now you reallocate your portfolio primarily for income (see the conservative model portfolio in Chapter 5). You have the interest payments sent to you, which fund about half of your mortgage payment, thereby significantly reducing your biggest monthly expense. In 8 more years, at age 70, your mortgage is fully paid off, and you still have the entire principal from your mortgage empowerment account.

STUDENT LOANS

If you carry student loans from your undergraduate or graduate school days, you may want to consider consolidating them. The U.S. Department of Education maintains an informative website (*http://loanconsolidation.ed.gov*) with many tools, calculators, and comprehensive information about student loan consolidation. With the consolidated loan program, a lender pays off your old student loans and generates a new loan for you with federally mandated provisions and guarantees. PLUS, Perkins, Health and Human Services, and Health Professions loans may all be consolidated.

As with credit card debt and mortgages, the principle to keep in mind is that you want to pay off maximum principal so that you pay off the loan in its entirety in a reasonable amount of time. Debt consolidation can help you simplify the process of paying your student loans. You may consolidate several types of student loans, possibly lower your interest rate, and restructure your repayment to more favorable terms.

Four types of repayment plans exist: standard, extended, graduated, and income contingent. The standard repayment plan requires a fixed monthly payment of at least $50 for up to 10 years. This plan has higher monthly payments but a shorter repayment period, which means your total interest paid will be lower. The extended plan stretches out the loan over 12–30 years. Monthly payments are lower, but because of the extended term of the loan, total interest paid will be higher.

The graduated repayment plan starts with lower payments and gradually increases. This is meant to mirror a career path on the part of the borrower wherein income is lower in the early years and increases over time. Generally borrowers pay more over the term of the loan with the graduated repayment plan.

The income-contingent plan bases the monthly payment on the borrower's annual adjusted gross income, family size, and total amount of direct loans. The borrower signs a disclosure document with the IRS, which allows the IRS to communicate with the Department of Education to determine payments. The maximum period for the income-contingent plan is 25 years. If the direct consolidation loan is not repaid after 25 years, the unpaid portion is discharged. This is an interesting provision, particularly if your income is low and you anticipate that it will stay that way. For example, a social worker who is a single parent and works for a nonprofit agency making a relatively small income may be well advised to pay a minimum based on his or her income and simply discharge the balance after 25 years.

You may change your repayment plan at any time and as many times as you like. In general, if your income is good, we suggest that you get the lowest interest rate you can find and pay off the loan in as short a time as possible so as to pay the lowest total interest. If you have a hardship, then it may be in your interest to switch to the income-contingent plan for the period during which you are having financial difficulty and then switch back to the standard plan when your income improves.

AUTOS AND AUTO LOANS

If you are not particularly image conscious about your car, then you can focus on safety and your budget with regard to auto ownership. If car image is important to you for personal or professional reasons, then you will probably need to support higher auto expenses in your budget. In either case, there are always ways to save money.

All other things being equal, you are almost always better off financially buying a used car rather than a new one and buying from a private party rather than from a dealership or a used car lot. Check out the Consumer Reports website (*http://www.consumerreports.org*) for rankings of used cars, and buy one ranked high for safety and low for rate of repairs. (My last car purchase was a 4-year-old Honda Accord, which had the safety and reliability rankings we wanted.) From a financial perspective, the best bet is to save up and buy a used car with cash. If you need to finance your car, shop around. You might be surprised at the amount you can save by taking a little extra time to shop a loan. Even if your credit is less than perfect, you may have more leverage then you think, so take the time to shop for the best car loan you can find. *http://www.Bankrate.com* has excellent tools and resources for shopping car loans.

If, for whatever reason, you choose to get a new car, then you will be faced with the decision to lease or to buy. If we were writing this book for real estate agents, who really do need a good-looking car as a tool of their trade, we might recommend leasing under certain circumstances. The one true advantage of a lease over ownership is that you can drive around in a nicer car for fewer dollars up front. However, most therapists need not go in over their heads for a car, and purchasing is almost always a better choice than leasing from a purely financial point of view.

When you purchase with a traditional auto loan, you are building equity in the car. If you keep the car, you will eventually own it free and clear. On the other hand, leasing a car is analogous to renting a house rather than buying it. The leasing agent will take possession of the car after your contract expires. The lure is usually low up-front costs and the opportunity to drive an upscale car for a manageable monthly payment. However, before you sign on the dotted line of a lease agreement, please consider the following words of caution:

You are building no ownership in the car.

Getting out of a lease prior to its termination date can be expensive; leases are usually written to levy heavy fees on early returns.

Leases commonly charge fees if you accumulate more than the specified number of miles.

You will need to return the car in clean shape; the leasing agency will likely charge a hefty fee for any cosmetic or mechanical damage.

Leases are written by lawyers who work for the leasing agency. The fine print of the contract may favor the leasing agency in ways that are not immediately apparent to you.

You may do well to shop for auto insurance also. A wide range of premiums are available for similar coverages. The Internet is a fantastic medium for doing this kind of comparison shopping. To compare auto insurance premiums simply enter "compare auto insurance premiums" in a search engine and you will find a plethora of websites. *http://www.Insure.com's* auto section will generate quote comparisons for you.

CONCLUSION

One's long-term financial success is as much dependent on keeping spending in line as it is on generating a healthy income. Therefore, controlling spending, and managing debt properly are essential to your financial wellbeing. Staying conscious of spending, and doing plenty of consumer research into the particulars of any loans you enter into are both fundamental to your long term financial health.

CHAPTER 20

An Insurance Primer

Insurance can be a confusing subject in that there are many varieties of it, the products can be complicated, and your needs will necessarily change in relation to your life phase and circumstances. The purpose of this chapter is to help you clarify your needs and to provide you with consumer information that will help you make sound choices.

LIFE INSURANCE

Who Needs It?

If someone depends on you for income, you wish to continue to provide for that person in the event of your death, and there are not sufficient assets in your estate to provide for that person, then you probably need life insurance. The classic case for life insurance is a young family wherein the children will need continued support in the event of the death of one or both parents. As we discussed in the previous chapter, this is all the more true when the surviving parent is a clinician in private practice, because the increased parental responsibilities may well decrease the surviving parent's availability to work clinical hours. Another issue for therapist families is that therapists often have a moderate income but are highly educated, with high hopes and expectations for their children's higher education: a major life expense.

How Much Do You Need?

There are a variety of ways to calculate one's life insurance needs. Feedback from a financial planner may in fact be the best way for you to arrive at a figure, as he or she should know your financial situation in detail. However, here is one approach that can be useful:

Determine your family income.
Multiply that number by .8.
Divide that number by a reasonable rate of return on the life insurance proceeds. (Many planners assume an 8% return on investment, although we prefer the more conservative figure of 6%.)
Subtract savings and investments currently owned.

The above steps will provide you with a ballpark figure on what it will take to replace current income. If you expect increasing expenses, such as higher education for the kids or care for an elderly parent, then this figure may be too low. If you expect your expenses to remain relatively constant, this figure should be more helpful.

Consider the case of Steve and Jessica. Steve makes $160,000 in his psychiatry practice and Jessica makes $65,000 in her clinical social work practice. They have two children: Amy, a 9th grader, and Bradley, who is in the 4th grade. Steve and Jessica have $250,000 in investments and savings. Let's see how much life insurance they might need. We will start with the amount of insurance Jessica will need in the event of Steve's death:

Combine their income and multiply the total by .8.
     Steve and Jessica's combined income is $225,000. This number is discounted by 20% because the family will no longer need to support Steve after his death.

$$225,000 \times .8 = $180,000$$

Because Jessica will continue to work but may be less available for full-time practice, her continuing income is assumed to be

$50,000. Subtract her ongoing income from the income needed to replace it with insurance.

$$\$180,000 - \$50,000 = \$130,000$$

Divide this figure by a reasonable rate of return on the investments they make with the insurance proceeds. A conservative rate of return estimate is 6%. This calculates the amount of principal needed to generate income sufficient to meet the survivor's income needs.

$$\$130,000 \div .06 = \$2,166,666$$

This figure is reduced by the amount they have in savings: $250,000.

$$\$2,166,666 - \$250,000 = \$1,916,666$$

Therefore, a ballpark figure for the amount of life insurance Jessica will need on Steve's life: $1,916,666.

Let us turn now to Steve's needs in the event of Jessica's death:

Reduce the combined income by 20%, because the income needed to support Jessica is no longer necessary in the event of her death.

$$\$225,000 \times .8 = \$180,000$$

Steve will continue to work but is less available to earn a full-time income due to increased parental responsibilities. His continuing income is assumed to be $130,000, which is then subtracted from the figure above.

$$\$180,000 - \$130,000 = \$50,000$$

Divide this figure by a 6% presumed rate of return.

$$\$50,000 \div .06 = \$833,333$$

Subtract their current investments from the above figure.

$$\$833,333 - \$250,000 = \$583,333$$

We now have a ballpark idea about the amount of insurance Steve needs on Jessica's life: $583,333.

Please bear in mind that these figures include many assumptions and should therefore be considered only an approximation of the amounts that will be needed. Again, we suggest you work with a financial planner on these need analyses. He or she should have software that can do a more sophisticated analysis than the one provided above. In any event, the above approach should give you a rough estimate of the coverage you need. For further help in calculating your life insurance needs, go to our website (*http:// www.insightfinancialgroup.com*) and follow the links to "Calculators" and then to "Insurance Calculators."

What Kind of Life Insurance Is Right for You?

Two basic types of life insurance exist: temporary and permanent. Temporary, or term, insurance does not build up a cash value and simply provides a death benefit for a given period of time. Permanent insurance, on the other hand, is designed to last until the death of the insured, and it does build up a cash value. Varieties of permanent insurance include whole life insurance, universal life insurance, and variable universal life insurance. For the present discussion, let us focus first on whether term insurance or permanent insurance is right for you. Next, we consider the question of which type of term or permanent insurance you may find most advantageous.

The rule of thumb for going with term insurance is that if one's need is temporary, then temporary life insurance should do the trick. A case where this might apply would be a family with two working parents and young kids. Should one or both die, the children will need additional support. However, unless the parents feel it is necessary to support the children into the income generating years of adulthood, that need might fall off when the children finish college—say, at age 25. If the youngest child were 15, then perhaps a 10-year term policy might be sufficient to meet the temporary need of supporting that child.

The rule of thumb for permanent insurance is a permanent need for insurance. A case where this might apply would be if there is an ongoing need for income for the surviving partner. Such situations are common for private practitioners because they are self-employed and therefore not usually part of a traditional pension plan that pays lifetime benefits.

Say, for example, that Judi and Anne are domestic partners. Judi is a marriage and family therapist in private practice. Anne is a public school teacher. Although Anne has a pension through the school district, her district does not allow same-sex domestic partners to be included in joint and survivor benefits. They have no children. If Judi predeceases Anne, then Anne will be okay because of her pension. On the other hand, if Anne predeceases Judi, Judi will have an ongoing need for retirement income.

Another example of a situation with permanent need is Dave and Alice. Dave is an LCSW and Alice is an MFT. Alice works for a family service agency with a minimal 403(b) plan. Dave is in private practice. They have not built up sufficient retirement funds, and neither can make it financially without the income of both.

One last example of a couple who chose permanent insurance is Michael and Clarissa. Michael is an attorney making $500,000+ per year. Clarissa is a psychiatrist making $200,000+ per year. They have extensive securities investments and real estate holdings and expect to inherit several million more when Clarissa's mother dies. Their need for insurance is driven by the fact that they will owe extensive estate taxes and do not want to put their children in a position to have to come up with a large amount of money to pay taxes when they die. Their situation is complicated by the fact that the estate tax laws are in flux. Despite many unknowns with future estate tax rules, they have opted for permanent insurance that will pay estate taxes if Congress has put them in place in the year that the second of them dies. If the proceeds are not needed for estate taxes because the estate tax has been eliminated, then they are happy to have the proceeds enhance the value of the estate.

If you determine that permanent life insurance is right for you, then you will need to decide which kind to use. Whole life insurance provides a fixed rate of return on the savings portion of the insurance and has a fixed premium. Ordinary whole life insurance allows the policyholder reasonable payments on the assumption that the premiums will be paid until the person dies. However, as the owner pays into the policy over the years, he or she may have options other than retaining the policy until death. For example, the policyholder may be able to use dividends to pay off the policy in a shorter amount of time, surrender the policy in favor of an annuity, or trade in the policy for a smaller amount of paid-up insurance. Whole life insurance provides permanent insurance for the lowest premium dollar and has limited but important flexibility as one's life circumstances change.

Another approach to permanent life insurance is universal life insurance. Universal life insurance offers flexible premiums and allows the policy owner to take money out of the account without taking a loan. With universal life, one does not direct the investments in the cash value. Instead, the insurance company gives the owner a fixed rate of return. With universal life, the owner can choose a level death benefit or an increasing death benefit. The level death benefit maintains the same death benefit while the amount owned in the cash value increases. Therefore, as one owns more and more in the cash value, the amount that the insurance company has put at risk decreases, thereby decreasing the amount of the premium dollar that goes to pay for the death benefit. With an increasing death benefit, the death benefit rises as the amount one owns in the cash value rises. Universal life insurance offers flexible premiums and allows the policy owner to take money out of the account through loans or partial withdrawals. As previously noted, any withdrawals or loans will reduce your cash value and/or death benefit. If you are looking for more flexibility than a whole life policy offers but want a fixed rate of return on your cash value, then universal life insurance may work well for you.

Yet another approach to permanent insurance is variable universal life insurance. In Chapter 15 we briefly discussed variable universal life insurance as a vehicle for tax-deferred investing. Variable universal life provides permanent insurance along with cash value, like whole life or universal life. A unique feature of variable universal life is that the owner directs investments in the cash balance with stocks and bonds in separate accounts that pool the resources of many investors and are professionally managed. The money management firms that run many of these separate accounts are leading investment companies. Most variable universal life policies offer a fairly wide range of investment choices, typically with a variety of familiar money management firms. Some variable universal life insurance policies even have a variety of socially responsible investment choices available in the subaccounts. If you are looking for maximum flexibility in permanent insurance, a variable universal life policy may be an investment to consider.

With any permanent insurance, it is important that the owner of the policy makes a serious commitment to keeping the policy over the long haul. Canceling a policy after just a few years can be quite costly, because the money in the cash value or separate account typically has steep surrender charges, meaning that the insurer will likely hit the owner with charges that reduce the cash-out value of the policy. If permanent insurance helps you meet your financial planning and/or estate planning goals and you plan on sticking with it long term, then permanent insurance may play an important role in your financial life. If, on the other hand, you have only a limited need for life insurance—say, for example, insuring your life until your children are of an age where you expect them to support themselves—then relatively inexpensive term insurance is probably right for you.

Good health and life insurance can have a problematical relationship to each other. If you are in good health, then you might feel as though life insurance is an unnecessary expenditure. On the other hand, once your health fails, it may be prohibitively expensive or impossible to get the coverage needed. We suggest that you try to think of your need for life insurance dispassionately; consider whether there are others who depend on your income and will be harmed financially by your death. Consider how long you would want to provide protection for that dependent. Is it necessary to provide for that person permanently or temporarily? We again suggest that you consider these issues while you are in good health, because if you wait too long, you may close out options for yourself.

LONG-TERM CARE INSURANCE

Long-term care costs an average of $150 per day, or $55,000 per year, in our home state of California. The California Department of Health Services reports, "Of those who enter nursing homes, 55% will have a lifetime use of at least one year, 24% will stay between one and five years, and 21% will have a total lifetime use of five years or more." The report goes on to say that, "More than 40% of those who turn 65 will spend some time in a nursing home."[1]

Clearly, the danger of a devastatingly expensive stay in a long-term care facility is real. Long-term care insurance can be sensible and even extremely important for many therapists in private practice, but it is not for everyone. Many in the psychotherapy professions fit into the income category of people who may benefit from long-term care insurance; in other words, people with a middle range of assets—between $150,000 and $1.5 million. A little background will explain why this is true.

Americans cannot rely on Medicare for long-term care coverage. Medicaid (Medi-Cal in California), on the other hand, currently pays for long-term care, but only if one has extremely limited assets. Think of long-term care insurance as insurance for your assets, so that you do not have to spend down your assets in order to qualify for Medicaid/Medi-Cal to pay for a long-term care bed.

Long-term care insurance may not be necessary if you have a high net worth; but if your assets are less than $1.5 million and more than $150,000 you might want to consider it. If your assets are high enough, then you probably will not need the coverage because you could pay the expenses yourself out of pocket and still protect sufficient assets for your heirs. If your net worth is low enough, then you may be able to spend down your assets such that Medicaid/Medi-Cal can kick in.

---

[1] California Partnership for Long Term Care: Consumer Information. <*http://www.dhs.cah-wnet.gov/cpltc/html/consumer.htm*>.

One of the nation's best-known personal finance writers and media personalities has been pitching long-term care insurance on the QVC television channel lately. We find this distasteful, wrong-headed, and a disservice to consumers. No one should buy long-term care insurance from a TV commercial. It is a complicated decision and a major financial commitment.

Some long-term care guidelines follow. The younger you are and the better your health, the lower your premiums will be. The downside is that these same favorable health conditions mean you may well be paying into your policy for many years and never need it. We sometimes counsel our clients to purchase long-term care insurance in their mid-50s. Another issue is home care and assisted living care. If you want these options, make sure they are written into your policy. Some policies cover only skilled nursing facilities, which, for many consumers, is their last choice.

In addition to waiting until your 50s to buy long-term care insurance, another sensible way to save money is to increase the elimination period, which is a waiting period before the benefits kick in. Do not save money on a long-term care policy by eliminating the inflation coverage. We recommend to all of our clients that they choose a 5% compound inflation coverage so that spiraling healthcare costs do not overtake the coverage in the long-term care policy. Make a few calls to the better long-term care facilities in the area where you would want to be should you need long-term care. Then design your policy around what you will need. With the 5% compound inflation rider, today's coverages should keep pace with inflation. A client of mine knows that if she were ever to need coverage, it would be at the finest facility in New York City—the same facility her mother was in for 7 years. We called their intake worker to find out cost: the facility charges a whopping $400 per day, or $146,000 per year! As you can imagine, we designed a very high-end policy for her. On the other hand, if you are in a lower cost part of the country, your costs will be lower and your premiums should be too.

Look for a company with solid financial ratings that has been in the long-term care business for at least 10 years. Some newcomers to the field may charge low premiums in the beginning; but you are more likely to deal with insolvency or premium hikes if you do not go with an established player in the field. The California Department of Social Services has entered into contracts with the following companies for long-term care partnership policies:[2]

---

[2] The California Partnership for Long Term Care is for California residents only and is a cooperative program between the California Department of Human Services and the private insurers. We list these companies not to promote their partnership policies (although they may be worth looking into), but to let readers know that the companies listed have been vetted by the State of California.

CNA	(800) 262-1037
GE Financial Assurance	(800) 354-6896
John Hancock Life Insurance	(800) 377-7311
New York Life Insurance	(800) 224-4582
Transamerica Occidental Life Insurance	(800) 797-2643
CalPERS Long-Term Care Program[3]	(800) 205-2020

These companies have been vetted by the State of California for sound business practices. Although the list is by no means exhaustive, it is a good place to start if you are looking for long-term care insurance. Your financial advisor should also be able to help you find the right company and design an appropriate policy.

A source of independent insurance ratings is available through Standard & Poor's at *http://www.standardandpoors.com*. Standard & Poor's provides financial solvency information that is important in choosing an insurer. You obviously want your insurer to be around and able to pay claims if and when the time comes, so do your research!

DISABILITY INSURANCE

As discussed in Chapter 14, a common financial mistake therapists in private practice make is not obtaining adequate disability insurance. If you have money in your family of origin that you can call upon, if you have significant investments that generate income, or if your spouse or domestic partner can support your household, then you may be able to do without replacing your practice income in the event of disability. However, if you cannot manage, over the long haul, to live without the revenue that your practice pulls in, then disability and business overhead insurance may be an important investment.

If you depend on your practice income, and will do so for the foreseeable future, disability insurance is usually more important to your financial well-being than long-term care insurance. Think of disability insurance as a basic coverage for your private practice working years and long-term care insurance as a basic coverage for the years when you are transitioning to retirement and in retirement. If you can afford both when you are in your mid-50s and beyond, that may be best, because both kinds of coverage are important.

A number of our clients confuse disability and long-term care insurance, so let us take a moment to discuss each of them. Long-term care insurance covers the cost of care if you become unable to

---

[3] Open only to California state employees and their families.

take care of the activities of daily living such as bathing, dressing, and ambulating. The classic case for long-term care is a Ronald Reagan scenario, where Alzheimer's renders the individual unable to care for himself or herself, and that person lives on for many years. Disability insurance, on the other hand, is income replacement insurance for people who had been working and cannot now return to work. The classic disability case is the private practitioner who has a stroke and cannot return to work for a number of years while rehabilitating.

Disability insurance has complicated underwriting and policy provisions. We suggest you work with a financial planner who has experience in designing these policies, because they vary widely in their quality. Things to look for in a disability policy include:

Definition of disability. Some policies use a definition of disability as restrictive as Social Security: the insured cannot work at any occupation. This restrictive definition of disability would be problematic for the therapist in private practice. Say a therapist had a stroke and needed to rehabilitate her speech before she could function again in her practice, but she could do some other kind of work. She would likely want disability insurance that defines disability as the ability to function in one's "own occupation." In recent years, most disability carriers have stopped offering long benefit duration periods for "own occupation" disability, and have shifted to a dual definition of disability wherein the insured is covered for 2–5 years in his or her "own occupation" and after that to "any occupation."

Partial disability benefits. Say a therapist had a heart attack and was rehabilitating. Furthermore, he has a small number of long-term patients who must continue to see him if they are to function, but he cannot work more than a few hours a day. Partial disability benefits cover either partial or residual disability following a total disability. Such benefits may be desirable for the private practitioner. Residual disability benefits are designed to make up the difference between income prior to disability and income earned during disability. Look for a policy that allows the definition of prior income to be the greater of two base periods so that you are not penalized by a single base period during a slump in your practice.

Guaranteed renewability. You do not want a policy that will weed you out if you begin to develop a medical problem that could result in disability, so it is best to avoid disability contracts that are not either guaranteed renewable or noncancelable. Also, avoid policies that can raise premiums on an individual rather than a class basis. Some companies will offer guaranteed renewability to age 65 and then conditional renewability to age 75. Many therapists continue to work into their 70s, so this feature may be worth seeking.

Elimination period. Disability policies usually have an elimination period, or waiting period, before benefits kick in. Of course, you can save on your premium with a longer elimination period. Typical options are 30, 60, 90, and 120 days. If you have savings or other sources of short-term income, you can save premium dollars with a longer elimination period.

Duration of disability. How long your policy pays for disability is of course a key provision. Obviously the longer the benefit duration, the higher the premium will be. Many companies will offer duration periods ranging from 2 years to age 65. Some companies offer a lifetime duration period. We suggest you consult with your financial planner on this issue, because the choices you make with this provision may have a lasting impact on the financial health of yourself and your family.

Cost-of-living adjustments. Many insurers offer cost-of-living adjustments as an option and allow the owner of the policy to decide the percentage rate used to calculate the adjustment. As with other features in a disability policy, there is a trade-off between level of benefit and premium. As with other features of a disability policy, we suggest you consult with a financial planner on this issue; there is a trade-off between premium dollars spent and potential benefit derived that depends on many individual factors such as your age, present and future financial responsibilities, and state of health.

BUSINESS OVERHEAD INSURANCE

If you were to become temporarily disabled, you would likely have ongoing expenses associated with keeping the infrastructure of your private practice in place while you recover. Business overhead insurance is designed to cover one's fixed practice expenses such as rent, secretarial services, utilities, and so forth, in the case of short-term disability. Business overhead insurance is commonly written in conjunction with disability insurance and can be a cost-effective adjunct to it. It is usually written for a benefit period of 1 or 2 years with a short elimination period. Because a private practitioner's fixed cost of doing business is relatively low, business overhead insurance can be quite affordable as an adjunct to disability insurance.

CHAPTER 21

Estate Planning: Financial Planning for after a Death

Dealing with issues of your own mortality inevitably arouses anxiety. This anxiety can be even greater when you consider the possibility that your partner may predecease you. Therapists are no different from their clients in their wish to avoid anxiety. Understandable though this may be, it is imperative that therapists make thoughtful, practical decisions about end-of-life issues. Whatever your net worth, estate planning is a vital piece of a well thought-out financial plan. The last gift a person can offer loved ones is an estate plan that protects them after his or her death. Likewise, therapists owe it to themselves to ensure that their own financial well-being is protected should their life partner predecease them.

Estate planning is a complex area of law and financial planning. We strongly recommend that you implement your estate plan with the help of a qualified financial planner and attorney. The purpose of this chapter is not to replace professional help, but rather to give you a general orientation to some basic estate planning issues and techniques.

The first step in making an estate plan is to establish your over-arching estate planning goals. You can then begin to work with your attorney and financial planner on implementing strategies designed to accomplish your goals. The next section lists some common estate planning goals. Hopefully, the list will serve as a trigger to help you think more specifically about your personal goals.

COMMON ESTATE PLANNING GOALS

Providing for your children and partner
Protecting your assets from creditors
Making plans for your practice and other businesses
Minimizing estate and income taxes
Minimizing or bypassing the probate process
Ensuring that your home will be available to your partner during his
    or her lifetime and then pass to your children
Providing for bequests of special items for specific people
Ensuring that assets are divided fairly, thus minimizing animosity
    among surviving family members
Providing for children and/or grandchildren's higher education
Putting advanced medical directives in place
Making provision for guardianship of minor children
Providing direction should you become incompetent
Protecting your own financial security should your partner die
    before you

Take a moment, if you would, to think about your estate planning goals. What are your concerns? What are your hopes and dreams? What are your core responsibilities? The answers to these questions will give you the beginning of your estate plan. You can then bring this to your attorney and financial planner. They will use what you bring as a starting point for the process of setting up a formal estate plan that reflects your priorities.

Estate planning is an ever-dynamic and changeable topic because, as tax laws change, the strategies one uses to minimize the tax burden on one's estate must necessarily change in response. As we write this, Congress and the president are negotiating changes in the tax code that will undoubtedly have a bearing on what we write. Nevertheless, certain techniques of estate planning should remain valid for many years to come.

The next section discusses estate planning techniques typically used to accomplish the goals you identified above. We consider each one in turn to familiarize you with basic estate planning terms and techniques. Once you have developed some familiarity with the basics of estate planning, you will be able to begin thinking creatively about your personal estate planning goals and how to best accomplish them.

COMMON ESTATE PLANNING TECHNIQUES

Living Trusts

The living trust is an effective method of efficiently passing on many assets according to your wishes. A living trust is established and operates while the creator of the trust is still alive. In most cases, the living trust is revocable, meaning that it can be rescinded, amended, or terminated by the person who created it. The most typical arrangement is that you create the trust and appoint yourself as the holder of the property, or the trustee. Once you create the trust, you change the title of the property from your own name to the name of the trust. Within the trust, you appoint a trustee who will take over in the event of your death or incompetence. Please note that living trusts do not change the tax picture for the grantor or for the estate.

For an example of retitling property in the name of a trust, let us assume that Jane Simon, PhD, has a brokerage account in her own name. She establishes the Jane Simon PhD Revocable Living Trust Dated April 25, 2003 and subsequently changes the registration of her brokerage account to Jane Simon PhD Revocable Living Trust Dated 4-25-03. She also changes the titles of her primary residence, vacation home, and car to the living trust.

The arguments in favor of a living trust include the following:

Property passes from the grantor to the beneficiary without the need for probate. Probate is the process of proving a will's validity in court and executing the provisions of the will under the guidance of the court. Probate can be costly and time consuming. Even uncomplicated estates can take 6 months or more to sort through. The living trust allows you to bypass the probate process, because the property in the trust passes to the beneficiary by operation of law.

If you operate your practice as a sole proprietorship, you may pass on your practice through a revocable trust to avoid termination of the practice. Say, for example, that you are a psychologist in private practice and so is your partner. You may leave the practice to your partner so that she can either continue to treat your patients or at least wrap up the billing and other loose ends prior to closing your practice.

If you own property in more than one state, you can avoid having to go through probate in two or more states by putting the property in your living trust in the state where you reside. You avoid ancillary jurisdiction of out-of-state property by titling it in your living trust.

When property goes through probate, the records are made public. With a living trust you avoid probate and the public record of private financial information.

A living trust is relatively easy to set up and change. Numerous self-help books (notably from Nolo Press) are available, but we strongly recommend that you use an attorney. There are many nuances to estate planning, and tax laws are a constantly moving target.

Living trusts are difficult to contest, whereas, in general, wills are more vulnerable to being contested.

Living trusts may help you consolidate your assets and get better organized. As you add property to the trust, you must think about its disposition and management.

The types of property commonly transferred into a living trust include:

Real estate
Bank accounts
Brokerage accounts
Stock and bond certificates
Vehicles and boats

Pour-Over Will

The revocable living trust allows you to detail the disposition of property that is titled in the name of the trust. However, property that is not specifically owned by the trust is not included in the trust. Therefore, you need a will to direct property not already owned by the living trust to be bequeathed either to the trust or to the individuals to whom you want the property to go. This is where a "pour-over" will comes into play. A pour-over will is so named because it instructs the executor of the estate to place the assets not titled in the trust to be poured into the trust after your death.

It is virtually impossible to title everything you own in the name of your living trust. Much property such as jewelry, clothes, your favorite lamp or vase, or that special book of poetry is quite difficult to title at all. You may detail in the pour-over will who gets what that is not titled in the name of the trust. All items that are not otherwise named in the pour-over will or titled in the name of the trust can be directed to pour into the trust, to be divided among your heirs according to its provisions.

Probably the most important issue in any will is the appointment of guardianship for minor children. This issue can be addressed in the pour-over will. We suggest that parents discuss the matter of guardianship with the future guardian and have a frank discussion about the emotional issues and financial responsibilities involved. It is easy to dismiss the possibility that death or incompetency may take you away from your children, but of course such scenarios are being played out each and every day. It is best to prepare for these unwanted and unforeseen circumstances so that your children are well taken care of. If the best people to care for the children will need financial help to do so, then life insurance held by a trust for the benefit of the children may well come into the picture as a way to finance their future needs.

PROPERTY OWNERSHIP: CHOOSING THE BEST METHOD

A variety of property titling options exist. Each has a different legal definition that affects the disposition of one's property after death. Let us take a look at the advantages and disadvantages of several methods of ownership.

Fee Simple Estate

A fee simple estate or fee simple ownership of property is an interest in property that belongs to one individual. Most property is owned in this way. The owner has individual and absolute ownership of the property. He or she can give the property to another person, persons, or entity during his or her lifetime or bequeath it to anyone at death. Table 21.1 details the pros and cons of fee simple ownership.

TABLE 21.1
Fee Simple Ownership

Advantages of Fee Simple Ownership	Disadvantages of Fee Simple Ownership
Easy to establish Absolute ownership and control Appreciation of real estate and individual securities are generally untaxed and may receive a step-up at death, meaning that the appreciation in the property is untaxed to inheriting party	Property is subject to probate Property held fee simple in your name will be included in your estate and subject to estate taxes If not specified in a will, property is passed on by the rules of state law at the time of your death. If you become incompetent, a court could decide who will control the property

Joint Tenancy with Rights of Survivorship (JTWRS)

When property is held in joint tenancy with right of survivorship, it is held by two or more people: most commonly, a couple. When one person dies, the survivor or survivors take the entire property by operation of law. Real estate, bank, and brokerage accounts are commonly held in this manner.

Although JTWRS ownership is common in the United States, it has many drawbacks and should be carefully considered as a form of ownership. One problem is that JTWRS ownership supersedes a will. An example from Peter's practice is Lisa, a social worker in Sacramento. Lisa's father was a self-made man, an immigrant who arrived penniless from Russia and did well in the plumbing business through dedication and hard work. His dream was to leave a legacy for Lisa that she would use to give her children the finest education money can buy. Lisa's parents owned a valuable home and a substantial stock portfolio held in JTWRS. When her father died suddenly of a heart attack, her mother became sole owner of the home and stock portfolio.

A few years later, Lisa's mother married a man with two children of his own. Having been accustomed to JTWRS ownership, the mother put the house and stock portfolio in JTWRS with her new husband. Lisa's mother died in the aftermath of a stroke 2 1/2 years later. Although her will specified that the house and stock portfolio should pass to Lisa, the property went to the new husband instead because JTWRS ownership supersedes a will and the husband was the joint tenant. The stepfather, whom Lisa has never gotten along with, will not return her calls. Lisa feels certain that the property her father worked so hard to accumulate will now pass to her mother's second husband's two children. She is distraught about this turn of

TABLE 21.2
Joint Tenancy with Right of Survivorship

Advantages of Joint Tenancy with Right of Survivorship	Disadvantages of Joint Tenancy with Right of Survivorship
Not subject to probate until the death of the second joint tenant	Property could pass to unintended heirs
Easy to set up	A variety of estate tax and income tax pitfalls exist
	Loss of control in your lifetime; if your joint tenant becomes incompetent, you could end up with a court-appointed conservator as your joint tenant
	Precludes having property to pass to a QTIP or credit shelter trust (discussed later in the chapter)

events. For a review of the advantages and disadvantages of JTWRS, see Table 21.2.

Tenancy in Common

Tenancy in common is the holding of property by two or more people, usually a couple, each of whom has an undivided interest in their portion of the property. A brokerage account, for example, could be registered as "Douglas Jones and Janet Jones, Tenants in Common." With this form of ownership, neither Douglas nor Janet own 100% of the property. They each have an undivided interest in 50% of the property. Either Douglas or Janet can sell or gift their portion of the property at any time. Property does not pass automatically to the tenant in common as it does with joint tenancy with right of survivorship. Instead, the property is passed according to the deceased tenant's will or, if there is no will, by state law. There are no survivorship rights for the remaining co-tenant when one tenant dies. Table 21.3 reviews the advantages and disadvantages of tenancy in common.

Community Property

Community property law recognizes property ownership by a husband and wife. There are currently nine community property states: Arizona, California, Idaho, Louisiana, Nevada, New Mexico, Texas, Washington, and Wisconsin (Wisconsin uses a different terminology than "community property"). Each state's law is somewhat different,

TABLE 21.3
Tenancy in Common

Advantages of Tenancy in Common	Disadvantages of Tenancy in Common
Easy method of titling property Each co-owner has control of his or her portion of the property; each owner's portion can be sold or gifted to another without the co-owner's permission	If your co-tenant passes his or her portion to someone else, you may not be well suited to share property with the new person You never have full control of the entire property—just your portion of it If your co-tenant becomes incompetent and has a court-ordered conservator appointed, you could end up owning property with a conservator Interest in the property becomes part of the estate at death and could be subject to estate taxes

TABLE 21.4
Community Property

Advantages of Community Property	Disadvantages of Community Property
You may will your portion of your property to whomever you choose; your portion does not have to be left to your spouse You receive a step in basis of the entire property when your spouse dies and leaves you his or her half of the property[a]	The property belongs ½ to the husband and ½ to the wife. The decedent's half must pass through probate. Property owned by one party before the marriage and then retitled in community property is now ½ owned by the new spouse. This may look appealing in the honeymoon period of a marriage but less appealing if the marriage seems to be heading for divorce.

[a] In JTWRS title, the deceased's portion is stepped up, but the survivor's basis remains the same. "Basis" refers to the value used to calculate the capital gain on the sale of property.

but the essential idea is that in a marriage, some property is considered separately owned whereas other property is considered community owned. Community property is property that was purchased after the marriage or owned by husband or wife before the marriage but retitled after the marriage. Your portion of community property passes to whomever you wish when you die. It does not automatically pass to the co-tenant, as with joint tenants with right of survivorship property. When the husband or wife dies, the tax basis of the property is "stepped up" to its current value. This can save on taxes for the surviving spouse if he or she sells the property. See Table 21.4 for a breakdown of the pros and cons of community property.

Credit Shelter Trusts

At death, a tax is imposed on all the property the decedent is passing on to loved ones. The values of all property, including the decedent's home, accounts, personal property, and so forth are totaled. The exclusion amount is an amount on which the estate does not have to pay taxes. The Economic Growth and Tax Relief Reconciliation Act of 2001 has temporarily increased the exclusion amount an estate can contain before estate taxes are due. The exclusion amount in 2001 was $675,000. In 2002–03 it is $1 million, for 2004–05 it is $1.5 million, for 2006–08 it is $2 million, and for 2009 it is $3.5 million. As the law currently reads, in the year 2010 the estate tax will be repealed entirely. However, in the following year, 2011, the estate tax repeal sunsets, and the estate tax credit reverts to $1,000,000. In other words, the amount of the credit increases gradually from 2002 to 2010 and then reverts to the 2002 level again in the year 2011.

If this all sounds confusing, it is because it is very political. Many Republicans (but far from all!) would like to repeal the estate tax altogether. On the other hand, many Democrats and Republicans both feel that the estate tax is sound public policy and is necessary to avoid deficit spending. We believe that the passing of wealth from one generation to the next is not a divine right of the wealthy, but a privilege that should be fairly taxed so as to benefit the whole of our country. Apart from our opinion as to what comprises good public policy, however, our opinion about what will happen in the future with the estate tax is that it will not be eliminated. We think that rising deficits and increasing disparity between the rich and poor in our country will make the elimination of the estate tax politically unfeasible.

So, how does one plan for a moving target? Does one assume that the law will just sunset as written and revert in 2011 to a $1,000,000 credit? Or does one assume that the estate tax will be permanently eliminated? No one knows, but again, our guess is that Americans will need to plan for future estate taxes.

Please allow us a word of caution here. If you think your estate will be too small to exceed the credit, then you might want to consider two factors. First, all of your property is included in your estate valuation, including your house, personal property, life insurance owned by you, and all accounts including retirement accounts. The combined value of these assets may surprise you. The second thing to keep in mind is the effect of inflation, particularly on the valuation of your home. In the year 2011, your home may well appraise for much more than it does today.

This leads us to a classic problem in estate planning with a classic solution. Because one can leave one's spouse an unlimited amount of money with no estate tax, many people pass all of their assets to their spouse. The problem results when the second spouse dies and assets are then transferred to the children. At that point, the estate tax credit comes into play. Let us assume that Jane's father left his entire $2,000,000 estate to Jane's mother when he died 5 years ago. His money passed to Jane's mother without any estate taxation due to the unlimited marital deduction. Then Jane's mother died in 2002, leaving $2,000,000 to Jane. The tax on $2,000,000 in the year 2002 was $780,800. From this we subtract the credit of $345,000, making the estate tax $435,000 and reducing Jane's inheritance to $1,565,000.

If Jane's father and mother had planned better, they could have avoided paying that $435,000 in estate tax. Here's how. The assets are split evenly, so that $1,000,000 is in his name and $1,000,000 is in her name. When he dies, his $1,000,000 goes to a credit shelter trust, not to his wife. The estate tax is $345,800, but he has a unified credit of $345,000, so the taxes due on his estate are $0. Jane's Mom's separate estate is worth $1,000,000. At her death, her taxable estate is $1,000,000, which is taxed at $345,000. The $345,000 due is reduced to $0 by the unified credit. So, the upshot of the estate planning is that the net estate that passes to Jane is $2,000,000.

The $1,000,000 that went into the credit shelter trust assets grows outside of the estate of the surviving spouse but is reasonably accessible to the surviving spouse for her economic well-being and protection. Typically in a credit shelter trust, the income from the trust goes to the spouse, with the principle or corpus going to the children.

Charitable Remainder Trusts

Many therapists would like to leave a legacy for the charitable organizations they have been committed to throughout their careers. A client of ours, for example, was a well-to-do social worker who volunteered much of her time to a clinic for homeless veterans. After a long bout with cancer, she passed away and left a substantial bequest to the clinic under a charitable remainder trust we had helped her establish. Leaving money to a nonprofit group one cares about can be good for more than the soul. It can make a great deal of sense with regard to taxation, particularly if one's estate will be large.

In the following discussion we explore a commonly used estate-planning device called the charitable remainder trust (CRT). CRTs are used to achieve several important goals for larger estates: (1) reduce estate tax liability, (2) provide support to a worthy charity,

(3) reduce capital gains taxes on highly appreciated investments, and (4) create a charitable contribution tax deduction in the year of the donation—even though the benefits of the trust do not go to the charity until the death of the grantor.

The person who establishes the trust is called the grantor. The grantor retains an income interest in the trust. The CRT pays the grantor an income generated by the trust for the lifetime of the grantor and his or her spouse. At the time of the second death (once both the grantor and spouse have died) the corpus of the trust goes to the charitable organization. Therefore, the grantor, grantor's spouse, and charitable organization all have an interest in the trust. When a stock is placed in a CRT, it can be sold without generating capital gains taxes. Therefore, in situations where there are substantial holdings of a highly appreciated stock that would otherwise trigger capital gains taxes upon sale, the CRT can be especially effective.

Ten years ago, Steven Dillar, MD, bought a substantial amount of stock in a tech company that has appreciated in value to a significant degree. The stock does not pay dividends, and Dr. Dillar, who is 65, would like to retire soon with income from his investments. This one stock holding represents a large percentage of his overall portfolio, subjecting the portfolio to significant risk should the stock lose value. He would like to sell the stock and balance his portfolio in a more appropriate asset allocation that is conservative and income producing. He could simply sell his tech stock and invest in income-producing securities. However, if he did so, he would have to pay substantial capital gains taxes. He pursues a CRT. With the stock moved to the CRT, it can now be sold without paying capital gains taxes. The CRT will pay an income from the sale of the stock to Dr. Dillar and his wife until the second of them dies. At the second death, the corpus of the trust will go to the charitable organization he has chosen.

To make up for the loss to his children's inheritance, Dr. Dillar purchases a life insurance policy that will pay his children the approximate amount they would have received from the stock had it not gone into the CRT. The insurance, a "second to die" permanent life insurance policy, pays once both Dr. and Mrs. Dillar are dead. The insurance is held in an irrevocable life insurance trust, and its proceeds are not included in Dr. or Mrs. Dillar's estate. When the death benefit is paid, it does not generate income taxes for Dr. Dillar's children.

In summary, then, a charitable remainder trust can provide a variety of benefits for the therapist with higher net worth and a wish to support a charitable organization. Under the right circumstance, and when utilized in conjunction with an irrevocable life insurance trust, there can be benefits to the charitable organization, to the grantor, and to the grantor's heirs.

QTIP Trusts

Earlier in this chapter, we discussed how, when using joint tenancy with right of survivorship, one can lose control of seeing to it that one's property passes to one's children. This can be particularly problematic with second marriages, when spouses may have differing loyalties as to which children will inherit property. These differing loyalties can become accentuated after the death of one of the spouses, thereby increasing the chances that the deceased spouse's children could get disinherited. The qualifying terminal interest property trust (QTIP trust) deals with this problem by allowing you to designate who, in the end, will receive your property when your spouse dies. Your attorney writes the trust so that your spouse can live in the house according to the terms of the trust. However, although your spouse has the benefit of the property, he or she does not control its disposition at his or her death; that control lies with the terms of the trust document that you have written. One attractive feature of a properly written and executed QTIP trust is that the property can qualify for the unlimited marital deduction although you do not have to give control to your spouse as to who will eventually inherit the property. You can see how this might be quite appropriate for second marriages.

To qualify for the unlimited marital tax deduction, the QTIP trust must include certain provisions. The surviving spouse must receive all income from the property at least annually. He or she must be given a life estate, meaning that the spouse has the benefit of the property until his or her death. The property cannot be directed to another person as long as the spouse is alive. The property must end up in the spouse's estate on the spouse's death—this ensures that the property will, eventually, be subject to estate taxation.

Advanced Medical Directives

Peter worked for several years at the University of California Davis Medical Center as a social worker in the hospice program. Here is just one story of many that underlines the importance of setting up advanced medical directives. The patient was a 40-year-old man with Lou Gehrig's disease. He was gradually losing motor control in his body, but he was quite intact cognitively. Peter discussed with him on several occasions the importance of clarifying his wishes should he need to be put on life support. The man told his family and Peter that he did not want extraordinary measures taken if there was no chance of recovery, but he avoided putting his wishes into a legal document. At one point, he was rushed, in a semiconscious state, to the hospital and put on life support. His treating physicians all agreed that there was no chance of recovery; his family did not want him to suffer further; and even his minister asked that no heroic medical measures be taken. However, because he did not have an advanced medical directive, he was placed on life support. He died 4 months later, and his family was hit hard by the medical bills and the emotional toll of this unnecessary prolongation of his suffering.

An advanced medical directive is your chance to give instructions about the level of treatment you want in case you are rendered unconscious or incompetent but could be kept alive by modern medical technology. Say, for example, you are in a car crash and are brought to the emergency room brain dead with no chance of recovery. We know this is a gruesome thought, but of course these situations occur every day. Would you want to be kept alive indefinitely with machines without regard to the cost to your family? Would you want to appoint someone to act as your agent? You can address these questions in an advanced medical directive so that your family has the peace of mind and legal standing they need to carry out your wishes.

Living Wills

The living will addresses the individual's wishes should he or she become terminally incapacitated or unconscious. In such a situation there can be a conflict between the physician's oath to preserve life and the individual's right to self-determination. Your living will provides legal protection for your physician to carry out your wishes. In many states, the law requires that one or two physicians certify that death is imminent, because the living will is applicable only when the patient's condition is terminal. The living will usually states in legal language that the individual does not want to prolong a dying process that is painful, fruitless, and financially devastating for the family.

Durable Power of Attorney for Healthcare

Whereas the living will is limited to terminal medical conditions, the durable power of attorney is applicable under broader medical circumstances. You appoint an agent to carry out your wishes. You may also appoint a co-agent and/or a successor agent. Choose an agent whose judgment and good will you really trust, as he or she will have a great deal of power and responsibility over life and death decisions.

When Peter worked in the hospice at the UC Davis Medical Center, he had a patient who was diagnosed with terminal cancer. Her husband was pushing hard for information on euthanasia and assisted suicide, which Peter did not provide, as providing such information was outside of the hospice code of ethics. The husband wanted to be appointed as her agent as well, but she instead appointed her sister to act as her healthcare agent. As the social work unfolded with this couple, it turned out that before she was diagnosed with cancer, she was involved in an extramarital affair about which he was absolutely enraged. He wanted her dead—not out of compassion but out of a jealous rage!

We share the above cautionary tale to emphasize that your agent should be a person who you deeply trust to act in your best interest. A durable power of attorney may also provide direction in medical issues other than those involving terminal illness, such as incompetence due to dementia or psychiatric disability.

A living will and durable power of attorney are by no means mutually exclusive. Many estate planning attorneys suggest that both be implemented. Table 21.5 provides a general comparison of what each entails.

Life Insurance

One of the principal goals of estate planning is to limit the amount of money in one's taxable estate so as to ensure that a maximum of one's hard-earned dollars go to loved ones rather than to the IRS. Life insurance policies have an owner, beneficiary, and of course the insured party. If you have a life insurance policy that pays on your death then you are the insured party. Just because it is your life that is insured does not mean that you are necessarily the owner of the policy. For example, the insured party (you), your spouse, or anyone with an insurable interest in you could conceivably own a policy that pays upon your death. If there is an insurance policy that pays on your death, it will be included in your taxable estate if you

TABLE 21.5
Comparison of Living Will and Durable Power of Attorney

Living Will	Durable Power of Attorney
Applicable only in terminal illness	Addresses broader medical decisions, including incompetence due to dementia or psychiatric illness
Involves only the author of the living will and his or her physician	Involves a third party who acts as agent for the patient

are the owner of the policy. It will also be included in the taxable estate if the estate itself is the designated beneficiary of the policy or if the beneficiary is a person whose charge it is to use the proceeds for the benefit of the estate. One way to avoid inclusion of your life insurance proceeds in your taxable estate is to have someone else own the policy (usually a spouse or adult child) and make certain that the policy proceeds are not earmarked to pay for any estate-related obligations, including the payment of estate taxes.

If you are married, it can make sense to have cross-ownership of the life insurance policies. Recall, for example, Steve and Jessica Smith. Both are in private practice. Steve is a psychiatrist who makes a higher income than Jessica, who is a social worker. Steve makes $160,000 per year and Jessica makes $65,000. They have two dependent children. They have a strong need for life insurance because they depend on two incomes and two parents to take care of the kids. If one were to die, not only would a large chunk of income be lost, but there would be a loss of available time to generate new income because the parenting responsibilities would greatly increase. In this circumstance it might make sense for Mary to own a policy on Steve's life and for Steve to own a policy on Mary's life. Let's say that Steve dies. The general rule of life insurance death benefits is that they are excluded from the gross income of the beneficiary. Therefore, when Steve dies and Mary receives the life insurance proceeds, they will be excluded from Mary's income tax. Furthermore, if Mary is the owner of the policy on Steve, then the death benefit is also excluded from his taxable estate.

Another method of avoiding the inclusion of one's life insurance proceeds into one's estate is to establish an irrevocable life insurance trust. This trust can be established so that the income is for the benefit of the spouse, with the corpus (principal) to go to one's children. An attorney draws up the trust, which is then funded with money to make premium payments. The next step is to have an attorney write a letter to the beneficiaries of the trust stating that they have a legal right to request a distribution of the funds for 30 days. Typically the beneficiaries will be your children, so you need to explain to them that the idea is to forfeit the right to withdraw the money that is intended to pay the insurance premiums. Now that the children have been given notice of their right to withdraw money from the trust, the premium payment qualifies for the annual gift tax exclusion from income taxation. At the time of death, the insurance death benefit goes to the trust. The trustee follows the terms of the trust to either provide for the beneficiaries or pay estate taxes. Because the irrevocable life insurance trust is a separate entity held outside of one's estate, the death benefit does not become a part of the taxable estate.

ESTATE PLANNING ISSUES FOR GAYS AND LESBIANS

Gay and lesbian couples are excluded from the unlimited marital deduction, a fundamental estate planning technique. The unlimited marital deduction allows spouses to leave property to each other without triggering estate taxes. Furthermore, same-sex couples are also excluded from the unlimited gift tax marital deduction, which allows couples to move property from one to the other in order to equalize their estates.

For example, Tara is a psychologist and her partner Barbara is a surgeon. Barbara is concerned about her professional liability as a surgeon and would like to gift a substantial portion of her assets to Tara so as to protect them from a potential future lawsuit. If she gifts substantial assets to Tara, the gift is subject to the gift tax, whereas if the gift were to a legally recognized spouse, she could utilize the unlimited gift tax marital deduction. To work around this unfair and discriminatory application of law, Tara and Barbara consulted with an attorney who specializes in estate issues for same-sex couples. In this case, the attorney suggests creating a limited liability company along with a trust to help move assets out of Barbara's name and to alleviate gift taxes.

Same-sex couples must define contractually the property rights that are recognized by law for heterosexual marriages. Same-sex couples who wish to leave property to each other should, with the help of a qualified attorney, create contractual agreements to ensure that this occurs.

It is especially important that the estate plans of same-sex couples be contractually sound, so as to fend off challenges from relatives who, either for reasons of greed or prejudice, challenge the passing of assets to a partner. When Peter worked at the hospice program, he cared for a patient named Ben, who was dying from AIDS. Ben owned a small house and car that he wanted to pass on to his life partner, "Dave," but he had not made legal arrangements to do so. Ben and Dave had lived together for 5 years. Dave had tended to

Ben throughout Ben's protracted illness. Ben's family of origin lived in Louisiana, were religious fundamentalists, and were very hostile to Dave. By the time Peter entered the scene, Ben was not mentally fit to sign a contract leaving the property to Dave. After Ben died, Dave had to move out of the house he had lived in for 5 years and the property went to Ben's family of origin against Ben's expressed wishes. This could have been averted if Ben and Dave had created a contractual cohabitation agreement.

In brief, it makes a great deal of sense for same-sex couples to be very conscious of their estate plans. Whereas heterosexual couples can often rely on law to make common-sense determinations about the passing of property in an estate, the same is not true for gay and lesbian couples. Same-sex couples must spell out everything, and do so in a legally sound way, so as to fend off challenges to the estate plan. For more information, please turn to Addendum I, where we have listed several estate planning books for gays and lesbians.

Your Money Pages

CHAPTER 22

Introduction to a Lifetime Plan for Your Financial Well-Being

We have looked at emotional issues, clinical issues, the therapist lifecycle, and some practical financial steps you can take. This section offers you an opportunity to put together your own personal financial plan. We provide you with a variety of worksheets to assist you in developing your plan.

This task requires that you bring together:
Your rational thinking function
Your creative imagination
The courage to contain your anxiety
A willingness to look at your shadow

Going through the worksheets in this chapter may stir up unpleasant feelings—impatience, anxiety, perhaps even dread. However, we think you actually can have an interesting time with this material. The trick is being willing to activate your creative imagination around the issues in your financial life. If you can move into a creative space, you may well find yourself enjoying the exercise and experience surprising pathways to resolution emerging. You will notice that we have provided "Process Pages" for you to journal in. We hope you will use these pages to record your feelings, reactions, and images as you complete the worksheets. By integrating your "right brain" process responses with the "left brain" financial information you are compiling, you will be doing the "integrative money work" that will allow you to move toward a new sense of financial mastery and empowerment.

Each person's financial plan must reflect the particular and complex realities of his or her individual situation. There really is no substitute for sitting down with a qualified financial planner who can help you shape a plan that is right for you. Our goal in the following chapter, however, is to provide you with useful tools designed to give you an in-depth analysis of where you are and where you are heading financially. The worksheets offer a structured framework to help you conceptualize your financial situation and goals.

The first set of worksheets is aimed at clarifying your financial objectives. First, we gather personal financial information and look at your financial objectives. Then we take a snapshot of your private practice with "Your Psychotherapy Practice: Basic Worksheet." Next, we take a broader look at your total family income. Our next task is to help you analyze your net worth by completing a balance sheet of your assets and liabilities. Next, we provide you with some tools to take charge of your cash flow, with a detailed expenses worksheet as well as a cash flow worksheet. We also look at your debt and debt maintenance.

The next set of worksheets will assist you in looking toward your financial future. We start by asking when you would like to retire. Then we look at your risk profile as an investor, your life insurance values, and the resources you have for retirement, including pension and Social Security. Next, we detail any special income you may expect such as inheritance income or divorce settlement income. We then look at any special expenses such as caring for a dependent parent or disabled relative as well as higher educational expenses for your children. Finally, we move on to information and input about the basic benefits package for your practice, including health insurance, disability insurance, saving for retirement in your qualified plan, long term care insurance, and life insurance.

We also provide you with tools to estimate your retirement savings needs and present funding levels.

CHAPTER 23

Financial Worksheets and Process Pages

In this chapter, we intersperse worksheets for your personal financial planning with "Process Pages" to give space to reflect, reduce anxiety, and stimulate your creative imagination. It is our hope that working with this material will help you gain a greater sense of financial mastery.

TABLE 23.1
Personal Information Worksheet

Today's Date _____

Your Name _____

Your Age _____

Spouse's Name _____

Spouse's Age _____

Process Pages

An open space for journaling your feelings, thoughts & emotional responses.

Object of Contemplation

Do you avoid dealing with financial issues?
If so, how does your avoidance work against you?

"We are here because there is, finally, no refuge
from ourselves."
Scott Rutan

FIGURE 23.1.

TABLE 23.2
Lifetime Financial Planning Objectives Worksheet

In the space below, please check off and write down your objectives for lifetime financial planning:

☐ Maintain practice and other income at a level sufficient to maintain an agreeable lifestyle.

☐ Accumulate sufficient assets to maintain an agreeable lifestyle in the elder phase while working only as much as I desire.

☐ Accumulate sufficient assets to pay for the educational needs of my children.

☐ Reduce debt.

☐ Reduce tax burden.

☐ Ensure that my family will have sufficient income in case I become disabled.

For disposition at death:

☐ Ensure that my family has sufficient assets in case of my premature death or that of my spouse.

☐ Avoid unnecessary taxes at my death or that of my spouse.

Additional Lifetime Financial Objectives

Process Pages

An open space for journaling your feelings, thoughts & emotional responses.

Question

"What feelings arise as you write down your financial goals?"

_____

_____

_____

_____

_____

_____

_____

_____

_____

_____

"Know your garden. It is time to speak your truth."
Hopi Elders

FIGURE 23.2.

The worksheet in Table 23.3 is designed to be a snapshot of your practice. It asks that you think of your practice as a business in which one of the business expenses is your remuneration. The business of your practice must support not only your current lifestyle, but also the expenses of the business itself, along with funding your other life objectives. For more on this, please see Chapter 14, where we discuss putting yourself on a salary.

TABLE 23.3
Private Practice Basic Worksheet
YOUR PSYCHOTHERAPY PRACTICE: BASIC WORKSHEET
Revenues Psychotherapy: Individuals and Couples

Ave. No. of Client Hours per Month	Ave. Fee per Session	Ave. Monthly Revenue from Individuals and Couples
A	B	(A*B)
	$	$

Other Sources of Private Practice Revenue
(e.g., groups, consulting, teaching, interns, etc.)

Source of Revenue 1 Description	Source of Revenue 2 Description	Source of Revenue 3 Description	
Approx. Monthly Income $	Approx. Monthly Income $	Approx. Monthly Income $	Total Monthly Revenues from Other Sources $

Monthly Expenses

COMPENSATION	
Your monthly remuneration	$
BENEFITS	
Health insurance	$
Disability insurance	$
Retirement investing	$
TAXES	
Federal taxes	$
State taxes	$
Local taxes	$
GENERAL BUSINESS EXPENSES	
Liability insurance	$
Rent	$
Furnishings	$
Business equipment	$
Cont. ed., consultation	$

Profit or Loss

Projected Revenues (monthly) $	Projected Expenses (monthly)	Profit or Loss (monthly)
$	($)	=

Process Pages

An open space for journaling your feelings, thoughts & emotional responses.

Creative Imagining

"How can you manifest more fulfillment and prosperity with your psychotherapy practice?"

_____

_____

_____

_____

_____

_____

_____

_____

_____

_____

_____

"The million little things that drop into your hands.
The small opportunities each day brings ... "
Helen Keller

FIGURE 23.3.

Now let's analyze your current financial situation. The information we gather next encompasses your financial life in a broader spectrum, beyond your practice, including the financial contributions of your spouse as well as other sources of revenue such as real estate, investments, trust income, and so forth. We suggest you use these worksheets not only as a snapshot of where you are, but also as a tool for thinking creatively about increasing your income, reducing expenses, and adding to your net worth.

First, we work with an income worksheet (Table 23.4), which will detail all your sources of income as well as income tax deductions. Next, we take an in-depth look at your assets and liabilities (Table 23.5) to determine your net worth. Next, we look in detail at your personal expenses (Table 23.6), including servicing any debt you may have (Table 23.7). This is where we look at how you spend your money. After that, we analyze your cash flow (Table 23.8).

TABLE 23.4
Income Worksheet

Earned Income	Annual
Your private practice remuneration[a] (annual)	$
Salaried income (e.g., work at a hospital, agency, or clinic)	$
Spouse's primary earned income	$
Spouse's secondary earned income	$
Additional Income	
Bonus from your practice profit over and above your regular remuneration (annual)	$
Other nonsalaried sources of income (income that will generate IRS form 1099) such as consulting, teaching, etc.	$
Other income from spouse	$
Total Annual Earned Income	$

Interest, Dividends, Income from Investments, and Trust Income	Annual Interest, Income, or Dividends
CDs or money market funds	$
Bonds or bond funds	$
Stocks or stock funds dividends	$
Limited partnerships	$
Investment property income	$
Total annual trust income	$
Total annual income from interest, dividends, investments, and trusts	$
Deductions for Federal Tax Liability	
Charitable 50%	$
State tax paid	$
Property taxes	$
Home mortgage	$
Gross deductions	$
Standard deduction	$
Allowed deductions	$
Personal exemptions	$
Total deductions for federal tax liability	$

[a] Please note that your private practice remuneration is not synonymous with your private practice revenue. Your remuneration is money specifically earmarked from your revenue for your salary.

Process Pages

An open space for journaling your feelings, thoughts & emotional responses.

Top Dog & Underdog

Write from the voice of self-criticism about your financial situation.

_____

_____

_____

_____

_____

Now respond to the critical voice with self-compassion and self-acceptance

_____

_____

_____

_____

_____

_____

_____

FIGURE 23.4.

TABLE 23.5
Balance Sheet

1	**Liquid Assets** (do not include retirement plan assets)	
2	Cash in bank—checking	
3	Cash in bank—savings	
4	CDs	
5	Money market	
6	Total value of stocks and stock mutual funds (not in a retirement plan)	
7	Total value of bonds and bond mutual funds (not in a retirement plan) Description:	
8	Cash value in life insurance	
	Nonliquid Assets	
9	Your retirement plan assets	
10	Spouse's retirement plan assets	
11	Your automobile	
12	Spouse's automobile	
13	Real estate (home) equity	
14	Real estate (investments) equity	
15	Furnishings—home	
16	Furnishings—office	
17	Other hard assets (e.g., jewelry, precious stones)	
18	Art	
19	(add lines 1 thru 18) **Total assets**	$
	Liabilities	
20	Mortgage on home Total due	$
21	Mortgage on investment property Total due	$
22	Total credit card debt (you and spouse combined) Total due	$
23	Total auto loan debt (you and spouse combined) Total due	$
24	Total student loan debt (you and spouse combined) Total due	$
25	Other misc. loan 1 (you and spouse combined) Total due	$
26	Other misc. loan 2 (you and spouse combined) Total due Description: Account #: Total due	$
27	(add lines 20 thru 26)**Total Liabilities**	$
28	**Your Estimated Net Worth**	
29	(from line 19) Total Assets	
30	(from line 27) Total Liabilities	
	(line 29 minus line 30) **Your Estimated Net Worth**	

Process Pages

An open space for journaling your feelings, thoughts & emotional responses.

Please journal about feelings that arise for you as you
enter the information that comprises your balance sheet.

_____

_____

_____

_____

_____

_____

_____

_____

_____

_____

_____

_____

_____

FIGURE 23.5.

EXPENSES

When dealing with your expenses, you must separate the business expenses from the personal expenses to keep things organized. So, let us refer to the basic worksheet (Table 23.3) for your practice to keep these expenses straight.

Business Expenses

- Your monthly remuneration
- Health insurance
- Disability insurance
- Retirement investing
- Taxes on your practice income
- Liability insurance
- Office rent
- Business equipment
- Furnishings
- Continuing education
- Consultation
- Bonuses to you over and above your remuneration

You can see from the above list that your private practice has a lot to support—both your life and the practice itself. You might think about keeping this list in mind next time you are tempted to undercharge for your services. Remember, your time is a precious commodity; you cannot afford to give it away or undercharge for it!

Remember, it is okay to think like a businessperson *and* like a therapist. In fact, if you are in private practice, you have to. So, keep in mind that a basic rule of business is to reduce expenses while increasing revenue. Creative businesspeople are always asking themselves how they can reduce expenses. Look with fresh eyes at your business expenses, and see if there are ways that you can reduce them, even a little bit!

Personal Expenses

All of these expenses come out of your monthly practice remuneration or other sources of your or your spouse's take-home income. List personal expenses in Table 23.6. Nobody likes to look at their spending with a fine-tooth comb. However, looking at your spending habits is not unlike looking at your eating habits, or other activities you sometimes do quite unconsciously. People are encouraged in modern society to spend unconsciously, without regard for consequences to their financial health, just as they are encouraged to eat junk food without regard for their physical health. The goal in looking at expenses is to find a balance between spontaneous support of what gives you pleasure and paying attention to what is in the interest of your long- and short-term financial health. Staying conscious about how you spend may not be a lot of fun, but then again, neither is excessive credit card debt.

TABLE 23.6
Personal Expenses Worksheet

Rent	$
Groceries	$
Home phone	$
Cell phone	$
Car maintenance	$
Mortgage or rent	$
Clothes$	$
Domestic help	$
Restaurants	$
Movies	$
Other entertainment	$
Vacations	$
Childcare	$
Alimony and child support	$
Furnishings for the home	$
Gifts	$
Medical expenses	$
Therapy	$
Health club	$
Massage	$
Other (description)	$
Other (description)	$
Other (description)	$
Total	$

Process Pages

An open space for journaling your feelings, thoughts & emotional responses.

A space to journal as you work with your expenses.

_____

_____

_____

_____

_____

_____

_____

_____

_____

_____

_____

"Out of clutter, find Simplicity.
From discord, find Harmony.
In the middle of difficulty lies opportunity."
-- *Albert Einstein*

FIGURE 23.6.

TABLE 23.7
Debt Maintenance Worksheet

Mortgage	Monthly Payment $	Years to Pay	Interest Rate %
Variable Rate Fixed Rate		Total Due $ _____	
Favorable PrepaymentTerms[a]? yes no			

Credit Card 1	Description:	Account #	Monthly Payment $
Total Due $	Interest Rate	%	
Credit Card 2	Description:	Account #	Monthly Payment $
Total Due $	Interest Rate	%	
Credit Card 3	Description:	Account #	Monthly Payment $
Total Due $	Interest Rate	%	
Credit Card 4	Description:	Account #	Monthly Payment $
Total Due $	Interest Rate	%	

Auto Loan 2	Description:		
Monthly Payment $	Total Due $	Interest Rate %	

Student Loan 1	Description:		
Monthly Payment $	Total Due $	Interest Rate %	
Student Loan 2	Description:		
Monthly Payment $	Total Due $	Interest Rate %	
Other Loans	Description:		
Monthly Payment $	Total Due $	Interest Rate %	
Other Loans	Description:		
Monthly Payment $	Total Due $	Interest Rate %	
Total Monthly Payment for Debt Maintenance $			

[a]See our discussion on mortgage prepayment in Chapter 6.

Process Pages

An open space for journaling your feelings, thoughts & emotional responses.

What comes up for you as you detail your debts?

_____

_____

_____

_____

_____

_____

_____

_____

_____

_____

"Self-criticism or self-judgment is self-hatred. It will always hurt you. There is no exception to that."

-- Dick Olney

FIGURE 23.7.

Now that we have established a worksheet for your expenses, we can plug in some important values. Let's look at your cash flow.

TABLE 23.8
Cash Flow Worksheet

1.	Idle cash on hand	$
Sources of Cash (inflow)		
2.	Total annual earned income (from Personal Income Worksheet)	$
3.	Total annual interest, dividends, income from investments, and trust income (from Personal Income Worksheet)	$
4.	**Total Cash Inflow** (add lines 1 + 2)	$
5.	**Total Cash Available** (add lines 1 + 2 + 3)	$
	Uses of Cash (outflow)	
6.	Total personal expenses (from Personal Expenses Worksheet)	$
7.	Total Debt Maintenance (from Debt Maintenance Worksheet)	$
8.	Federal taxes paid	$
9.	State taxes paid	$
10.	Property taxes paid	$
11.	Liability insurance	$
12.	Office rent	$
13.	Office furnishings	$
14.	Business equipment	$
15.	Cont. ed., consultation, personal therapy	$
16.	Health insurance	$
17.	Disability insurance	$
18.	Retirement investing	$
19.	Other/misc. uses of cash	$
20.	Total Cash Outflow	$
21.	END OF YEAR Cash Balance (line 5 + line 20)	$

Note: All values are annual and include both you and your spouse.

Process Pages

An open space for journaling your feelings, thoughts & emotional responses.

A space to journal as you work with your expenses.

_____

_____

_____

_____

_____

_____

_____

_____

_____

_____

When all the doing is done, I have to face myself in my naked reality.
-- *Marion Woodman*

FIGURE 23.8.

At this point you should have a pretty good idea of where you stand financially. If the picture looks good then you should be pleased. Congratulations on doing things well! For those of you for whom the picture looks discouraging, do not lose heart! Money is like any other issue in life—it can and will respond to your intention to work with it.

YOUR FINANCIAL FUTURE

Now let's look forward—into your financial future. First, take a moment to read through the overview on Social Security benefits and do some inquiry into what you can expect when you reach retirement age.

Social Security and the Private Practitioner

The most common sources of income for retired therapists are social security, qualified retirement accounts, individual retirement accounts, annuities, and cash values in life insurance policies. Other sources of income might derive from other investments such as real estate or other businesses. It is not uncommon for therapists to continue to work past the traditional retirement age of 65. Many therapists love their work and do not want to give it up entirely in retirement. Other older therapists continue to work due to a continuing need for income. A combination of these two factors keeps many therapists working well into their 70s. Please see a more detailed discussion of this in Chapter 5.

Whatever your sources of income may be, it is important that you plan ahead for a comfortable retirement income. A good place to begin is by estimating your Social Security benefit. You should receive an annual estimate of your projected Social Security benefits from the Social Security Administration. This data is mailed to all participants who are 25 and older. The data sheet typically arrives about 3 months before your birthday. File form SSA-7050-F3 or Form SSA-07004-PC-0P1 to request a current estimate. You can find forms, addresses, phone numbers, and other important Social Security information online at *http//:www.ssa.gov.*

When you look at your data sheet and projected monthly Social Security benefit, you will see that Social Security is not designed to provide an adequate retirement income by itself. Instead, it is designed to provide a safety net that is supplemented with other retirement funds. You become eligible for Social Security payments through credit for qualifying quarters worked. Not all work is covered by Social Security, so you will need to clarify exactly what work you have done that qualifies. The yearly data sheet from the

Social Security Administration should be helpful in clarifying the number of qualifying quarters you have worked.

How You Qualify for Social Security as a Solo Practitioner

If you are like most people in private practice, you probably run your practice as a sole proprietorship. The term "sole proprietorship" basically means that you are self-employed and not organized as a corporation or other entity such as a limited liability partnership. You are simply in business for yourself. As a sole proprietor, your business income is reported on IRS schedule C. You pay self-employment tax based on your self-employed income. The self-employment tax is a Social Security and Medicare tax similar to those withheld from most wage earners. You figure your self-employment tax using schedule SE (Form 1040). By the way, wage earners cannot deduct Social Security and Medicare taxes whereas sole proprietors may deduct half of self-employment tax in figuring their adjusted gross income.

The self-employment tax rate is 15.3%. The rate consists of two parts: 12.4% for social security (old age, survivors, and disability insurance) and 2.90% for Medicare (hospital insurance). Only the first $87,000 of your combined wages and net earnings in 2003 is subject to any combination of the Social Security part of the self-employment tax. All your combined wages, tips, and net earnings in 2003 are subject to the 2.9% Medicare part of self-employment tax. Again, you can deduct half of your self-employment tax in figuring your adjusted gross income. This deduction affects only your income tax. If does not affect either your net earnings from self-employment or your self-employment tax.

You must be insured under the Social Security system before you begin receiving Social Security benefits. Paying your self-employment tax makes you eligible for Social Security as a solo practitioner. You are insured if you have the required number of quarters of coverage. You can earn a maximum credit of four quarters per year. For 2003 you earn one credit for each $890 of income subject to Social Security taxes. You need $3,560 of self-employment income and wages to earn four credits.

Estimating Your Social Security Benefit

Some very useful tools are available on the *http://www.ssa.gov* website. You can estimate your Social Security payments with a calculator on the site. You can look at your estimated benefits in today's dollars and in future, inflated dollars. For example, we inputted the following information and got an estimated benefit amount from the calculator. We inputted an income of $100,000 for a 62-year-old individual. In today's dollars, the monthly benefit at age 65½ would be $1,797; with inflation counted in, the monthly benefit at age 65½ would be $1,908. This amount would be difficult for most therapists to live on, and it underscores the importance of supplementing your Social Security benefit with other sources of retirement income.

Now let's move on to the next set of worksheets, all of which in some way deal with retirement financial concerns (Tables 23.9–23.17.

TABLE 23.9
Social Security Worksheet

	You	Your Spouse
Age benefit starts	$_____	$_____
Anticipated annual increase rate	$_____	$_____
Anticipated benefit	$_____	$_____

TABLE 23.10
Retirement Age Worksheet

Your projected retirement age _____
Spouse's projected retirement age_____

TABLE 23.11
Worksheet for Yearly Living Expenses[a] Now and in Retirement

Now	$_____
Current surviving household	$_____
During retirement	$_____
Single retiree survivor	$_____

[a] Not including taxes. In today's dollars. For your household.

Process Pages

An open space for journaling your feelings, thoughts & emotional responses.

Feelings may arise as you think about the age at which you want to retire, and the money you will need to be comfortable.

_____

_____

_____

_____

_____

_____

_____

_____

_____

_____

Now we are changed, making a noise greater than ourselves.

-- *Kathleen Norris*

FIGURE 23.9.

TABLE 23.12
Risk Profile Worksheet (Please circle the word that best describes your attitude about risk with your investments.)

Conservative

Moderately conservative

Moderate

Moderately aggressive

Aggressive

TABLE 23.13
Life Insurance Worksheet

	You	Your Spouse
Permanent life insurance	$_____	$_____
Term life insurance	$_____	$_____
Cash values (minus loans)	$_____	$_____

TABLE 23.14
Pension Worksheet

	You	Your Spouse
Defined benefit pension plan	$_____	$_____
Anticipated annual amount	$_____	$_____
Starting age	$_____	$_____
Increase rate before retirement	$_____	$_____
Increase rate after retirement	$_____	$_____
Survivor benefit	$_____	$_____

Process Pages

An open space for journaling your feelings, thoughts & emotional responses.

Pension and Social Security
A place to journal your emotional response.

_____

_____

_____

_____

_____

_____

_____

_____

_____

_____

Where does the lotus grow?
In the mud.

-- Marie Stuart

FIGURE 23.10.

TABLE 23.15
Special Income Worksheet[a]

Description	Annual Amount	Annual Increase	Starting Year	Number of Years

[a] Include any sources of expected future income (e.g., inheritance or divorce settlement).

Process Pages

An open space for journaling your feelings, thoughts & emotional responses.

What comes up for you as you think about future income such as an inheritance? Feelings may arise in response to lack of inheritance as well.

_____

_____

_____

_____

_____

_____

_____

_____

_____

We do not see things as they are; we see things as we are.
-- *Talmud*

FIGURE 23.11.

TABLE 23.16
Special Expenses Worksheet[a]

Description	Annual Amount	Annual Increase	Starting Year	Number of Years

[a] Include any future expenses such as vacations, down payment on real estate, care for a dependent family member, and so forth (not including education expenses).

Process Pages

An open space for journaling your feelings, thoughts & emotional responses.

Special expenses may be for things that you
really value and want to make room for in your life.

_____

_____

_____

_____

_____

_____

_____

_____

_____

_____

You must ask for what you really want. Don't go back to sleep.

-- Rumi

FIGURE 23.12.

TABLE 23.17
Higher Education Expenses[a] Worksheet

Name of Child	Years Until College	Cost per Year	Number of Years	Current College Fund Amount

[a] For dependents. In today's dollars.

Process Pages

An open space for journaling your feelings, thoughts & emotional responses.

A financial gift such as paying educational expenses can make a profound difference in the life of a young person. Were you given this gift? What feeling, memories and associations come up around this?

_____

_____

_____

_____

_____

_____

_____

_____

_____

_____

We must be diligent today. To wait until tomorrow is too late.
-- *Buddha*

FIGURE 23.13.

BASIC BENEFITS PACKAGE AND OTHER FINANCIAL ISSUES

If you have worked with the worksheets provided, you now should have a sense of your current financial standing and some of the financial issues for which you need to prepare. Now let's look at various issues that affect the financial life of your practice. In this section we discuss important business issues for your practice:

Federal tax deductibility issues for sole proprietors
Qualified plans of deferred compensation
Business overhead insurance
Medical and disability insurance
Personal liability insurance

Tax Deductions

If you are structured as a sole proprietorship, many of your business expenses are deductible. Most therapists work under a structure the IRS denotes as "Sole Proprietor." In today's environment, if you are working individually, setting up your business as a sole proprietorship is both the most common business form and usually quite sensible. The main issue we have with the sole proprietorship structure is that there is no separation, from the IRS's point of view, between your business and you as an individual. Our thrust throughout this book is that your practice must be run like a business that will provide you, its owner, with a good living and benefits. In this sense you are both the employer and the employee. Therefore, it may be best for you to set up your practice as a sole proprietorship but to think like a corporation, in the sense that your practice should be conceptualized as a business that stands on its own, provides you with your remuneration, and provides you with benefits including a retirement plan, health plan, and disability insurance.

Before the Economic Growth and Tax Relief Reconciliation Act of 2001 (EGTRRA), some therapists created professional corporations in order to gain higher maximums on qualified retirement plans. However, since the passage of EGTRRA, sole proprietors have much more liberal maximums on tax-advantaged investing plans.

Below is a list of practice expenses that are generally deductible if you are organized as a sole proprietorship:

Employees' pay
Reimbursement for employees' expenses

Depreciation on business equipment
Fire, theft, flood, or similar insurance
Health insurance premiums (100% starting in 2003)
Tax-qualified long-term care insurance (100% starting in 2003)
Interest on debts related to your business
Legal and professional fees
Tax preparation fees
Pension plans
Rent expense
Entertainment to a customer or client
State income taxes directly attributable to your business
Employment taxes
State unemployment fund
State disability fund
Self-employment tax
Personal property tax on property directly related to your business
Travel meals and entertainment when traveling for business
Business use of your home if you see patients in a home office
Advertising
Donations to business organizations
Education expenses
Licenses and regulatory fees
Repairs to keep your office in normal operating condition
Subscriptions to trade or professional publications
Supplies and materials
Utilities

Solo practitioners have many financial difficulties and challenges, but they also have a wide array of deductions. Use them! These deductions are your right as a sole proprietor, and they are absolutely essential to keeping your practice in good financial shape. Remember our social contract in the United States—we have limited services provided by the government compared with the rest of the developed world. On the other hand, we have lower taxes. Nowhere is this clearer than in private practice. You can take significant deductions as a sole proprietor—and you need them, because it is costly to buy your own social safety net with private health insurance, long-term care insurance, disability insurance, retirement savings, and education savings.

Health Insurance

Let's start with health insurance. You need it! If you do not have it, then you should seek it out immediately. You may be able to find a policy through your professional organization. Otherwise, look on the Internet or in the yellow pages. A good national resource is *http://www.bluecares.com*, a national website of Blue Cross and Blue Shield organizations with links for health coverage in 50 states.

You also might want to check into starting a medical savings account (MSA). You purchase a high-deductible insurance plan that is specifically designed to be compliant with MSA rules (*http://www.bluecares.com* can provide links to Blue Cross/Blue Shield plans that are MSA compliant). Each year, you may put pre-tax money into your MSA account, which can be invested in a variety of investment instruments. Then, you pay your deductible expenses by withdrawing funds from the account. If you reach your deductible, then your insurance kicks in. If you do not spend down your MSA account in a given year, you can use it in future years or for retirement savings. You must pay a 15% penalty (which is withdrawn from your account) for withdrawals for any use other than medical expenses before age 65. Many therapists are oriented to alternative healthcare, which may not be covered under traditional insurance; in this case the MSA makes even more sense.

Whether you go with a traditional policy or one of these new MSA accounts, it is vital that you do not "go bare" with regard to health insurance coverage. The cost of healthcare is devastatingly expensive, and unless you are extremely wealthy, you cannot afford to be without coverage.

Disability Coverage

The next vital issue is your disability coverage. As we discussed earlier in this book, your earnings power is probably your main source of income and livelihood, and likely your most valuable asset. Build disability coverage into your practice right from the start. As you move through the stages of your practice, with aging, the possibility of disability will likely feel more and more real. If you are faced with a health challenge that prevents you from working, you will be relieved that you are not also faced with financial failure. Some coverage guidelines are presented here.

If your state has short-term elective disability coverage, then you may want to look into purchasing the maximum coverage for the short term (in California, go to *http://www.edd.ca.gov* and follow the links to elective disability coverage). Additionally, you may want to purchase business overhead coverage, which will allow you to pay your office expenses in the event of illness or injury. By the way, if you are a sole proprietor, your business overhead coverage is deductible from your federal taxes. The third piece in the puzzle is to purchase disability insurance that will cover you for an extended period of time and will kick in after your short-term coverage has ended.

Two leading providers of private disability coverage and business overhead coverage are UnumProvident insurance and Principal Insurance. You can find UnumProvident online at *http://www.unumprovident.com* and Principal Insurance online at *http://www.principal.com*. If you have a financial planner, he or she should be able to assist you in finding and designing appropriate coverage.

As we discussed earlier, make sure your disability policy defines disability as an inability to return to your own profession, so that the insurer cannot force you to go into a new line of work or refuse to pay you. We suggest also that you purchase coverage to the maximum allowable age and that you replace the maximum of your income allowable. One problem therapists face is that their expenses are high and therefore their taxable income tends to be low. Because disability coverage is based on your taxable income, you will want to maximize the percentage of income being replaced. Although disability coverage is not generally a tax-deductible expense for a sole proprietor, business overhead coverage is. In most cases, benefits from your privately purchased disability coverage should be tax-free.

Saving for Retirement

Okay. Now we have taken a look at your practice and its profitability, determined where you stand financially, your net worth, your income, your expenses, and your cash flow. We have discussed the vital importance of health and disability insurance to your financial well-being as a private practitioner. Now, we shall analyze how much you need to retire and then how much you need to put away now in order to get there. These calculations are rather complex and are usually done with computers. The program we use for our clients is called MoneyTree. You can find various calculators for retirement on a number of websites. To get a rough snapshot of your retirement savings needs, we have posted a financial calculator programmed for that purpose on our website: *http://www.insightfinancialgroup.com*. From our home page, go to the "Calculators" link and choose the "Retirement Resources" calculator. Again, this calculator is not designed to give you the in-depth information you will get from a program like MoneyTree, but it should give you a ballpark idea of what you need to save now in order to reach your retirement savings goal.

Long-Term Care Insurance

If you are in your mid-50s to mid-60s, it is time to think about long-term care insurance. We discussed this coverage earlier in the book, but in this section we get down to brass tacks and discuss how much coverage you need. Please review the Long Term Care section in Chapter 20 that covers whether long-term care is appropriate for you. If it is, then the first step is to call nursing homes in the area where you plan to retire. Find out how much a bed would cost in your geographical area on a daily basis. Next, you will want a policy that is designed to meet those needs. Make sure you purchase a policy with inflation protection and coverage for assisted living as well as home care. Finally, make sure that you have a tax-qualified policy so that you can deduct your premiums from your taxable income.

Just to give you a rough idea, Peter ran a long-term care quote with a major insurer for a 55-year-old person rated as a "preferred risk" in the state of Illinois for a 6-year policy for $125 per day, 100% home care coverage, assisted living coverage, 5% compound inflation coverage, and a 60-day waiting period. The premium came to $128 per month. The same policy for a 60-year-old came to $162 per month. For a 65-year-old, the premium is $212 per month. Obviously, your costs will vary, but we offer this to give you some idea of the cost of long-term care insurance. As we mentioned in the earlier section on long-term care, we usually advise our clients to purchase long-term care insurance in their mid-50s, but of course your individual circumstances determine what is most sensible for you.

Let's take an overall look now at the major items you will need as a basic benefits package for yourself (Table 23.18).

TABLE 23.18
Basic Benefits Package in the Life Cycle of Your Practice

	Launching Phase Ages 30–35	Establishing Phase Ages 36–40	Prime Phase Ages 41–65	Elder Phase Ages 66–?
Health insurance	Needed	Needed	Needed	Medicare Parts A & B will provide your basic coverage; Medicare supplemental insurance is often a good idea.
Retirement savings	Fund according to estimates on calculator	Fund according to estimates on calculator	Fund according to estimates on calculator; make up for any shortfalls in earlier funding	Hopefully you have put away enough at this point that no further funding is necessary.
Disability insurance	Usually can wait until establishing phase	Needed—usually replace 80% of net schedule C income	Needed until about age 60, when resources can flow to long-term care insurance instead	Not applicable; most disability policies pay the benefit only to age 65 or 67
Long-term care insurance	Usually not recommended until mid-50s	Usually not recommended until mid-50s	Recommended in mid-50s	Usually recommended unless you have very few assets, have a very large estate, or do not care about leaving an estate to your heirs

TABLE 23.18
Basic Benefits Package in the Life Cycle of Your Practice
(Continued)

| Life insurance | Only needed if you have dependents; getting an early start with permanent insurance may be a very smart move | A must if you have a family that depends on your income; it will enhance your estate and provide a savings vehicle, whereas term insurance will provide basic coverage | A must if you have a family that depends on your income; evaluate your needs, because they may change as you have more in retirement and your children are on their own financially | If you have maintained a permanent policy, then you may want to let the cash value pay for the death benefit at this point so you do not have to keep paying a premium |

Process Pages

An open space for journaling your feelings, thoughts & emotional responses.

Object of Contemplation:
If life were teaching you certain lessons by placing you in your current financial situation, what might those lessons be?

_____

_____

_____

_____

_____

_____

_____

_____

Of course there is no formula for success except perhaps an unconditional acceptance of life and what it brings.

-- *Arthur Rubinstein*

FIGURE 23.14.

CHAPTER 24

Looking Forward

WHERE TO GO FROM HERE

If you have worked your way through this book, then you are now ready to move forward toward implementing your financial plan. You are armed with knowledge about your practice, investing, retirement planning, insurance planning, and estate planning. At this point, you can either implement your own plan based on the information you have gathered here or consult with a professional financial planner. Our bias is that professional consultation can be a worthwhile investment. Probably the strongest financial plans are developed when the client is deeply involved and informed about the issues and seeks out professional consultation in the design and implementation of the plan. This is not unlike effective psychotherapy with an informed, interested patient who is willing to invest in treatment with a professional psychotherapist rather than going it alone.

A sound plan will address:

Marketing and developing your practice
Implementing a retirement plan
Implementing appropriate investments within the plan

Creating a sound tax strategy to limit taxation
Risk management with appropriate insurance coverage
Estate planning issues
Support for insight into the emotional material that colors your
  financial life

SOME FINAL THOUGHTS

Really working with the material in this book is not easy. We congratulate you on facing issues that can be so challenging and yet are so critical to your financial well-being.

You can take charge of your practice and financial life at any stage of the game, but the truth is the earlier in life you begin the process, the easier it is. If you are in the launching phase and reading this book, then you can put the time value of money to work for yourself, develop good financial habits, and start saving now for your future. You will thank yourself later in life if you do.

If you are in the establishing phase, then you still likely have plenty of time to put your financial plan in order. You may need to be a bit more aggressive if you have not done any saving up to this point. On the other hand, your income should be improving at this phase, hopefully giving you extra latitude in putting away more money for retirement.

If you are in the prime phase, then hopefully you have been taking care of business in the earlier phases and just need to stay on track. If, however, you have not done a lot up to this point, then you may need to be aggressive in the funding of your retirement plan to make up for lost time. Again, your earnings at this phase will hopefully give you the latitude to invest larger sums.

If you are in the elder phase, then you really have gotten to where you have been heading. If you took care of business, then you are likely in good shape and enjoying your life and practice as a labor of love. If you did not put enough away, for whatever reason, there still may be some options for you. One option is to do a reverse mortgage on your home, so that the bank pays you for your home in exchange for taking title of the home on your death. Hopefully you can work during this phase as much or as little as you like.

Thinking holistically—that is, recognizing the connection between affect, thinking, and behavior—could be described as the essence of psychotherapy. We encourage you to use your understanding of your own affective responses to enhance your financial self-care. Throughout Chapter 23, we provided you with space to write down your thoughts, feelings, and associations to the material in the worksheets. We encourage you to look back on those process pages with a sense of creativity and openness.

If feelings have come up for you around issues such as looking at the cash flow of your practice (e.g., fear or self-deprecating thoughts), then we encourage you to look at the connection between your process and your financial outcomes. The financial dimension is no different than any other aspect of your life in that your affective responses may have a profound influence on your effectiveness. If, for example, you were working with the "Special Income" planner and it triggered feelings about your family of origin with regard to your inheritance or lack thereof, these feelings are important and may be influential in how you deal with the nuts and bolts of financial planning issues.

Psychotherapy is more than a profession, more than a behavioral science. It is a way of life that most of us find incredibly meaningful, heartfelt, and rewarding. Those of us who love our profession feel there is something deeply important to be gained when a person learns to be true to him or herself. The work we do with individuals ripples out into the larger world, helping to humanize an increasingly dehumanized world. Our mission in this book has been to help helpers take good care of themselves. We hope we have succeeded in being helpful to you.

A Buddhist approach to working with the financial issues in our lives and practices would embrace a feeling tone of compassion, self-acceptance, and self-exploration. If you can embrace such a feeling state, then the financial dimension of your practice can transform from a source of anxiety to a source of excitement, self-care, creativity, and self-development. We hope you will find new energy for your practice and financial life as you work with the materials in this book.

May your financial path be filled with learning, discovery, and fulfillment.

Further Resources

PSYCHOTHERAPY MARKETING AND PRACTICE DEVELOPMENT

Ackley, Dana. (1997). *Breaking free of managed care.* New York: Guilford Press.

Covers how to move one's practice from third-party payers to private pay; valuable discussion of marketing and positioning.

Barnes, Dorothy. (1999). *Independent practice for the mental health professional.* New York: Brunner-Routledge.

Solid information about marketing, how to set up an office, and how to position yourself professionally.

Grodski, Lynne. (2000). *Building your private practice.* New York: Norton.

An inspirational and practical guide to marketing and building your private practice.

Kolt, Laurie. (1997). *How to build a thriving fee-for-service practice: Integrating the healing side with the business side of therapy.* New York: Academic Press.

Covers how the field of therapy is changing, how to choose a specialty and market oneself, and how to write a business plan and track one's business progress. The tone is practical and motivational.

Poynter, William. (1996). *Marketing for therapists: A handbook for success with managed care.* San Francisco: Jossey-Bass.

Covers marketing and best business practices for therapists who work in managed care. If you are just launching your practice and want the help of managed care to provide that boost to get started, this is an excellent resource.

Poynter, William. (1994). *The preferred provider's handbook: Building a successful private therapy practice in the managed care marketplace.* New York: Brunner-Routledge.

A guide to working with managed care, with useful information on marketing.

Psychotherapy Finances. A magazine and website (*http://www.psyfin.com*).

Provides information on practice building, marketing, and niche marketing. A useful resource for current information on trends and issues in the psychotherapy marketplace.

GAY AND LESBIAN COUPLES: FINANCIAL AND ESTATE PLANNING

Berkery, P. M. (2000). *J.K. Lasser's gay finances in a straight world: A comprehensive financial planning handbook.* New York: John Wiley & Sons.

A comprehensive guide to estate and financial planning issues for gays and lesbians. The J.K. Lasser imprint is well respected among financial publications. This book provides sound, reliable information.

Curry, Hayden, Clifford, Denis, & Hertz, Frederick. (2002). *A legal guide for lesbian & gay couples* (11th ed.). Berkeley, CA: Nolo Press.

Nolo Press is a leading publisher of self help legal books. This book, although comprehensive, is rather dense. Thus it is more suited to legal do-it-yourselfers than to readers who want merely a general orientation but who will rely on an attorney to implement the particulars.

Lustig, Harold L. (1999). *4 steps to financial security for lesbian and gay couples.* New York: Random House.

Provides solid information and a supportive tone.

LIVING AND RETIRING SIMPLY

Dominguez, Joe, & Robin, Vicki. (1999). *Your money or your life.* New York: Penguin.
Emling, Shelly. (1996). *Your guide to retiring to Mexico, Costa Rica and beyond: Finding the good life on a fixed income.* New York: Avery Penguin Putnam.
Goldstein, Margaret J. (Ed.). (1999). *The world's top retirement havens.* Berkeley, CA: Publishers Group West.
Knorr, Rosanne. (2001). *The grown up's guide to retiring abroad.* Berkeley, CA: Ten Speed Press.

PUBLISHED BY PETER COLE

Cole, Peter. (1995). Resistance to awareness: A Gestalt therapy perspective. *The Gestalt Journal, XVII*(1).
Cole, Peter. (1996). Boundary disturbances in hospice work. In Yaro Starak, Ann Maclean and Anna Bernet (Eds.), *More Grounds for Gestalt.* New Zealand: Foreground Press.
Cole, Peter. (1998). Affective process in psychotherapy. *The Gestalt Journal, XXI*(1), 49–72.

ONLINE RESOURCES

Independent Financial Websites

The Motley Fool, *http://www.fool.com*

Offers objective financial information with a solid, common-sense approach.

MSN Money, *http://www.moneycentral.com*

Another general website, by Microsoft, with solid financial information and excellent investment tools including comprehensive reviews of stocks and mutual funds.

CNN Money, *http:// www.cnnmoney.com*

Similar to MSN Money with excellent tools, columns, and unbiased information.

Socially Responsible Investment Forum, *http://www.socialinvest.org*

A clearinghouse of information on all aspects of socially responsible investing.

Yahoo Finance, *http://finance.yahoo.com*

Another excellent general financial website with lots of tools and information.

Financial Services Companies

Insight Financial Group, *http://www.insightfinancialgroup.com*

The website for our company, Insight Financial Group. We post a series of articles called "Clinicians' Money Update," written specifically for therapists. We also provide links to most of the sites listed here. You can access quotes, IRS publications, links to Social Security and Medicare, and a variety of calculators to help you make informed financial decisions.

Pacific Life, *http://www.pacificlife.com*

Pacific Life is a leading provider of life insurance and other investments. Use their "educational information" link for lots of solid, user-friendly information on a variety of financial planning, insurance, and estate planning issues.

Real Estate Investment Trusts

National Association of Real Estate Investment Trusts, *http://www.investinreits.com*

Information on real estate investment trusts from the National Association of Real Estate Investment Trusts.

ReitNet, *http://www.reitnet.com*

A clearinghouse of information on real estate investment trusts.

Disability Insurance Carriers

Principal Financial Group, *http://www.principal.com*

Principal is a major provider of disability insurance.

Unum Provident, *http://www.unumprovident.com*

Unum Provident is another major provider of disability insurance.

Government Agencies

State of California Employment Development Department, *http://www.edd.ca.gov*

The state of California provides short-term disability insurance. Follow the links to elective disability coverage for information on this coverage.

Medicare, *http://www.medicare.gov*
Housing and Urban Development, *http://www/hud.gov*

The official website of the U.S. Department of Housing and Urban Development. Follow the links to reverse mortgages for a thorough review of HUD's reverse mortgage program.

Social Security Administration, *http://www.ssa.gov*

The official website of the Social Security Administration. Full of useful information.

Bookkeeping

QuickBooks®, *http://www.quickbooks.com*

The official website of QuickBooks®, a leading accounting package used by many therapists.

Safeguard, *http://www.gosafeguard.com*

For therapists who do not want to use a computerized accounting program, Safeguard is the leading provider of noncomputerized "one write" accounting systems.

Debt Management and Credit

Cardweb, *http://www.cardweb.com*

A great website for comparing credit card rates and features.

U.S. Office of Federal Student Aid, *http://loanconsolidation.ed.gov*

This website provides information on consolidating your student loans.

Bankrate.com, *Bankrate.com*

A great resource for comparing rates on any sort of consumer loan including credit cards, auto loans, and mortgages.

Equifax, *Equifax.com*

Obtain your credit report here.

MyFico.com, *MyFICO.com*

Find out your FICO score here. Your FICO score is a numerical assessment of your credit standing.

Consumer Information

Consumer Reports, *http://www.consumerreports.org*

The venerable consumer magazine is now online.

Insurance Information

Insure.com, *Insure.com*

Allows you to compare auto insurance quotes.

Standard & Poor's, *http://www.standardandpoors.com*

The official website for Standard & Poor's. Obtain an independent rating of the financial solvency of insurance companies. A good place to visit before you commit to an insurance policy.

Historical Data for Stocks, Treasury Bills, and Treasury Bonds: 1928–Present

The following graph shows annual returns from 1928 to the present in stocks, Treasury bills (short-term U.S. Government bonds), and Treasury bonds (long-term U.S. Government bonds). We have reproduced this data to provide a historical context for understanding the role of stocks and bonds in your portfolio. If you look from year to year you will see much greater volatility in the price of stocks than in the price of bonds. However, the arithmetic average growth of stocks from 1928 to 2002 has been 11.6%, whereas the arithmetic growth in bonds has been less than half that amount. These historical data underscore the strategy that stocks provide growth in your portfolio but also entail more risk and volatility. We use bonds to steady a given portfolio with the trade-off that we typically do not expect high returns from the bond portion of the portfolio.

TABLE A.1
Historical Data: Stocks, Bonds, and Treasury Bills (Value of $100
Compounded)

Year	Stocks	T. Bills	T. Bonds	Stocks	T. Bills	T. Bonds
1928	43.81%	3.08%	0.84%	$143.81	$103.08	$100.84
1929	−8.30%	3.16%	4.20%	$131.88	$106.34	$105.07
1930	−25.12%	4.55%	4.54%	$98.75	$111.18	$109.85
1931	−43.84%	2.31%	−2.56%	$55.46	$113.74	$107.03
1932	−8.64%	1.07%	8.79%	$50.66	$114.96	$116.44
1933	49.98%	0.96%	1.86%	$75.99	$116.06	$118.60
1934	−1.19%	0.30%	7.96%	$75.09	$116.41	$128.05
1935	46.74%	0.23%	4.47%	$110.18	$116.68	$133.78
1936	31.94%	0.15%	5.02%	$145.38	$116.86	$140.49
1937	−35.34%	0.12%	1.38%	$94.00	$117.00	$142.43
1938	29.28%	0.11%	4.21%	$121.53	$117.12	$148.43
1939	−1.10%	0.03%	4.41%	$120.20	$117.16	$154.98
1940	−10.67%	0.04%	5.40%	$107.37	$117.21	$163.35
1941	−12.77%	0.02%	−2.02%	$93.66	$117.23	$160.04
1942	19.17%	0.33%	2.29%	$111.61	$117.62	$163.72
1943	25.06%	0.38%	2.49%	$139.59	$118.06	$167.79
1944	19.03%	0.38%	2.58%	$166.15	$118.51	$172.12
1945	35.82%	0.38%	3.80%	$225.67	$118.96	$178.67
1946	−8.43%	0.38%	3.13%	$206.65	$119.41	$184.26
1947	5.20%	0.38%	0.92%	$217.39	$119.87	$185.95
1948	5.70%	0.95%	1.95%	$229.79	$121.01	$189.58
1949	18.30%	1.16%	4.66%	$271.85	$122.41	$198.42
1950	30.81%	1.10%	0.43%	$355.60	$123.76	$199.27
1951	23.68%	1.34%	−0.30%	$439.80	$125.42	$198.68
1952	18.15%	1.73%	2.27%	$519.62	$127.59	$203.19
1953	−1.21%	2.09%	4.14%	$513.35	$130.25	$211.61
1954	52.56%	1.60%	3.29%	$783.18	$132.34	$218.57
1955	32.60%	1.15%	−1.34%	$1,038.47	$133.86	$215.65
1956	7.44%	2.54%	−2.26%	$1,115.73	$137.26	$210.79
1957	−10.46%	3.21%	6.80%	$999.05	$141.66	$225.11
1958	43.72%	3.04%	−2.10%	$1,435.84	$145.97	$220.39
1959	12.06%	2.77%	−2.65%	$1,608.95	$150.01	$214.56
1960	0.34%	4.49%	11.64%	$1,614.37	$156.75	$239.53
1961	26.64%	2.25%	2.06%	$2,044.40	$160.28	$244.46
1962	−8.81%	2.60%	5.69%	$1,864.26	$164.44	$258.38
1963	22.61%	2.87%	1.68%	$2,285.80	$169.16	$262.74
1964	16.42%	3.52%	3.73%	$2,661.02	$175.12	$272.53
1965	12.40%	3.84%	0.72%	$2,990.97	$181.84	$274.49
1966	−9.97%	4.38%	2.91%	$2,692.74	$189.81	$282.47
1967	23.80%	4.96%	−1.58%	$3,333.69	$199.22	$278.01
1968	10.81%	4.97%	3.27%	$3,694.23	$209.12	$287.11
1969	−8.24%	5.96%	−5.01%	$3,389.77	$221.59	$272.71

1970	3.56%	7.82%	16.75%	$3,510.49	$238.91	$318.41
1971	14.22%	4.87%	9.79%	$4,009.72	$250.55	$349.57
1972	18.76%	4.01%	2.82%	$4,761.76	$260.60	$359.42
1973	–14.31%	5.07%	3.66%	$4,080.44	$273.81	$372.57
1974	–25.90%	7.45%	1.99%	$3,023.54	$294.21	$379.98
1975	37.00%	7.15%	3.61%	$4,142.10	$315.24	$393.68
1976	23.83%	5.44%	15.98%	$5,129.20	$332.39	$456.61
1977	–6.98%	4.35%	1.29%	$4,771.20	$346.85	$462.50
1978	6.51%	6.07%	–0.78%	$5,081.77	$367.91	$458.90
1979	18.52%	9.08%	0.67%	$6,022.89	$401.31	$461.98
1980	31.74%	12.04%	–2.99%	$7,934.26	$449.63	$448.17
1981	–4.70%	15.49%	8.20%	$7,561.16	$519.28	$484.91
1982	20.42%	10.85%	32.81%	$9,105.08	$575.62	$644.04
1983	22.34%	7.94%	3.20%	$11,138.90	$621.32	$664.65
1984	6.15%	9.00%	13.73%	$11,823.51	$677.24	$755.92
1985	31.24%	8.06%	25.71%	$15,516.60	$731.83	$950.29
1986	18.49%	7.10%	24.28%	$18,386.33	$783.79	$1,181.06
1987	5.81%	5.53%	–4.96%	$19,455.08	$827.13	$1,122.47
1988	16.54%	5.77%	8.22%	$22,672.40	$874.86	$1,214.78
1989	31.48%	8.07%	17.69%	$29,808.58	$945.46	$1,429.72
1990	–3.06%	7.63%	6.24%	$28,895.11	$1,017.59	$1,518.87
1991	30.23%	6.74%	15.00%	$37,631.51	$1,086.18	$1,746.77
1992	7.49%	4.07%	9.36%	$40,451.51	$1,130.39	$1,910.30
1993	9.97%	3.22%	14.21%	$44,483.33	$1,166.79	$2,181.77
1994	1.33%	3.06%	–8.04%	$45,073.14	$1,202.49	$2,006.43
1995	37.20%	5.60%	23.48%	$61,838.19	$1,269.83	$2,477.55
1996	23.82%	5.14%	1.43%	$76,566.48	$1,335.10	$2,512.94
1997	31.86%	4.91%	9.94%	$100,958.71	$1,400.65	$2,762.71
1998	28.34%	5.16%	14.92%	$129,568.35	$1,472.93	$3,174.95
1999	20.89%	4.39%	–8.25%	$156,629.15	$1,537.59	$2,912.88
2000	–9.03%	5.37%	16.66%	$142,482.69	$1,620.16	$3,398.03
2001	–11.85%	5.73%	5.57%	$125,598.83	$1,712.99	$3,587.37
2002	–21.98%	1.80%	15.12%	$97,996.61	$1,743.82	$4,129.65

Arithmetic Average				Risk Premium	
				Stocks – T.Bills	Stocks – T.Bonds
1928–2002	11.60%	3.93%	5.35%	7.67%	6.25%
1962–2002	11.19%	6.03%	7.53%	5.17%	3.66%
1992–2002	10.73%	4.40%	8.58%	6.32%	2.15%
Geometric Average				Stocks – T.Bills	Stocks – T.Bonds
1928–2002	9.62%	3.89%	5.09%	5.73%	4.53%
1962–2002	9.90%	5.99%	7.14%	3.90%	2.76%
1992–2002	9.09%	4.40%	8.14%	4.69%	0.95%

Table by Aswath Damodaran, PhD, Professor of Finance, Stern School of Business at New York University. Reprinted with permission. *http://pages.stern.nyu.edu/~adamodar/pc/datasets/histretSP.xls*

Bookkeeping with QuickBooks®[1]

GETTING STARTED

QuickBooks® by Intuit has become standard bookkeeping software for small businesses. It is quite adaptable and can readily be set up to help you with your private practice. We use QuickBooks® Pro for Windows. In this addendum we will provide basic information for setting up QuickBooks® for a private practice that is organized as a sole proprietorship. This brief overview is in no way meant to be comprehensive, but is just a thumbnail presentation of how Quick-Books® can be applied to a therapy practice. Other excellent accounting software programs include Peachtree Accounting by Best Software and ACCPAC Simply Accounting. We recommend you find one that works for you and adapt it to your needs.

One reason we recommend using an accounting system such as QuickBooks® is that it forces you to organize the financial dimension of your practice. Properly assembling your current practice information will help you get a handle on your financial situation. Although QuickBooks® is designed to be user friendly, you may experience

---

[1] The authors would like to thank bookkeeper extraordinaire, Ms. Jayne Miller of Reno, Nevada, for her help with the QuickBooks® information we have provided in this addendum.

some confusion at first. Do not despair. QuickBooks® will eventually become second nature once you learn to work with it.

When you first open QuickBooks® Pro for Windows (Edition 2003), you will be prompted to go through an "interview" to create a new company. Many people find the interview confusing, so we suggest skipping it. To do so, hit the "next" button until you get to the screen where you can hit the "skip interview" button. This should take you to the "Creating a New Company" screen. Fill in your practice information here, and in the "Income Tax Form Used" field, enter "Form 1040 (Sole Proprietor)" if your business is set up as a sole proprietorship.

At the next screen, choose "Service Business." The Service Business template works nicely for therapists in private practice. Next, just move forward through the screens and QuickBooks® will save and set up your practice as a new business. If the program asks if you want industry-specific forms, say no. Now you are ready to add your patients.

ADDING YOUR PATIENTS AND OTHER SOURCES OF REVENUE

At the top of the screen you should see the following menu options: Invoice, Customer, Item, Mem Tx, Vend, Check, Bill, Reg, Acct, Rmnd, Find, Support, Backup. Go to the Customer pull-down menu and click on "Customer Navigator." On the Customer Navigator screen, click on the button labeled "Customers" with an icon of two people inside a file folder. You should now be in the "Customer:Job List" screen. From here you can set up all your patient accounts.

In the Customer:Job List screen, you will see a button on the lower left of the window that says "Customer:Job." Click on that button and a pop-up menu will appear. To add a new patient click on "New." This takes you to the "New Customer" screen, where you fill in your patient information. If the patient has a balance due, input that balance in the "Balance Due" screen. After you enter the patient information, hit "OK." Repeat this procedure until all your patients are entered into the Customer:Job List. If you have sources of revenue other than patients, add them as customers as well. Let's say you work with a youth services agency as a 1099 contract consultant. You can add the youth services agency as a customer just as you would a new patient.

Another income source to account for in many practices is managed care, EAP, or insurance revenue. In this case, set up each company as a separate customer and each patient treated under that contract as a subaccount. For example, let's say the Acme Managed

Care Corp. has authorized five sessions for Mrs. Smith and five sessions for Mr. Jones. Go to your Customer Navigator and hit the Customers button. At the bottom left of the Customer:Job List, select "New" and fill in the Acme Managed Care Corp. information.

Now Acme is a customer. Go back to your Customer:Job List screen and highlight "Acme." Right-click on Acme and click on "Add Job" from the pull-down menu. You can now add Mrs. Smith as a sub-account of Acme. Do the same to add Mr. Jones. Now you have Acme as a customer, and the patients that Acme pays for are listed as subaccounts for that customer. If Mrs. Smith completes her five managed care sessions and continues therapy as a private-pay patient, then you will set up an account for her as a private-pay patient, separate from her account under Acme. All sessions billed directly go under her private account and all sessions billed to Acme go under her Acme account. Once you have entered all your private-pay patients, managed care accounts, and other sources of revenue, you are well on your way to being set up with QuickBooks®.

ADDING THE PEOPLE YOU PAY EACH MONTH

Your next task is to add the people your business must pay each month. QuickBooks® calls them "Vendors." From the main page, go to the Vendors pull-down menu and click on "Vendors Navigator." From the Vendors Navigator, hit the Vendors button — it has the icon with three people inside a file folder on the bottom left of your screen. Now you will add your vendors by hitting the Vendors button on the bottom left of your screen and clicking on "New." You can then fill in the pertinent information about the people your practice pays. Typical vendors in a therapy practice might include a landlord, utility companies, secretaries, and consultants. Setting up your vendor accounts allows to see your practice expenses all in one place — which is of course a critical issue to monitor in any business.

SETTING UP YOUR BANKING

From the main QuickBooks® screen, go to the "Banking" pull-down menu and choose the "Banking Navigator." Choose "Create a New Account" from the top right-hand side of the Banking window. Enter your bank information including the current balance. Do this for all bank accounts you use in your practice. You have now set up all the essentials to use QuickBooks® in your practice!

ENTERING INFORMATION ABOUT YOUR DAILY ACTIVITY

Let's say you see six patients on a given day. You will have already entered them into QuickBooks®. At the end of the day, go to the main QuickBooks® screen. Click on the Customers pull-down menu and choose "Create Invoices." If QuickBooks® asks if you want assistance in choosing a sales form, say no. (You have set yourself up as a service business, and that sales form should work well for private practice billing to clients.) From the Customer:Job pull-down menu, choose the first patient for whom you want to enter information. Now you are ready to invoice the patient for the hour of therapy received today.

Go to the row that says "Item" and click on the pull-down menu. You will now add the category. Click on "Add New." This will take you to the "New Item" menu. From the "Type" pull-down menu, choose "Service." For the "Item Name," type "Ind" for individual therapy. Under "Description," type "Individual Therapy." Under "Rate," put the hourly fee you are charging this patient, and from the "Account" pull-down menu, choose "Fees." Enter all patient account activity for the day.

ENTERING PAYMENTS RECEIVED

To enter payments received from your patients, choose Customer Navigator from the QuickBooks® main screen. Click the "Receive Payments" button, which appears as an icon with bundled money. On the "Received From" pull-down menu click on the patient's name. Fill in the payment method and amount and click on the dates of service this payment applies to in the "Invoices Paid" field. On the bottom left of the screen you will see a pull-down menu to choose the bank account where you will deposit this check. It is good business practice to deposit into the bank all money you receive, even if it is cash, and then withdraw the money you need.

MAKING A DEPOSIT

Go to the Banking Navigator and hit the "Deposit" button, with the vault icon. This screen will walk you through depositing your funds into the bank account of your choice. If you want to hold onto cash given to you by a patient, go to the "Cash back goes to" pull-down menu at the bottom of the "Make Deposits" screen. Choose "Owners Capital:Draw." Under the "Cash Back Memo," write "kept cash," and enter the amount under "Cash Back Amount." Once you have entered your deposit information, save and close.

CREATING STATEMENTS AND BILLING

You can create monthly (or other) statements for each patient with the Customer Navigator. In the Customer Navigator you will find a button labeled "Statement" with the icon of a printer. That will take you to the "Create Statements" screen. From there you can choose the dates you want the statement to cover and select the patients you want to generate statements for under the "Select Customers" portion of the screen. You can use the Intuit Standard Statement or customize your own statement.

WHY QUICKBOOKS®?

We like QuickBooks® because it is a well-conceived program and because it is a standard accounting program for small businesses and therefore has readily available support and lots of resources. The program comes with a comprehensive manual, but it may be worthwhile to find a consultant to help you get set up properly. Your accountant can very likely help you with setting up and using QuickBooks®. If, however, you need help finding a qualified Quick-Books® consultant, go to our website, *http://www.insightfinancial-group.com*, and e-mail or call us. We will be happy to help you find someone in your area.

Once QuickBooks® is up and running it will really help you to be organized, and getting organized is a huge step in treating your practice as a business. Additionally, you will be able to run reports that will allow you to analyze your income and expenses. Remember, all successful businesses are continually engaged in issues of increasing revenues while reducing expenses. QuickBooks® reports that show you how you spend and how you earn will help you think creatively about making your practice more profitable.

Glossary of Financial Terms

401(k)	A retirement plan that is funded by employee contributions and often with matching contributions from the employer. Contributions are made on a pre-tax basis and grow tax-free until money is withdrawn. [See "Individual 401(k)."]
403(b)	A retirement plan for public schools, colleges, and certain nonprofits. Such plans are self-directed. The employee makes a contribution that is sometimes matched by employer contributions. Tax-sheltered annuities are 403(b)s.
529 plan	A state-sponsored college savings plan that provide tax-advantaged college investing. Each state has a 529 program—your state may provide state income tax advantages if you use its plan. You can use any state's plan for the federal income deferral.
Amortization	The repayment of a loan (frequently used in reference to a mortgage) by the systematic repayment of interest and principal. In the early years of a mortgage, most of each payment goes toward the interest. An amortization schedule shows the breakdown of the pay-down of principal versus the payment of interest with each mortgage payment over the life of the mortgage.
Annual percentage rate (APR)	The Truth in Lending Act requires that lenders show the total finance charges associated with a loan. The APR allows consumers to compare loans offered by competing lenders on equal terms, taking into account interest rates, points, and other finance charges.
Annuitant	When an annuity contract is set up to make a regular payment to the policyholder, the policyholder who receives the annuity payments is referred to as the annuitant.
Annuity (fixed)	A contract with an insurance company that can guarantee fixed payments to the annuity owner over the life of the annuity. The annuitant can rely on a fixed stream of income, with the insurance company assuming the investment risk. The annuity provides for tax-deferred growth on savings in the funding phase. When the annuitant is ready to retire, the contract is then "annuitized," meaning that regular payments are made to the annuitant.

Annuity (variable)	These annuities provide for tax-deferred growth in separate accounts during the funding phase and payment on growth in the annuity when paid out. Variable annuities invest the policy-holder's money in securities such as stocks and bonds that vary in value.[a]
Appreciation	The increase in the value of an asset. For example, a stock that you bought at one price a year ago may have appreciated to a higher price today. Appreciation also commonly refers to real estate values.
Asset	Something one owns that has value, such as a stock, a bond, real estate, or an automobile.
Asset allocation	A mixture of investments of various types that is designed to match the goals and preferences of the investor. Asset allocation models are frequently categorized as conservative, moderately conservative, moderate, moderately aggressive, or aggressive.
Asset class	A category of investment (e.g., stocks, bonds, real estate, or cash).
Bear market	A period during which stock prices are declining. A bear market can last months or even years.
Blue chip stocks	Equity issues of highly regarded companies that are well established. Many blue chip companies pay dividends in both bull markets and bear markets.
Bonds	A formal certificate of debt issued by a government entity or corporation. Most bonds make a fixed payment at regular intervals; this payment is normally a fixed percentage of the face value of the bond. The face value is repaid when the bond matures.
Bull market	A period during which stock prices are rising. A bull market can last months or even years.
Cash	Not just the money you have in your wallet or in the bank. As an asset class, cash refers to Treasury bills, short-term commercial paper, high-quality municipal debt, high-quality short-term corporate debt, and other high-quality short-term securities. Cash has the lowest volatility of all asset classes. (See "Money market funds.")

Cash equivalents	Examples include money market funds, Treasury bills, and CDs.
Cash surrender value	The value of funds returnable at any given time to the insured person upon the immediate surrender of a policy. Most life insurance and annuity contracts have significant deferred sales charges, making the cash surrender value less than the cash value. For this reason, such contracts make sense only if one intends to stay in for the long haul.
Cash value	The value of the savings element in permanent insurance.
Certificate of deposit (CD)	A low-risk investment offered by banks for varying durations up to 5 years. CDs are generally insured by the FDIC for up to $100,000 per depositor and banking institution. Fees are usually assessed for early withdrawal.[b]
Charitable remainder trust (CRT)	An irrevocable trust with one or more living income beneficiaries and one or more qualified exempt charitable organizations to receive the remainder of the trust upon expiration of the income interest. CRTs are often used with highly appreciated securities. A properly structured CRT permits the donor to receive income, estate, or gift tax advantages.
Chartered financial consultant (ChFC)	The ChFC designation has been conferred on more than 40,000 financial professionals since its inception in 1982. ChFC designees have completed a comprehensive curriculum in financial planning and have met specific experience and ethical requirements.
Common stock	A security that represents ownership in a corporation. Shares are bought by the stockholder who can, in turn, sell the share in a stock exchange.
Compounding	A process whereby the value of an investment increases by using the principal plus the previously earned interest to calculate interest payments. Compound interest contrasts with simple interest, which bases interest payments simply on the original principal, without including previously earned interest to calculate present interest payments.

Conservator	A guardian and protector appointed by the court to protect and manage the financial affairs and/ or the daily life of an individual who is not capable of managing his or her own affairs due to physical or mental limitations.
Consumer debt	Debt that is incurred in the purchase of consumer goods such as credit card debt, auto loans, and store-financed debt. Unlike most mortgage debt, most consumer debt is not deductible.
Corporate bond	A formal debt security issued by a corporation. Most corporate bonds are offered with a $1000 face value. Generally corporate bonds pay a higher coupon (intereset payment) than government bonds because of higher risk. Corporate bonds are rated for risk by independent rating agencies. As a general rule, the higher the risk, the higher the coupon rate of the bond.
Corporation	Legal structure for a business to act as an artificial person that can sue or be sued. A for-profit corporation may issue shares of stock to raise funds.
Custodial care	A term used in long-term care and long-term care insurance. Refers to care that provides for personal needs such as walking, bathing, dressing, eating, or taking medicine. Medicare does not pay for custodial care.
Debt markets	The exchanges where debt securities such as U.S. government bonds, municipal bonds, and corporate bonds are bought and sold.
Decedent	A legal term used in life insurance and estate planning to refer to a person who has died.
Defined benefit pension plan	A pension plan in which the employer assumes investment risk and specifies the amount that will be paid to the employee in retirement. Such plans commonly provide a formula for the amount paid in retirement as calculated by the number of years served in relation to salary received. Such plans are expensive for employers and are becoming less common in the private sector than they were in years past, although such plans are still common in public employment.

Defined contribution plan	In such plans, the employee assumes investment risk. The employer does not guarantee a given amount of income in retirement. Instead, contributions are made into the plan and benefits are received based on those contributions, the performance of investments made by the plan, and vesting. These plans are considered less costly for employers than defined benefit plans.
Depreciation	An accounting principle that represents the decline in value of an asset over time. For tax purposes, a business owner writes off the cost of an asset over a period of time with charges made against earnings.
Disability insurance	A policy designed to pay benefits based on a percentage of earned income if the insured becomes unable to work. Disability insurance is distinct from long-term care insurance and does not cover the same risks.
Disposable income	Income that is available for spending or saving, after taxes have been paid.
Diversification	An investment strategy to spread risk among a variety of investments such as stock mutual funds, bonds, real estate, individual stocks of a variety of companies, etc. The goal of diversification is to not put all your eggs in one basket, so that factors that may adversely affect one of your holdings will not have an adverse effect on all of your holdings. For example, concerns about terrorism and security may be bad for the airline industry but lead to brisk business for companies that specialize in providing security.[c]
Dividends	A portion of a company's profit that are distributed to its shareholders. Dividend paying companies are frequently large and well established.
Dollar cost averaging	A method of investing a fixed amount of money into an investment such as a mutual fund. Frequently, the money is transferred directly from a bank account into the investment on a monthly basis without regard to the price of the investment. Thus, the investor buys more shares when the price is low and fewer shares when the price is high. This may result in lowering the average cost per share.[d]

Dow Jones Industrial Average (DJIA)	A widely used indicator of the stock market, the DJIA has been computed since 1896. It is a price-weighted average of 30 blue chip companies chosen by the *Wall Street Journal.* The DJIA currently includes GE, GM, HP, Coca Cola, Microsoft, and Exxon/Mobile.
Durable power of attorney for healthcare	Empowers the person you appoint to make healthcare decisions for you. The designated person makes medical decisions for you if you are unable to make them for yourself due to illness or incapacity. Most people choose a family member or close friend.
Equity	In the context of stocks, equity refers to an ownership interest in a corporation in the form of common stock or preferred stock. In a real estate context, equity refers to the difference between the amount owed on the mortgage and the value of the property.
Estate	All that a person owns. Upon death, "estate" refers to the total value of the decedent's assets. The estate value includes all funds, interest in businesses, real property, real estate, stocks, bonds, notes receivable, and any other asset the person may have possessed.
Estate planning	The orderly and thoughtful preparation of a plan to administer and dispose of one's property so that after death the people and/or institutions that the decedent favors will receive maximum benefit with minimum loss of assets to taxes.
Estate tax	Tax levied on the transfer of property from the decedent to his or her beneficiaries and heirs. It is based on the value of the decedent's estate and can include insurance proceeds.
Executor	The person named in a will and appointed to carry out the desires of the decedent. Responsibilities include gathering and protecting estate assets, ensuring that heirs and beneficiaries are treated according to the terms of the will, arranging for estate debts to be paid, and managing the calculation and payment of estate taxes.
Face amount	The amount to be paid upon death or upon maturity of a life insurance policy.
Face value	In the context of a debt security, it is the amount paid to the bondholder when the bond matures.

Fair market value   The amount an asset would bring   in the open market if put up for sale.

Fiduciary   A party who occupies a position of trust such as a trustee, executor, or retirement plan administrator. Fiduciaries must follow the "prudent person rule," which states that those with responsibility to invest money for others should act with prudence, discretion, intelligence, and regard for the safety of capital as well as income.

Financial planner   A professional who assists individuals, families, and organizations in carrying out their financial goals.

Fixed annuity   See "Annuity (fixed)."

Fixed investment   An investment such as a bond, certificate of deposit, or note that pays a given rate of interest.

Fixed-rate mortgage   A property loan with interest terms that are set and do not change over the life of the loan.

Fluctuation   The variation in prices of stocks and other securities traded in secondary markets.

Fund manager   A person (or team) who is responsible for making investment decisions related to a mutual fund or other formal portfolio such as a pension or insurance fund.

Fundamental analysis   A method of stock valuation that studies the company's financial statements, operations, earnings, competition, and management strength. Fundamental analysis focuses on the company itself and is contrasted by technical analysis.

Future value   A calculation relating to the time value of money. It calculates money's value in the future given the present value of the money, the number of years it will be held, the percentage rate at which it will grow, the number of times interest will be compounded per year, and the amount and number of payments that will be added over the years it is to be held. Inflation reduces money's future value, whereas compounding of interest increases money's future value.

Group insurance   Insurance issued to a group, such as employees of a company or members of a credit union.

Growth stock	A common stock whose price is considered likely to increase because the issuing company's business is poised for growth. Growth stocks generally do not pay dividends.
Guardian	A term used in connection with wills and estate planning, it refers to a person named to care for another person, usually a minor.
Healthcare advance directive	A document that expresses your general wishes about your medical treatment in the event that, in the future, you cannot speak for yourself. (See "Durable power of attorney for healthcare.")
Home equity loan	A loan that is collateralized with the equity the borrower has in the home. The interest paid on home equity loans is sometimes deductible as mortgage interest.
Illiquid	Assets that are not readily converted to cash, such as real estate, collectibles, and limited partnerships.
Illustration	A projection of how a specific permanent insurance policy or annuity is expected to perform over time, given certain inputs such as rate of return, premium payments, and length of time that premium payments are made.
Income stock	A stock that historically has paid high dividends consistently.
Individual 401(k)	New 401(k) plans established with the 2001 tax law. These plans allow individuals in solo practice and their spouses to establish a 401(k) with greatly reduced administrative requirements. [See "401(k)."]
Inflation	An economic term that describes a set of conditions in which there is an increase in the price of goods and services that causes a decline in purchasing power.
In-force policy	An insurance policy that is sufficiently paid up as to be currently in effect and valid.
Insurability	The degree to which an insurance company is willing and able to insure a particular person given his or her health status and other risk factors.
Insured	The person whose life is covered by life insurance and upon whose death, a life insurance policy pays.

Interest rate risk	In a fixed investment, the risk that the interest being paid will be less than the going rate at a future date.
Intestate	To die intestate is to die without a will. In such cases, state law determines the disposition of an estate.
Investment portfolio	A mixture of securities and other assets that is designed to meet the needs of the investor. Refers to looking at the entire collection of holdings in their totality.
Investment strategy	The approach an investor employs in making investment decisions.
IRA	Individual retirement account. If one meets certain requirements set forth by the IRS, an individual may fund a traditional IRA with pre-tax dollars that will grow tax deferred and will be taxed when spent in retirement.
IRA rollover	Certain retirement accounts may be "rolled over" into an IRA held at a financial institution. For example, an individual who separates from service with a school district may be eligible to roll the 403(b) retirement account into a rollover IRA. The IRS has specified certain rules and penalties with regard to IRA rollovers, so be sure to consult with a financial professional before you make such a move.
Junk bonds	Bonds issues by entities that receive a below-investment-grade rating from independent rating agencies such as Standard & Poor's. Junk bonds must pay higher coupon rates than investment-grade bonds to attract investors.
Keogh	A tax-deferred retirement plan for self-employed individuals and the employees of sole proprietors. The Keogh is frequently used by sole proprietors for retirement saving.
Leverage	Debt. A company that is highly leveraged is utilizing borrowed money. Similarly, an investor using leverage is using borrowed money to invest. The use of borrowed money in investing increases risk and may magnify gains and/or losses.

Liability insurance	Insurance that covers the possibility of loss due to the insured being held responsible for another's injury, resulting from negligence or inappropriate action.
Life expectancy	Based on actuarial tables, an insurance company's estimate of the insured's life span. It is used in calculating life insurance premiums.
Life insurance	Insurance that pays a specified amount on the death of the insured.
Liquidity	The degree to which an investment is readily convertible to cash without penalty or loss.
Living will	Document that specifies one's wishes with regard to medical treatment in the event the individual becomes incapable of making his or her own medical decisions. Commonly, living wills state whether the individual would want artificial life support to be initiated or continued in the event that it is the only thing keeping him or her alive.
Long-term care	Custodial, intermediate, or skilled nursing care provided to an individual who does not need acute care but who cannot carry out daily living activities independently. Long-term care encompasses a broad range of help with daily activities that chronically disabled individuals need for a prolonged period of time.
Long-term care insurance	A type of health insurance specifically designed to cover long-term care expenses. Some policies cover home health care and assisted living expenses. Benefits are triggered when the insured cannot independently perform specified activities of daily living.
Medicaid (Medi-Cal in California)	Medical expense benefits for individuals and families deemed to be low-income and otherwise eligible by state and federal guidelines.
Medical power of attorney	A document giving an individual (agent) the authority to make medical decisions on behalf of the person assigning the power of attorney in the event that he or she becomes incapable of making his or her own medical decisions. The agent is usually a trusted friend or relative.

Medicare	Federal program that provides medical expense benefits for retired Americans. Medicare Part A provides coverage for in-hospital acute care. Part B provides outpatient coverage.
Medigap insurance	Insurance that covers some, but not all, areas of medical expenses not covered by Medicare (i.e., gaps). Medigap insurance does not cover long-term care expenses. Various levels of Medigap insurance have been standardized by state insurance commissioners.
Minimum distributions	In most tax-deferred retirement plans, there comes a point (age 70½ for most plans) when the retiree must begin to take money out of the plan and pay taxes on that portion. The minimum amount the retiree must take out is known as the minimum distribution.
Money manager	Investment professional who buys and sells securities on behalf of his clients for a fee.
Money market funds	Highly liquid and conservative funds that attempt to keep the value of one share to $1.00 with interest rates that vary. These funds invest in short-term debt obligations such as Treasury bills, commercial paper, and certificates of deposit. Money market funds are neither insured nor guaranteed by the U.S. government.
Mortality tables	Actuarial charts that insurance companies use to predict life expectancy of an applicant or insured individual.
Mortgage-backed securities	Securities that are backed by pooled mortgages. Government National Mortgage Association (Ginnie Mae), Federal National Mortgage Association (Fannie Mae), and Federal Home Loan Mortgage Corporation (Freddie Mac) issue such securities.
Municipal bonds	Debt securities issued by state, county, and local governmental entities, including water districts and school districts. "Munis" are typically not subject to federal income tax and therefore offer lower coupon rates than taxable bonds. Their lower coupon rate typically makes Munis inappropriate investments in tax-deferred accounts.

Mutual fund	An open-ended investment company that combines the investment dollars of many shareholders to manage a portfolio of securities: typically stocks and/or bonds. Mutual funds are used by small investors and large investors alike. They offer instant diversification, professional management, and the cost savings of sharing transaction fees among the shareholders. Mutual funds are sold by prospectus. The prospectus informs potential and current shareholders about the investment focus, fees, management, and performance of the mutual fund.
NASD	Established under federal law, the National Association of Securities Dealers (NASD) is a private, not-for-profit organization dedicated to bringing integrity to the markets and confidence to investors. Virtually every securities firm doing business in the United States is a member of the NASD. Among other responsibilities, the NASD acts as a provider of financial regulatory services to the U.S. securities industry.
Net asset value (NAV)	Mutual funds hold many securities. At the end of each trading day, mutual fund companies must compute the value of a single mutual fund share (the NAV). This computation involves adding up the total value of the underlying assets, subtracting the fund's liabilities, and then dividing by the number of shares outstanding.
Net worth	An individual's total assets minus total liabilities.
Pension plan	A qualified retirement plan. Defined benefit plans are more traditional pension plans that place the investment risk with the company and pay a specific amount in retirement based on factors such as years of service, previous salary, and vesting. Defined contribution plans, on the other hand, place the investment risk with the employee, and benefits are based on accumulated account balances rather than a promise by the company to pay a specified amount. Popular defined contribution plans are 401(k)s and 403(b)s.
Policy	An insurance contract between a policy owner and an insurance company that sets forth the terms and conditions of insurance.

Policy loan	In permanent life insurance, a loan to the policy owner by the insurance company that is secured by the cash value in the policy.
Power of attorney	A document placing decision-making power in the hands of a trusted person to act on behalf of the individual signing over this decision-making power.
Preferred stock	Dividend-paying stock that is primarily held by corporations. Preferred stock takes precedence over common stock in the event of bankruptcy and liquidation. Dividends are paid to preferred stock before they are paid to common stock.
Premium	The amount a policyholder pays the insurer to keep a life insurance policy in force.
Principal	In a mortgage or other loan, the outstanding amount owed other than interest. When a payment is made, principal is the part of the outstanding balance that is thereby reduced. In an investment account, principal is the amount originally invested. When investors say, "I am not touching the principal," they are referring to leaving the original amount invested in the account, but leaving open the option of taking dividends or interest payments as income.
Probate	Administration of the estate of a deceased person under the supervision of the court.
Profit-sharing plan	A qualified retirement plan that allows individuals in private practice to put away a portion of their income on a pre-tax basis for retirement. The funds will grow tax deferred and will be taxed when distributed in retirement. If you have employees, you will have to contribute for them as well.
Prospectus	In mutual fund and variable-product, separate-account investing: a document produced by an investment company that must meet the specific guidelines of the Securities & Exchange Commission in describing in detail the investment being offered. The prospectus provides terms, objectives, historical returns, costs, biographical information, and other information deemed useful in helping prospective investors make informed decisions.

Qualified retirement plan	Offered through one's employment, such plans are qualified by the IRS under section 401(a) to provide tax-advantaged retirement investing. For sole proprietors in private practice, a qualified plan such as a 401(k) or Keogh can be established, with the individual acting as both employer and employee. Qualified plans require strict compliance with IRS rules, so it is advisable to seek professional advice in establishing and maintaining them.
Refinance	To take out a new loan on a property (paying off the previous loan) presumably with more favorable terms to the borrower.
Registered representative	A person who has passed the appropriate NASD tests and is licensed in various states to sell securities as an agent through association with an NASD member broker/dealer.
Rider	An optional feature on an insurance policy. Policyholders may choose a rider in exchange for a higher premium. Example: On a permanent life insurance policy, an accelerated death benefit rider would allow for early partial payment of the death benefit to the insured during his or her lifetime if certain conditions are met.
Roth IRA	An individual retirement account that is funded with after-tax dollars. Money may be withdrawn tax free in retirement. In contrast, the traditional IRA is funded with pre-tax dollars and is then taxed when distributed in retirement.
Rule of 72	A way to approximate when your money will double given a fixed annual compound interest rate. Divide 72 by the expected rate of return to approximate the number of years it will take to double your money. For example, if you are earning 5% compounded annually and you reinvest all of your interest, you will double your money in approximately 14.4 years.[e]
S&P 500 index	Standard & Poor's identifies 500 well-established U.S. corporations for inclusion in this widely regarded measure of large-cap U.S. stock market performance. The S&P 500 attempts to include a representative sample of leading companies in leading industries.

Safety of principal	An investment objective emphasizing that the original amount invested be as protected as is feasible given the risk characteristics of a given portfolio. The more aggressive the portfolio, the less emphasis there is on safety of principal. Conversely, the more conservative the portfolio, the more emphasis is placed on safety of principal. Safety of principal is insured up to the limits of FDIC protection with accounts in depository institutions that are covered by the FDIC.
Second mortgage	A loan, collateralized by real estate, that is in addition to the primary mortgage. It carries rights that are junior to those of the primary mortgage.
Securities & Exchange Commission	The primary federal regulatory body for the securities industry. The SEC promotes full disclosure and is charged with preventing fraud and manipulative practices in the securities industry.
SEP-IRA	A tax-advantaged retirement vehicle. The Simplified Employee Pension (SEP)-IRA is commonly used by therapists in private practice because it allows those who are self-employed or own a small business to invest on a tax-deferred basis.
Skilled nursing care	In long-term care planning, refers to the level of care needed by a patient who requires the supervision of a registered nurse 24 hours a day.
Skilled nursing facility	A facility primarily engaged in providing skilled nursing care to its residents. Such facilities have at least one full-time registered nurse, the supervision of a physician, and a physician on call for emergencies.
Small cap	Stocks of smaller, publicly traded companies. This asset category is generally more aggressive and growth oriented than the stocks of more established companies with larger capitalization.
Stock dividend	The common stocks of certain companies regularly pay shareholders a portion of income earned, called dividends. Although some common stocks customarily and regularly pay dividends, corporations are not legally obligated to pay dividends on common stock.

Stock exchange	A market where stocks, bonds, and other equities are bought and sold. Major U.S. stock exchanges include the New York Stock Exchange, the American Exchange, and the Nasdaq.
Stocks	A stock certificate signifies an ownership position or equity in a corporation. The amount of ownership the stockholder has in the corporation is proportional to the percentage of the stock he owns relative to total stock outstanding.
Suitability of investment	An investment's appropriateness for a particular investor given the individual's risk tolerance, financial circumstances, and life circumstances. Registered representatives are required by the NASD and other self-regulatory agencies to only sell investments that are suitable for their client.
Surrender value	In variable life insurance or variable annuities: the cash value of the policy minus any deferred sales and surrender charges. Most variable life insurance and variable annuities have substantial surrender charges and are therefore only suitable for people who intend to hold the policy over the long term.
Tax credit	A dollar-for-dollar, direct reduction that offsets other income tax liabilities. Certain investments offer tax credits as their primary selling point.
Tax deduction	A reduction in total income relative to the individual's tax bracket. A tax deduction is subtracted from adjusted gross income in determining taxable income. Commonly used tax deductions include contributions to qualified plans, state and local taxes, and charitable gifts.
Tax-deferred	In tax-deferred accounts such as qualified plans, contributions are made on a pre-tax basis, with taxation deferred until the money is withdrawn in retirement.
Tax-sheltered annuity (TSA)	Offered by certain nonprofit organizations, school districts, and hospitals as tax-deferred retirement plans.

Tenants in common	Two or more people, usually a couple, who each have an undivided interest in their portion of a property that they hold jointly. One person may sell his or her share or leave it in a will without the consent of the other owner or owners. If a person dies without a will, his or her share goes to his or her heirs, not to the other owners.
Term life insurance	Life insurance that has no cash value and is time limited. Term life insurance is contrasted with permanent life insurance, which is priced to last until the insured's death, at which time it will pay a death benefit, and which carries a cash value. Term insurance is significantly less expensive than permanent insurance.
Testamentary trust	A trust created under the provisions of a will. It takes effect upon the death of the grantor.
Ticker symbol	A combination of letters that is shorthand for a security. Some famous ticker symbols include MSFT (Microsoft), GM (General Motors Corp.), JNJ (Johnson & Johnson), and GE (General Electric).
Time value of money	A calculation of compound interest over a given number of years with a given interest rate and given contributions. It refers to the concept that a given amount of money will be worth more in the future than it is now because of money's capacity to garner interest.
Total disability	Some disability insurance policies define total disability as the inability of the insured to perform any work for which he or she is qualified. Other policies define it as the inability of the insured to perform the duties of his or her own occupation. Some policies may change occupation definitions after a specified period of disability. When choosing a disability policy, you must understand how your insurer defines total disability.
Treasury bill	A debt security offered by the U.S. Department of the Treasury that has a duration of less than 1 year. Treasury bills are guaranteed by the government for repayment of principal and interest if held to maturity.

Treasury bond	A debt security offered by the U.S. Department of the Treasury that has a duration of more than 10 years. Treasury bonds are guaranteed by the government for repayment of principal and interest if held to maturity.
Treasury note	A debt security offered by the U.S. Department of the Treasury that has a duration of between 1 and 10 years. Treasury notes are guaranteed by the government for repayment of principal and interest if held to maturity.
Universal life insurance	A kind of permanent life insurance that offers flexibility of premium payments. Universal life offers a death benefit along with a tax-advantaged savings component. The policyholder may borrow against the cash value in the policy without paying taxes on the borrowed sum. As long as the policy stays in force, the loan may not need to be paid back. At the time of death, if a loan is outstanding, the death benefit will be reduced by the amount of the outstanding loan.
Unlimited marital deduction	In estate planning, this refers to the fact that married people can leave unlimited assets to their spouses without incurring estate taxes. The estate taxes are eventually collected when the remaining spouse dies. A common Estate Planning mistake is encountered when the deceased leaves everything to the spouse (employing the unlimited marital deductions) and, eventually, estate taxes are levied upon the death of the spouse who now has all the assets in his or her name alone. Estate planners employ a variety of strategies to avoid the mistake of creating excessive estate taxation when the second spouse dies.
Value stocks	Stocks that are thought to be a good buy primarily because the price of the stock is considered to be underpriced when subjected to fundamental analysis of the earnings and overall health of the issuing corporation.
Variable investment	An investment in a security that can gain or lose value. Stocks and bonds are variable investments in that their value can and does vary when sold in the secondary stock and bond markets.

Variable-rate mortgage (VRM)	A mortgage whose rate changes with interest rates. Generally, variable-rate mortgages are available at lower initial rates, because the borrower is assuming the risk that rates will rise. In contrast, fixed-rate mortgages are generally more expensive because the lender is assuming the risk that rates will rise.
Variable universal life insurance	Life insurance that combines a death benefit with a tax-advantaged investment component. The insured self-directs the investment among the separate accounts that are offered within the policy. The accounts typically are managed by the same money management firms that manage large mutual funds and pensions. The policyholder may borrow against the cash value in the policy without paying taxes on the amount borrowed. The amount borrowed may not need to be repaid as long as the policy remains in force. If the insured dies with the policy in force and with borrowed funds outstanding, the death benefit is reduced by the outstanding loan amount. Variable universal life policies typically have steep deferred sales charges that decline and disappear over time. These polices are appropriate only for long-term investors.
Vesting	Retirement accounts frequently include both employee contributions and employer contributions. Vesting refers to the schedule set out in the retirement plan by which the employee acquires ownership in the retirement funds contributed by the employer. Employee-contributed funds are always fully vested.
Viatical settlement	If a person with a terminal illness such as cancer or AIDS owns a life insurance policy, that policy may be sold in a viatical settlement that pays the insured an amount that is less than the death benefit, for use while still living. The purchaser of the policy pays the premium and receives the death benefit on the death of the insured now. At the height of the U.S. AIDS epidemic in the 1980s viatical settlements were commonly used by AIDS sufferers to meet their financial obligations.

| Whole life insurance | Permanent insurance that has both a death benefit and a cash value that accrues over time. |
| Zero coupon bonds | Bonds that do not make regular coupon payments but instead are sold at a discount and pay face value at maturity. |

[a] Variable annuities are sold by prospectus only. Investors should read the prospectus carefully before investing. Annuities are long-term investments designed for retirement purposes. Withdrawals of taxable amounts are subject to income tax, and, if taken prior to age 59½, a 10% federal tax penalty may apply. Early withdrawals may be subject to withdrawal charges. An investment in the securities underlying a variable annuity involves investment risk, including possible loss of principal. The contract, when redeemed, may be worth more or less than the original investment. The purchase of a variable annuity is not required for, and is not a term of, the provision of any banking service or activity. Guarantees are backed by the claims-paying ability of the issuer.

[b] CDs offer a fixed rate of return. They do not necessarily protect against a rising cost of living. The FDIC insurance on CDs applies in the case of bank insolvency but does not protect market value. Other investments are not insured, and their principal and yield may fluctuate with market conditions.

[c] Although diversification does not guarantee a profit, it may reduce the volatility of your portfolio.

[d] Dollar cost averaging neither guarantees a profit nor eliminates the risk of losses in declining markets, and you should consider your ability to continue investing through periods of market volatility and/or low prices.

[e] The rule of 72 does not guarantee investment results or function as a predictor of how your investment will perform. Returns will fluctuate and there is no guarantee that your investment will double in value.

Index